I064866 1

MIGRANTS IN EUROPE

PUBLISHED WITH ASSISTANCE FROM THE
ROGER E. JOSEPH MEMORIAL FUND FOR GREATER UNDERSTANDING OF
PUBLIC AFFAIRS, A CAUSE IN WHICH ROGER JOSEPH BELIEVED

MIGRANTS IN EUROPE

problems of acceptance and adjustment

by ARNOLD M. ROSE

THE UNIVERSITY OF MINNESOTA PRESS
Minneapolis

© Copyright 1969 by the University of Minnesota. All rights reserved. Printed in the United States of America at the Lund Press, Minneapolis. Published in Great Britain, India, and Pakistan by the Oxford University Press, London, Bombay, and Karachi, and in Canada by the Copp Clark Publishing Co. Limited, Toronto

Library of Congress Catalog Card Number: 76-76162

JV
6080
R65

PREFACE

In post-World War II Europe the attitude was widespread that peace and economic prosperity among nations could be realized best if steps were taken toward the integration of Europe. Integration as used here means establishing such a degree of political, military, economic, and social interdependency among a group of nations that international conflict among them becomes literally impossible, and economic development — through extension of the market and opportunities for economic cooperation — becomes practically inevitable. While the nations of the Near East, Black Africa, the Soviet bloc, and Latin America have held desultory discussions about integration from time to time, and have even taken some halfhearted steps toward it, various groups of nations in Europe have made definite progress toward integration since 1950. There have also been some setbacks, and it is still too early to say that Europe is so far along the road to integration that it cannot turn back. In a significant way, Europe was integrated in ancient times under the Roman Empire, in the Middle Ages under the Roman Catholic Church and the Holy Roman Empire, and in the nineteenth century under the Concert of Europe and the specialized international organizations that were created to meet specific needs (such as the International Postal Union). But the bonds did not hold and each time Europe broke up into smaller sovereignties and more provincial societies. The wave of integration during the post-World War II period has had the active support of the United States of America, whose government has seen European integration against the backdrop of a possible larger North Atlantic Community, and it has had the leadership of a number of devoted and expert statesmen. But has Europe passed the "point of no return" on the road to integration?

A number of European and American scholars have periodically described and analyzed the progress and the setbacks in the integration movement in Europe.[1] In 1964 a team of five social scientists was formed at the University of Minnesota to study once again the degree of integration in Europe in a scholarly and analytic fashion, this time combining the talents of men from five academic disciplines. I was the sociologist on the team and the others were: Robert H. Beck, professor of comparative edu-

v

282604

cation; Harold C. Deutsch, professor of contemporary European history (whose interests were the political and military aspects of integration); Philip M. Raup, professor of agricultural economics; and John G. Turnbull, professor of economics. We five gained the interest of Willard Cochrane, dean of the Office of International Programs (OIP) at the University of Minnesota, and of his policy committee. Dean Cochrane and his committee had charge of administering funds provided by the Ford Foundation to further international and comparative research, and they promised to make some funds available for the proposed research if a larger share of the necessary funds could be obtained from another source. The "other source" was found in the Louis W. and Maud Hill Family Foundation of St. Paul, Minnesota, which generously contributed 60 percent to the OIP's 40 percent of the estimated dollar needs. The contributions of the Hill Foundation and the Office of International Programs are gratefully acknowledged.

We five Minnesota social scientists began our field researches in the summer of 1966, and spent most of the academic year 1966–67 in Europe. We decided to present our work to the public in two forms — a summary, integrated volume written by all five of us and a series of specialized monographs detailing the research findings of the individual scholars. The present volume is one of the latter.

In discussing the integration of a heterogeneous, divided area such as Europe, it seems useful to distinguish three levels of integration. The first is the cultural-structural level: the development of a common economic, social, and ideational framework in which people of different countries can interact with one another in a meaningful way and can become economically dependent on one another. This common culture and structure has been developing in Europe for two thousand years, although the strength of political nationalism, economic autarchy, and local culture has been dominant for long periods.

The second level of integration arises from agreements among statesmen. In times past this occurred in the European hegemony of the Pope and the Holy Roman Emperor, of Napoleon, of the Concert of Europe, and during the period before World War I in a series of technical agreements to facilitate international communications and transportation. Since 1945 a number of powerful, cross-national institutions have been created — the European Coal and Steel Community, the North Atlantic Treaty Organization, and the European Economic Community — as well as weaker ones — the European Free Trade Association, the Council of Europe, and the Organization for Economic Cooperation and Development.

The third level of integration — which may be called the "integration of people" — is reached by direct interaction of people from different nations. It is characterized by the development among these people of attitudes and behavior of mutual acceptance as associates, neighbors, friends, fellow-citizens, and — above all — fellow Europeans. The three levels of integration in Europe have progressed at different speeds and have reached different stages, although it may be hypothesized that a development in any one of them facilitates a development in the other two.

This monograph concentrates on the third and least developed level of integration — the integration of people. More specifically, I have approached this topic by studying the cross-national migration of workers and their "acceptance" or "adjustment" in countries of immigration. This is a topic important in its own right as well as an aspect of the larger problem of the integration of Europe. Some attention has been devoted to the second level of integration — the agreements creating labor mobility and the Social Funds — and by implication I have also been concerned with the cultural-structural level of integration.

Much literature, published and unpublished, exists on this topic of research, and a significant amount of it has been summarized in the analysis that follows. Not all sources can be cited; some public officials made materials available, with permission to use their contents, provided the source was not named. The reason is that the material may irritate the sensibilities of some group or country, even though the contents are accurate.

I have tried to make an original contribution to the study of cross-national migration by using a combination of approaches, not all of which have been utilized together even in the many superb monographic studies previously published: (1) This study is comprehensive and systematic, although it does not go in depth into all of the many facets of the complicated problem. (2) This study is comparative, not for the purpose of making invidious distinctions among nations, but because comparison is the only satisfactory technique for making data on cross-national relations meaningful and measurable. It has not been possible to get every item of relevant information for every country studied, so there are some gaps, but nearly every fact is presented in a comparative context. (3) A framework of theory has been constructed for this study; that is, it is not purely descriptive, although description takes up the majority of its pages. (4) A great variety of data is used, including published and unpublished statistics, public opinion polls, direct and indirect case observations, historical and contemporary description from library materials, legal documents, interviews with specialists, and even some documents produced by the migrants themselves.

I wish to express appreciation to three assistants who helped me obtain basic data, particularly for the countries indicated: Jean Belden (Belgium and France), Ruth Rose (Greece, Luxembourg, the Netherlands, and Switzerland), and Volker Knoppke-Wetzel (Germany). Valuable criticisms of the first draft of the manuscript have been offered by Dr. G. O. K. Beijer (secretary of the Research Group for European Migration Problems, The Hague), Mme. Andrée Michel (of the Centre d'Etudes Sociologiques, Paris), members of the Minnesota team, Caroline B. Rose, Jean Belden, and Ruth Rose.

A.M.R.
July 1967

THIS *manuscript was complete when Arnold Rose returned from Europe in May 1967. Soon after, he submitted it to the University of Minnesota Press, and several months later it was accepted for publication. Arnold Rose died in January 1968, and the tasks an author is normally called on to perform when a book is in production were assumed by his wife, Caroline B. Rose.*

TABLE OF CONTENTS

LIST OF TABLES

MIGRANTS IN EUROPE

INTERNATIONAL ORGANIZATIONS REFERRED TO
IN THIS VOLUME

ECSC. European Coal and Steel Community (now merged with EEC and Euratom). HEADQUARTERS: Brussels. MEMBERSHIP: Belgium, France, Italy, Luxembourg, Netherlands, West Germany.

EEC. European Economic Community or "Common Market." HEADQUARTERS: Brussels. MEMBERSHIP: Belgium, France, Italy, Luxembourg, Netherlands, West Germany.

EFTA. European Free Trade Association or "Outer Seven." HEADQUARTERS: Geneva. MEMBERSHIP: Austria, Denmark, Norway, Portugal, Sweden, Switzerland, United Kingdom.

ILO. International Labor Organization. HEADQUARTERS: Geneva. MEMBERSHIP: practically all nations of the world.

OECD. Organization for Economic Cooperation and Development (formerly OEEC). HEADQUARTERS: Paris. MEMBERSHIP: Austria, Belgium, Canada, Denmark, France, West Germany, Greece, Ireland, Italy, Japan, Luxembourg, Netherlands, Norway, Portugal, Spain, Sweden, Switzerland, Turkey, United Kingdom, United States.

UNESCO. United Nations Educational, Scientific and Cultural Organization. HEADQUARTERS: Paris. MEMBERSHIP: practically all nations of the world.

1 *THE MEANING OF INTEGRATION*

◄───

The movement during the post-World War II era toward a more politically integrated Europe has been created largely by high-level policy-makers. Some were idealists who believed that economic development and political stability could only be achieved in larger-than-national units. Others were opportunists seeking more power for their nations or responding to American pressures to develop greater European strength. Probably both the idealists and the opportunists were reacting to the threat of Russian expansionism and sought to secure their safety and independence by joining forces. These and other factors at first influenced only the leaders and made little impact on most of the western European population; in no sense could the creation of the various international organizations in Europe be considered a mass movement with broad popular support. The economic benefits of reducing trade barriers and of economic collaboration were, however, soon felt by the European "man in the street," and he came to approve of such international arrangements as the Common Market and the European Free Trade Association.[1]

But economic integration involves only increasing the transfer of goods and services across international borders, while political and social integration requires the transfer of people across national borders. In addition, it ultimately requires that any national group be willing to have all other national groups participate in common elections or that it be willing to grant power to some supra-national agency. People need direct, personal contacts with others to accept them as their "own kind," suitable for living with in a common political community. Not all such contacts lead to acceptance — other conditions must exist for this to happen, but direct contacts are a necessary requirement.

Some of this transfer or interchanging of peoples is now going on in Europe, and thus experience with it today can provide some clues on the probable reaction to its expanded forms tomorrow. The problem of this study is to ascertain the extent of the integration of people across national boundaries in Europe today, describe its forms, indicate how far it has gone, suggest some of the problems it has involved, and draw some generalizations about factors in its development.

It seems reasonable to suggest that the integration of people is just as important for the creation of "Europe" as the agreements of statesmen; the latter will be able to go only so far without the further integration of people (although it must be recognized that certain agreements of statesmen can facilitate the integration of people). The achievements to date in the creation of "Europe" will be nullified or even reversed if there should be large-scale rejection of the integration of people. The agreements among European nations so far have been more or less opportune for all the signatory powers; they have not yet had to face the test of making sacrifices for the benefit of their "brother" Europeans. Only the integration of a "European people" will get them over that hump. Without basic integration, the promising international agreements of today will be as weak in the face of crisis as was the socialist ideology in 1914 in the face of war: all the talk about "class solidarity across national lines" did nothing to inhibit World War I, nor did the cross-national cousinly relationships limited to the aristocratic elite. In the face of test, the people of Europe did not think of themselves as the "people of Europe"; they thought of themselves as Frenchmen, Germans, Britons, and so on. Yet history shows that new nations *can* be born from an amalgamation of various peoples: the United States was born out of these same Britons, Germans, Frenchmen;[2] Germany was born out of Prussians, Bavarians, Hessians, and others; and Italy was born out of Piedmontese, Tuscans, Calabrese, to name but a few.[3] The question before us is whether Europe, in this sense, is being born today.

What is meant here by "the integration of people"? It means Europeans accepting each other as members of a common nation — that is, achieving a sense of belonging to the same "community." It does not mean complete abandonment of self-identification as Greek or Swede or Frenchman, but it does mean placing self-identification as "European" *above* being Greek or Swede or Frenchman. It does not mean the elimination of old national cultures and institutions, but it does mean allowing a new cross-national culture and set of institutions to be built parallel to the old. Americans are not less loyal to their family or church or ethnic background for being loyal to the United States and some are also loyal to their separate states. The individual countries of Europe will have to take on the psychological character of "states," in the American sense, or of ethnic groups, before there can be an integrated Europe. It is not necessary to go so far as to say that there must be the creation of a "United States of Europe," a new state, before there can be integration, but there must be a much stronger sense of mutual acceptance and of common "Europeanness" than Europe has ever had before, and probably some sort of political confederation will be needed.

4

Various other terms have been used which bear a close relationship to the "integration" discussed above. Eisenstadt speaks of the "absorption" of Jewish immigrants of various national and cultural backgrounds into Israel;[4] Zubrzycki speaks of the "accommodation" of the Polish refugees into Britain after World War II;[5] and American sociologists for several generations have spoken of the "assimilation" of at least the white-skinned immigrants into the United States. There will be no discussion here of whether "melting pot," "cultural pluralism," or "conformity to the dominant national culture" is the best relationship for nationality groups occupying the same territory to have toward each other, or even whether migration across national lines should be temporary or permanent. If there is to be an integration of people in Europe, economic factors will largely decide how temporary or how permanent a migration is to be, and sociological and psychological factors operating through individuals and families will decide whether there is to be "melting pot" or "cultural pluralism" or adherence to one dominant culture. Most migrant workers think of themselves as moving temporarily as a means of accumulating savings or vocational experience. Government or private organizational policies can affect the outcome of the migration of these workers by modifying the influence of economic, sociological, or psychological forces. It is not the purpose here to suggest either the value premises for giving direction to such policies or the techniques by which one or the other set of goals can most effectively be reached.

Not only have European countries been politically and economically divided; there are also considerable differences of culture and "national character" among them. The medieval synthesis provided by the Catholic Church and the Holy Roman Empire in much of Europe has long since disappeared, and national differences have become marked during the past several centuries. To encourage social integration along with political and economic integration after World War II, many enterprises have been initiated — for instance, cultural and educational exchanges, international meetings for all sorts of purposes, modification of school curricula to orient children toward Europe and the world as well as toward their individual nations,[6] the encouragement of tourism, businessmen's collaboration on common enterprises,[7] and special efforts to aid in the adjustment and assimilation of cross-national migrants. Some of these activities were not entirely novel and had antecedents going back before World War I, but the considerable extent to which they were planned and effectuated was a distinctive characteristic of the post-World War II era. If Europe is to have internal peace, if it is to act even in small ways as a unified whole, it must integrate its culture and people to some extent — at least so it is felt by those who think in terms of "Europe." It is the purpose of this study to examine the most extensive of these efforts — the encouragement of migration of people across national lines — and to test certain hypotheses concerning its success or lack of success. That is, this work is limited to a consideration of the contribution which cross-national migration is or is not making to the integration of Europe.

"CAUSES" OF MIGRATION

Migration, as discussed in this volume, applies only to situations in which persons move across international boundaries and take employment, sometimes permanently but at least for a "season" (usually nine months). Excluded are tourism, study abroad, international meetings, diplomatic missions, daily frontier-crossing for work, and other situations in which there is usually no motive for the person who crosses the border to think of himself as a part of the country to which he moves. Most migrants, in the sense of the word as used here, expect to return to their home countries, but, as will be shown later, practically all of them also entertain, intellectually, the possibility that they will remain permanently in the country to which they move.

Probably the major stimulator inducing migration is the economic factor — defined here as the absence of adequate job opportunities in the home country and their presence in the receiving country.[1] The role of this economic stimulator will be discussed briefly, but the main concern will be with noneconomic factors that facilitate the *adjustment* of migrants. This should not be construed to mean that the economic factor acts as a stimulator to migration and not as a facilitator to adjustment after migration; to do so would be wrong for two reasons. In the first place, a marked increase in the real income and standard of living of a migrant, especially if he has been unemployed and unable to achieve his material aspirations in his home country, will do much to ease his adjustment to the country of immigration. If he has the money, he can "buy" language and vocational training courses, decent housing, and other aids that facilitate his adjustment and acceptance. Furthermore, his happier economic condition may increase his desire to adapt himself to the country of immigration. Second, there are stimulants to migration other than differential income opportunities in the home and receiving countries.

The other important macroscopic stimulant to migration in addition to the economic factor is the political-ideological factor. East Germany lost people to West Germany until, in 1961, it built a wall and an aggressive police force to prevent further migration. It is estimated that 3,095,600 persons migrated to West Germany from East Germany and the Soviet sector of Berlin between 1950 and 1961.[2] A tiny proportion of these — estimated at between 5 and 8 percent — returned to East Germany. The old colonial powers — particularly France, the United Kingdom, Belgium, and the Netherlands — received back, as refugees, their former colonial administrators and other conationals who had migrated, sometimes generations earlier, to the former colonies. France, for example, had an influx of 710,000 French Algerians in 1962 and another 105,000 during the succeeding two years.[3] The Netherlands repatriated some 38,000 Dutch from Indonesia in 1958, and another 20,000 in 1962 when West New Guinea was transferred to independent Indonesia.[4] About 200,000 refugees from Hungary began to stream into western Europe after the abortive revolt of 1956, but it was not until some years later that those who fled first to Austria and Yugoslavia found their permanent homes.

It is difficult to say what effect possible future political upheavals may have on international migration, but it appears that the political-ideological motive and possibility for migration have declined. In May 1967 a report to the Executive Committee of the United Nations High Commissioner for Refugees stated that there were only 7,400 refugees in need left in Europe.[5] No doubt there will be a continuing small stream of those from eastern Europe seeking political asylum. It may be that there is an ideological element in the out-migration of some Spaniards, Portuguese, Yugoslavs, and Greeks, but rarely can these people be considered as refugees with a dominant political motive for migrating. As the political-ideological factor behind migration has declined, the economic factor has assumed a greater relative importance.

Without emphasizing them too much, the minor factors in migration must be mentioned: marital discord (in some Catholic countries where divorce is not legal, migration of one partner is a substitute for divorce), social freedom for women (especially from Turkey),[6] escaping revenge for a murder committed by a member of the family of a worker in a peasant society that still practices *vendetta*,[7] other personal dissatisfactions, desire for adventure and new experience, and idiosyncratic attraction (to a girl met on vacation, for example). The escape migration offers is often satisfying if discontent with the home environment is sociological in origin, often unsatisfying if psychological in origin. The many noneconomic, nonpolitical reasons for migrating may be impelling for some individuals, and their existence relates to the central problem of adjustment that is the main consideration in this study, but by themselves they account for a small proportion of the migrants. Rather, they tend to be accessory factors to the main economic factor. Many a migrant has relatives or friends in certain countries of immigration, and this not only encourages him to migrate, but also influences strongly his choice of a place to migrate to. After a detailed study of Dutch emigrants to overseas countries, N. H. Frijda [8] offers a "three-factor theory of emigration": "firstly, a background of dissatisfaction, predominantly but not solely of an economic nature; secondly, a special stimulus to leave the community, either through the pull of ties with emigrants or through the push arising from orientation which differs from that of the community, and a lesser degree of adhesion to that community and the people who comprise it; and thirdly, a more specific motive is sometimes present in the shape of longings which already contain the germ of 'somewhere else.' "

The economic factor — which by the middle 1960's was the major cause of migration — is perceived by the individual migrant as an improvement in job, business, or training opportunities, and in income. But it also has macroscopic interpretations involving supply and demand.

In countries of supply — that is, countries of emigration — the economic factor is expressive of demographic requirements. Where modern medical knowledge and techniques have achieved a rapid decline in the death rate, particularly the infant mortality rate, the subsequent increase of employable adults can seldom be absorbed by an economy all at once. Northern and western Europe in the late eighteenth and the nineteenth centuries, despite its rapid economic growth, had a surplus population which emigrated to North and South America, Australia, New Zealand, Algeria, and other parts of the "colonial" world. Gradually, the birth rate fell into a new balance with the lowered death rate, and western Europe no longer had such a pressing need to export population. Some of the countries of the Mediterranean basin did not have a fall in the birth rate until recently, and Turkey and parts of the Arab world have not had it yet, so they still have "excess" population to export. Of course, when these countries experience an economic growth rapid enough to keep up with population growth, they can absorb the increased population. As of the late 1960's, the demographic balance is rapidly changing in the Mediterranean basin: the countries with a "surplus" of population have (with the exception of Turkey and some Arab nations) brought their birth rates down so they no longer have much surplus of births over deaths.

In countries governing demand — that is, countries of immigration — the creation of new and better income opportunities is related to that complex of causes collectively called "economic growth." The demand for more labor is part of "economic progress": the transformation of a rural, peasant economy into a "modern" industrial economy, which involves a shift from Colin Clark's "primary" or extractive occupations to "secondary" manufacturing occupations and then to "tertiary" service occupations. [9] This transformation, this "progress," can take place in large countries — particularly the USA and the USSR — as internal country-to-city migration, but in much of Europe it takes place partly as international migration. Some countries, such as the Netherlands, Sweden, Belgium, Luxembourg, and United Kingdom, have very small rural populations from which to draw migrants for the industrial and service jobs available. Others, like France and Belgium, have drawn heavily on their rural populations in recent years but have not found them sufficient to fill all the secondary and tertiary positions available. This is especially the case when these countries have gaps in their working-age population, created by age-selective high death rates and low birth rates during World Wars I and II. The result is that all of these become "host" countries, receiving immigrants from the more "primitive" economies where agricultural peasant populations are still relatively large. A country like Italy, which has a large peasant population *and* a highly industrialized modern urban sector, is able to meet its manpower needs from within its own national boundaries. Until the present, Italy has had a surplus of rural population, and has been the major population-exporting country of Europe. Now it is modernizing its economy so rapidly (and the birth rate has fallen so rapidly) that its industrial-commercial sectors will very soon absorb all its excess rural population. Assuming that other population-exporting countries in Europe — Spain, Portugal, Ireland, Yugoslavia, Greece, and Turkey — move into the path of economic development, as they have already begun to do, it will be but a few years until they absorb their own excess manpower. The manpower-importing countries of northern and central Europe will then have to seek their foreign workers from more distant areas or "rationalize" their labor force.

By "rationalization" of a labor force, economists mean obtaining the maximum production from the existing potential labor force.[10] In the short run this can be done in several ways: (1) Techniques of production can be modernized so as to reduce rural labor. (2) Inefficient work practices and the number of unproductive workers can be reduced. In an underdeveloped country this often means increasing the number of unemployed who then either move to a more developed country which can employ them or are supported locally in some other way — by government relief, relatives, or marginal employment. In a developed country, eliminating inefficient work practices means releasing workers who can then be employed in more productive areas of the economy although they may need retraining and various aids and encouragement to move. (3) "Underemployment" in the service industries can be reduced. (4) Those persons hitherto considered unemployable can be introduced into the labor force. Typically these are women, the elderly, and the physically handicapped.

In the long run rationalization of manpower involves raising the ratio of machinery to labor and changing the organization of production so as to absorb the entire labor force and to make each worker as productive as possible. Whereas the short-run situation assumes the capital equipment and productive technology of the society to be relatively fixed, the long-run approach concentrates on changing them to make optimal use of the available resources of both capital and labor. Every country could move further along the road to rationalization than it now has, in both short-run and long-run terms, but some European countries have moved much further ahead on the road to labor force rationalization than others. Southern European countries have low degrees of rationalization in their labor force: they have a great number of underemployed workers and workers of low productivity; they use relatively little capital in production; they typically "waste" their unemployables from an economic standpoint. They are countries of emigration. Sweden provides an example of a country which already has rationalized its labor force: it has relatively few persons unemployed or underemployed; it uses capital equipment extensively and intensively; it has programs for bringing women, handicapped persons, members of the Lapp minority, and others traditionally excluded from the labor market into that market. Yet Sweden has a continuing labor shortage, and especially in relation to its small total population, it is a significant importer of labor.

While different degrees of rationalization of the labor force can affect migration, they are not always directly correlated with the amount of import or export of labor. Some countries in eastern Europe have low rationalization but will not allow their underemployed to leave, and Asiatic countries cannot find places which will accept their unemployed and underemployed. France is an example of a country which imports large amounts of labor, but compared to other northern European countries has a relatively nonrationalized labor force. As late as 1946, 36.5 percent of its laborers were in agriculture (including forestry and fishing), but there has been a considerable increase in agricultural efficiency since then, so that by 1965 only 18.2 percent were in these primary occupations.[11] It is in the tertiary occupations that one sees the great waste of labor today in France: there are innumerable little shops and restaurants (many of them attracting few customers), and selling is by weight and by small unitary items instead of in prepackaged form (so that several salesmen are required in tiny foodshops); there are large numbers of domestic servants, often using primitive household equipment; hand labor is used in cleaning streets and, to a considerable extent, in construction; two men are employed on each bus (sometimes a baggage handler in addition); a woman rents facilities in each public toilet; and a whole family (*concierge*) is

11

Table 1. Economic Indexes for European Countries of Immigration and Emigration

Country	Percentage of Civilian Occupied Manpower in Agriculture in 1965	Gross National Product at Current Market Prices per Capita in 1965 (US $)	Private Consumption Expenses per Capita in 1965 (US $)	Cars per 1,000 Inhabitants in 1965	Telephones per 1,000 Inhabitants in 1965	Index of "Real" Private Consumption per Capita (US in 1960 = 100)[a]
Countries of Immigration						
Belgium	5.7%	$1,780	$1,170	132	162	53.6
France	18.2	1,920	1,230	197	124	54.3
Germany (FR)	11.1	1,900	1,080	164	148	56.1
Luxembourg	13.5	1,700[b]	1,030[b]	185	243	[c]
Netherlands	9.5	1,550	900	103	188	45.0
Sweden	11.5	2,500	1,410	231	450	77.4
Switzerland	9.2	2,330	1,360	144	384	59.1
United Kingdom	3.5	1,810	1,160	167	188	61.7
Countries of Emigration						
Greece	54.7[d]	590[e]	420[e]	11	58	13.4
Ireland	32.4	920[e]	650[e]	99	75	22.0
Italy	26.1	1,100	690	106	116	30.8
Portugal	41.6[d]	420	310	25	60	17.0
Spain	35.1	570[e]	390[e]	25	87	19.5
Turkey	75.3[d]	250	[c]	3	12	9.8
Yugoslavia	56.9[f]	[c]	[c]	9	22	13.5

SOURCES. For all countries except Yugoslavia: *OECD Observer*, No. 26 (February 1967), pp. 19–26, 37. For Yugoslavia: Federal Institute for Statistics, *Statistical Pocketbook of Yugoslavia, 1966* (Belgrade, 1966), pp. 20, 26, 69–70.   [d] Estimate by OECD.   [e] 1964 data.   [a] The Beckerman method was used.   [b] 1963 data.   [c] Data are not available.   [f] 1961 data.

maintained to stand guard in each apartment house. (One could raise the question whether the huge bureaucracy and police force of France do not also belong in this category of nonrationalized tertiary occupations.) While French manufacturing has dramatically increased in efficiency since World War II by using modern machinery and managerial techniques, there is still a French tendency to keep repairing old things that could more economically be replaced with new items, and a tendency to favor nepotism in the employment of sub-managers which keeps the labor component in the cost of production comparatively high.

Sweden, with its relatively rationalized labor force, and France, with its labor force still not nearly so rationalized but gradually becoming more so, are heavy importers of foreign workers — in both countries 4–6 percent of their labor force is made up of nationals of other countries. So the macroscopic force stimulating migration today is not purely economic; if for some reason migration of foreign labor were to be cut off, France would probably make more use of capital, speed up the rationalization of its labor force, and thereby raise the average gross national product per capita. In this sense the steady immigration into France is slowing down economic progress. Obviously there are noneconomic factors on the macroscopic level encouraging the immigration of foreign workers. In the case of France, these are a traditional attachment to the lavish use of unskilled labor (just noted) and the policy of the French government to "normalize" the age composition of its population and to raise the birth rate. France also maintained an open-door policy toward Algerians from 1947 to 1962 as a political means of tying Algeria to it; the United Kingdom has had a similar policy toward Commonwealth nations, which it modified in 1962.

Even though the "pull" of a country for immigrants includes factors such as desire for demographic "health" or balance, political intentions of tying emigrant countries to it, or traditional demands for cheap non-rationalized labor, that country is not going to succeed in attracting immigrants unless it is economically much better off than the countries with labor surpluses and can pay higher real wages. In Table 1 are listed the chief European countries of emigration and immigration during the 1960's, with selected statistical indexes of standard of living to indicate the macroscopic economic reasons why they are countries of emigration and immigration. The countries of immigration are obviously much richer than the countries of emigration. Italy, long divided between a rich north and a poor south, provides a partial exception among the countries of emigration; as already noted, it is rapidly ceasing to be a country of emigration.

Migrants in Europe

Before turning to the central topic of the integration or acceptance of immigrants, the extent, directions, and history of cross-national migration in Europe should be examined. Some statistics on the extent of this migration are presented in Tables 2 and 3. The total net emigration reported in Table 2 is much lower than the total net immigration reported because (1) France and the United Kingdom drew a great number of their immigrants from outside the European countries of emigration listed, as did the Federal Republic of Germany before 1962; (2) some listed countries of immigration received Europeans from countries not listed as emigrant countries (e.g., Finns going to Sweden); (3) countries of emigration do not know about all the population they lost, since some emigrants leave clandestinely (notably from Portugal) and others leave as "tourists" rather than as emigrants. (However, countries of immigration quickly catch up with the presence of "tourists" who plan to stay permanently

Table 2. Migration Indexes for European Countries of Immigration and Emigration

Country	Net Immigration (+) or Emigration (−)		Active Occupied Foreign Population in 1964	
	Annual Average for 1960–65	Percentage of Total Estimated Population in 1965	Number	Percentage of Total Active Occupied Population
Countries of Immigration				
Belgium	+24,000	0.3%	350,000[a]	9.8%
France	+296,000	0.6	1,200,000	6.2
Germany (FR)	+318,000	0.5	1,058,000	4.0
Luxembourg ...	+2,000	0.6	30,000	21.7
Netherlands ...	+9,000	0.1	46,000	1.6
Sweden	+17,000	0.2	147,000	4.0
Switzerland ...	+74,000[b]	1.2	782,000	32.3
United Kingdom	+66,000	0.1	1,500,000[a]	6.0
Countries of Emigration				
Greece	−40,000	0.5		
Ireland	−26,000[b]	0.9		
Italy	−86,000	0.2		
Portugal	−52,000	0.6		
Spain	−135,000	0.4		
Turkey	−52,000[c]	0.2		
Yugoslavia	−80,000[c]	0.4		

SOURCES. For all countries except Yugoslavia and Turkey: *OECD Observer*, No. 26 (February 1967), pp. 19–26, 37 (first two columns); Robert Descloîtres, "Adaptation of Foreign Workers to Industrial Work and Urban Life," MS/S/66.167 (OECD, June 1966), pp. 22–24 (last two columns). For Yugoslavia: *Migration Today*, No. 5 (December 1965), p. 62. For Turkey: Turkish Employment Service.
[a] Estimate by OECD.　　[b] Annual average based on 1960–64 only.
[c] Net migration for 1965 only (see footnote c to Table 3).

Table 3. Trends of Immigration (+) and Emigration (−) in European Countries, 1950 to 1965
(net migration in thousands, with statistical adjustments)

Country	Annual Average 1950–54	1955–59	1960	1961	1962	1963	1964	1965
Countries of Immigration								
Belgium	+3.2	+10.6	+7.0	−1.0ᵃ	+19.0	+34.0	+49.0	+31.0
France	+27.8	+156.0	+140.0	+180.0	+860.0	+250.0	+195.0	+141.0
Germany (FR)	+221.4	+297.2	+336.0	+419.0	+283.0	+224.0	+302.0	+344.0
Luxembourg	+0.9	+0.6	+0.6	+2.4	+2.8	+1.6	+3.1	+3.0
Netherlands	−20.6	−3.2	−13.0	+6.0	+17.0	−8.0	+14.0	+19.0
Sweden	+9.2	+9.8	+11.0	+14.0	+11.0	+12.0	+23.0	+33.0
Switzerland	+22.8	+32.0	+76.0	+101.0	+88.0	+57.0	+48.0	−1.0
United Kingdomᵇ ...	−33.6	−3.2	+39.0	+198.0	+97.0	+43.0	+7.0	+10.0
Countries of Emigration								
Greece	−13.8	−25.0	−26.0	−19.0	−49.0	−56.0	−44.0	−43.0
Ireland	−34.8	−44.4	−41.0	−30.0	−16.0	−17.0	−24.0	−24.0
Italy	−100.8	−127.4	−192.0	−177.0	−137.0	−56.0	−81.0	−85.0
Portugal	−64.2	−68.0	−68.0	−32.0	−55.0	−47.0	−55.0	−53.0
Spain..........	−51.8	−104.0	−138.0	−133.0	−119.0	−126.0	−158.0	−135.0
Turkeyᶜ	ᵈ	ᵈ	ᵈ	ᵈ	−11.2	−30.3	−66.2	−52.1
Yugoslavia	ᵈ	ᵈ	ᵈ	−1.5ᵈ	−34.0	−34.0	−56.0	−80.0

SOURCES. For all countries except Turkey and Yugoslavia: 1950–59 figures from ILO Automation Programme, *International Differences Affecting Labour Mobility* (Geneva: ILO, 1965), pp. 12–14, and from OECD, *Manpower Statistics 1950–1962* (Paris, 1963); 1960–64 figures from OECD, *Manpower Statistics 1954–1964* (Paris, 1965), corrected by unpublished OECD statistics; 1965 figures from unpublished OECD statistics. For Turkey: Turkish Employment Service. For Yugoslavia: 1965 figure from *Migration Today*, No. 5 (December 1965), p. 62; earlier figures from *Ekonomska Politika* (Belgrade), October 15, 1966, p. 1320.

ᵃ Not including correction from census.

ᵇ Figures for the United Kingdom did not include migrants from Ireland and, before 1962, did not include migrants from Commonwealth countries. Thus the data indicate a net emigration for Britain during the 1950's when in fact it was experiencing very heavy immigration from India, Pakistan, and the West Indies.

ᶜ Net immigration figures for Turkey are not available; reported here are the 161,300 persons aided by the Turkish Employment Service from 1961 through 1965. However, few Turkish emigrants had returned permanently by 1965, and for these five years only some 20,000 Turks emigrated without using the facilities of the Turkish Employment Service. Hence, the Turkish figures are roughly comparable to the OECD figures given for the other countries.

ᵈ Data not available, but in any case very small.

15

through a process of "regularization": when those who enter as "tourists" find a place to live and a job, they must register for residence and work permits, and thereby they get into the immigration figures.)

Furthermore, countries have different methods of counting immigrants and foreign residents, so that exact comparability is impossible. An OECD report, written by Robert Descloîtres and one of the best available studies of foreign workers, has this to say about the lack of uniform statistics:

The statistical categories used for immigrant workers or the foreign population vary considerably from one European country to the other. The timing and scope of surveys of this type of population also differ widely. In one country a thorough census is made, four times a year, of the "controlled" foreign workers, while the number of foreigners classified as "permanently established" is only estimated, at irregular intervals, over periods which cannot be compared with the period chosen for the first category (Switzerland). In another country the number of frontier and seasonal workers is included with that of permanent workers (Germany [FR]), whereas in a neighbouring country (Switzerland), they are deducted. In another country, an annual count is made of foreign workers registered at the National Immigration Office, but not of those who leave the country, and some of the non-active immigrants, women and children, who accompany the migrant workers are not counted at all (France). In another case, only the "initial work permits" issued in the course of one year are added up, so that there is no way of knowing, except by rather hazardous guesswork, the total number of foreign workers employed at a given time (Belgium). At fairly long intervals, however, a national census provides accurate figures for both the total foreign population and the active foreign population in a particular country (Netherlands, Belgium, France).

The application of the principle of free movement of persons, introduced by the Treaty of Rome, as well as special provisions governing relations between various States with regard to migration (France and Algeria, United Kingdom and Ireland, Belgium and the Netherlands, etc.) are further obstacles to the statistical control of large numbers of foreign immigrants, so that it is difficult to build up a true picture of migratory movements in Western Europe. . . . the controls carried out by emigration countries do not always provide a means of making the necessary check and cross-check. Some of these operations are, moreover, conducted in a rather irregular manner. Indeed, emigrants frequently cross their country's frontiers not as "workers" but as "tourists." Finally, in some extreme and special cases the clandestine nature of the population movement (Portuguese into France) makes any counting impossible.

For all these reasons — and many others besides, since we can only give an outline here — it is impossible to assemble data that are all equally precise, broken down into identical categories and comparable in time.[12]

Despite these inadequacies in the statistics, Tables 2 and 3 permit one to make the following observations: (1) The European countries with the highest number of immigrants between 1950 and 1965 were the Federal Republic of Germany, France, and Switzerland. The United Kingdom also had heavy immigration during this period, although the figures do not indicate this. Figures for the United Kingdom did not include migrants from Ireland and, before 1962, did not include migrants from Commonwealth countries although during the 1950's Britain was experiencing a heavy immigration from India, Pakistan, and the West Indies. (2) Switzerland and Luxembourg have by far the highest *percentages* of foreigners in the active working force. Intermediate positions are held by Belgium, France, the United Kingdom, West Germany, and Sweden. West European countries with low percentages of foreigners in their active working force are the Netherlands (1.6 percent), Austria (1.2 percent, mostly seasonal workers), Norway (1.0 percent), and Denmark (0.5 percent). Among these countries with low percentages of foreign workers only the Netherlands since 1960 has been receiving a small flow of immigrants, and it will be considered a "country of immigration" for the purposes of this study, even though a significant small proportion of its own nationals emigrate overseas. (3) Beginning in 1963 Spain surpassed Italy as the leading European country of emigration in terms of absolute *numbers*. (4) In terms of *proportions* of their total population emigrating, Ireland, Portugal, Greece, Yugoslavia, and Spain are leading, in that order, while Italy has greatly reduced its net emigration.

The figures in Tables 2 and 3 are *total net* migration figures and hence do not reflect the dynamics of movement as well as do separate emigration and immigration figures. They also do not, for the emigrant countries, show the change in the direction of emigration toward Europe and away from the Americas. Thus Tables 4 and 5 are included to add to the picture of the dynamics of recent migration. Table 4 shows the great absolute and relative increase after 1959 in the Europe-bound emigration from Spain, Portugal, and Greece, and the peak that was reached by Italy in 1961. It also shows that, whereas Spain, Portugal, and Greece sent only a minority of their emigrants to European countries in 1959, Spain had 87 percent going in this direction by 1964, Greece had 80 percent, and Portugal had 69 percent. Table 4 also shows the huge increase in immigration for Germany, Belgium, and France between 1959 and 1964, the slower increase and stabilization of immigration for the United Kingdom and Switzerland, and the slight decline in immigration for Luxembourg. Table 5 shows the dimensions of the migration to certain European countries from non-European countries during this same time period: the United Kingdom received a huge wave of non-European immigrants that peaked in 1961–62; France received a smaller wave of Algerians that peaked in 1963; smaller but significant numbers of Africans and Asians went to Germany and Belgium.

Cross-national migrations are not new in Europe, although their direc-

Table 4. Intra-European Immigration (+) and Emigration (−),
1959 to 1964 (in thousands)

Country	1959	1960	1961	1962	1963	1964
Countries of Immigration						
Germany (FR)						
Number	+84.4	+250.5	+344.7	+379.6	+362.5	+428.2
Index[a]	100	313	429	474	456	531
Belgium						
Number	+6.8	+8.7	+11.9	+21.7	+29.7	+31.6
Index	100	128	175	319	427	462
France						
Number	+108.0	+157.8	+175.8	+208.2	+216.8	+275.0
Index	100	146	163	193	201	255
Luxembourg						
Number	+13.1	+13.3	+14.3	+9.1	+9.2	+10.6
Index	100	101	109	70	70	81
United Kingdom						
Number	+40.9	+47.2	+52.9	+48.6	+43.9	+60.8
Index	100	115	129	119	107	139
Switzerland						
Number	+273.9	+341.9	+422.6	+455.8	+445.1	+455.4
Index	100	125	154	166	159	166
Countries of Emigration						
Spain						
Number	−24.1	−40.8	−108.8	−149.9	−154.0	−185.3
Index	100	169	451	622	639	769
Percentage of total emigration to Europe	41%	51%	75%	85%	86%	87%
Greece[b]						
Number	−6.7	−26.9	−39.6	−60.8	−74.2	−79.5
Index	100	400	591	907	1,104	1,186
Percentage of total emigration to Europe	28%	56%	67%	72%	74%	80%
Italy						
Number	−169.3	−309.9	−329.6	−315.8	−258.7	−236.6
Index	100	183	195	187	159	140
Percentage of total emigration to Europe	72%	81%	85%	86%	86%	83%
Portugal						
Number	−3.7	−3.8	−6.0	−9.2	−17.1	−38.4
Index	100	103	166	243	462	1,038
Percentage of total emigration to Europe	11%	12%	18%	28%	44%	69%

SOURCE. Attilio Oblath, "Migration in Europe: Recent Trends and Prospects," in International Institute for Labour Studies, "Conference on the Migration of Workers to Europe" (Geneva, 1965), pp. 7–8.

[a] In all cases 1959 = 100, except for Turkey where 1961 = 100.

[b] Slightly higher emigration figures and a figure of 87,242 for 1964 are reported in Center of Planning and Economic Research, *Draft of the Five Year Economic Development Plan for Greece (1966–1970)* (Athens, December 1965), p. 44.

Table 4 — Continued

Country	1959	1960	1961	1962	1963	1964
Turkey[e]						
Number	0	0	−4.1	−10.9	−39.8	−71.1
Index			100	264	965	1,724
Yugoslavia[d]						
Number			−74.9	−33.7	−56.5	−63.0

[e] Since few Turks migrated overseas, the percentage of total emigration to Europe is practically 100 percent for all years. Very few Turks, mostly professionals, emigrated before 1961, so unknown figures for 1959 and 1960 are given as 0. It is estimated that between 1961 and 1966, 20,000 workers emigrated unknown to the Government Employment Office. In 1965, 51,520 emigrated from Turkey.

[d] No figures are available for years before 1961, but in January 1962 it was estimated that there were 74,850 Yugoslavs employed in other countries. The percentage of total emigration to Europe is practically 100 percent for all years. Yugoslav authorities estimated that 300,000 persons had emigrated from their country by October 31, 1966, practically all of them to countries in western Europe (*Ekonomska Politika,* November 12, 1966).

Table 5. Immigration[a] to European Countries by Nationals of Non-European
Countries, 1959 to 1964 (in thousands)

Country	1959	1960	1961	1962	1963	1964
Germany (FR)	5.0	8.9	15.7	17.0	15.0	14.2
Belgium	0.2	0.2	0.4	0.8	3.6	9.0
France[b]	18.0	16.0	33.0	25.1	50.5	40.0
United Kingdom[c]	21.1	57.8	123.2	92.5	66.0	75.5

SOURCE. Attilio Oblath, "Migration in Europe: Recent Trends and Prospects," in International Institute for Labour Studies, "Conference on the Migration of Workers to Europe" (Geneva, 1965), p. 9.

[a] Figures for Germany and Belgium report gross immigration; for France and the United Kingdom, net immigration.

[b] Figures refer to Algerians only, and from 1962 on include also civilian Moslem transients.

[c] Figures include only Commonwealth countries, but not the Federation of Rhodesia and Nyasaland.

tions are somewhat so.[13] In the years 1914–18, not only was there tremendous emigration from southern Europe overseas to the Americas, but numerous northern Italians moved across the frontier to Switzerland and France; neighboring Spaniards, Belgians, and Swiss, and more distant Poles also migrated to France; Austrians, Poles,[14] Serbians, Belgians, and Dutch went to Germany; Germans, Dutch, Italians, and Poles moved to Belgium. The early migrants to France and Germany were mainly agricultural workers; those to Belgium, mainly miners. While many of the worker immigrants were seasonal rather than permanent, their numbers were substantial. In 1910 foreigners constituted about 15 percent of Switzerland's population, only slightly less than the 17 percent attained in

1964; in 1907 the proportion of foreign workers in Germany's labor force was higher than in 1965. The proportion of foreigners in France did not reach a peak until 1931, but then it was significantly higher than today. France was the leading country of immigration during the interwar years of 1919–31, with most of its economic immigrants coming from Poland and Italy, and refugees coming from White Russia and Armenia (in Turkey). With the partial exception of France, Europe was much less permissive in allowing cross-national migration than it had been before World War I. Part of this was due to poor economic conditions, but part was due to growing nationalism and xenophobia.[15] The post-World War II years saw a resumption of the liberal policy, and there was an increase of immigration — mainly of refugees at first. For France this new policy included a liberalization of the law on naturalization, which caused the number of Frenchmen of foreign birth to rise sharply. By 1962 there were 1,266,680 naturalized persons and 1,815,740 foreigners — respectively 2.72 percent and 3.90 percent of the French population.[16]

The first decade after the end of World War II saw the relocation of many refugees in Europe.[17] French, Belgians, Dutch, and other Allied nationals who had been forced into the German "work camps" during the war now returned home, while Germans who lived in Prussia, the Sudetenland, and other eastern territories were expelled into a narrower Germany. Since most of Europe was still recovering economically from the war, there was little by way of strictly economic migration within Europe, although economic motives for migration were undoubtedly mixed with political and ideological ones. The chief direction of economic migration, and much of the refugee relocation also, was overseas. During the decade 1945–55, "The chief countries of emigration have been Germany, Austria, Italy, Greece, and the Netherlands; the chief non-European countries of reception, the United States, Canada, Australia, Israel, Argentina, Venezuela, and Brazil."[18] Table 6 shows that Europe was not the major destination of most of the European displaced persons or other migrants in the decade following World War II. Some eight million Europeans moved across international lines between 1946 and 1954, but only three of the ten countries leading in their reception were European, and these were near the bottom of the list. The leading European country of immigration in that period was the United Kingdom, which recovered economically from the war more rapidly at first than the other war-involved nations of Europe.

In the years following World War II the United Kingdom kept its doors open to natives of Commonwealth countries, and there began a wave of immigration from Asia (particularly Pakistan and India) and from the West Indies (particularly Trinidad and Jamaica). The United Kingdom imposed restrictions on immigration from Commonwealth colored nations in 1962, but the easy terms had at first only a temporary effect of reducing immigration: in 1960 there were 60,000 immigrants; 1961, 130,000; 1962, 30,000; 1963, 67,000; 1964, 100,000.[19] In 1965 the United Kingdom raised its barriers still higher against immigration from the Commonwealth colored nations, and from that time immigration began to fall.

During this time France was the major country in continental Europe to encourage immigration, and it had demographic and political reasons as well as economic ones for doing so. Alfred Sauvy of the Institut National d'Etudes Demographiques convinced high French officials that they should make up their demographic losses from war and a low birth rate. As part of this effort France made a strong attempt to retain Algeria as an integral part of the nation and permitted Algerians to migrate freely into European France.[20]

Table 6. Leading Countries of Immigration, 1946 to 1954

Country	Immigrants
United States	1,700,000
Canada	1,100,000
Australia	900,000
Israel	790,000
Argentina	760,000
Venezuela	500,000
United Kingdom	440,000
Brazil	410,000
France	390,000
Belgium	290,000

SOURCE. W. D. Borrie, *The Cultural Integration of Immigrants* (Paris: UNESCO, 1959), p. 17.

When Algeria achieved national independence in 1962, there was no decline of immigration but rather an increase. While the annual average immigration was 15,000 between 1954 and 1961, it rose to 25,000 in 1962, and to 50,000 in 1963.[21] In 1964 Algerians were made subject to labor and health controls, the same as France imposed on other non-EEC nationals, and immigration fell.[22] Black Africa — especially Senegal, Mali, and Mauretania — increased its emigration until by the end of 1964 about 35,000 black workers were in France (half in the Paris area).[23] From 1955 until 1962, 500,000 Asians, Africans, and Antilleans immigrated.[24] "In 1936 there were only 90,000 emigrants from the African continent living in France, 72,000 of them from North Africa; at the present time [1965] 700,000 are living in France (mainly), Belgium, Germany, Switzerland and Great Britain. There are also over one million persons from

21

Asia and the Americas living in Europe, three-quarters of them in the United Kingdom." [25]

The chief sources of cross-national migration in Europe in the 1960's were from within Europe itself, as shown by Table 7. West Germany drew from all labor-exporting countries of southern Europe, with the number from Greece, Spain, Turkey, and Yugoslavia growing each year. France, as already noted, kept receiving a stream of migrants from Italy, but its immigration from Spain and Portugal [26] became almost as large. Switzerland, while primarily relying on Italy for immigrant workers (although increasingly they were from southern rather than northern Italy), drew a growing number of migrants from Spain. In 1963 Switzerland adopted a policy of forcing its employers to cut down on their number of foreign workers, and in the succeeding years Switzerland became an exporter, rather than an importer, of foreign (non-Swiss) labor. Immediately after World War II, Sweden was the beneficiary of immigrants — both skilled and unskilled — from the Baltic countries (by then politically absorbed into the Soviet Union). Sweden's continuing labor shortage led to an agreement among the Scandinavian nations for free movement of labor, and it came to rely most heavily on Finland for unskilled labor, although significant numbers of workers came also from Italy, Greece, Yugoslavia, and Turkey. The Benelux countries came to draw on labor from all of southern Europe, as well as on a small stream from Asia and Africa. The United Kingdom kept its traditional reliance on Ireland for unskilled labor, but otherwise obtained very few workers from Europe; as noted earlier, the United Kingdom for a while also relied heavily for labor on the colored Commonwealth countries of India, Pakistan, and the West Indies. For over a century after 1841, Ireland's emigration was larger than its natural increase so that the country reduced its total population from 6,529,000 in 1841 to 2,818,300 in 1961; even after 1961 emigration absorbed most of Ireland's natural increase. [27]

The situation regarding intra-European migration as of early 1967 can be summarized from a survey prepared for the *New York Times* by Robert C. Doty. [28] According to this survey, based on interviews with government officials all over Europe, there were approximately five million European migrant workers in countries of Europe other than their own by the end of 1966. About 2,000,000 were Italians; 600,000 Spaniards; 400,000 Portuguese; 200,000 to 300,000 Yugoslavs; 250,000 Greeks; and 196,-000 Turks. They were located in France (2.2 million), West Germany (1.1 million), Switzerland (800,000), Belgium (650,000), Sweden (180,000), the Netherlands (75,000), and, in lesser numbers, in a half dozen other countries. "Britain provided no figures on workers from the Continent, but Italy alone lists more than 150,000 of her nationals there."

During the fall and winter of 1966–67, Doty reports, some 100,000 returned home because of unemployment, mainly from West Germany, Britain, Belgium, and the Netherlands (and some from Switzerland because of the restrictionist policy adopted there). These countries also were no longer accepting "tourists" from south Europe, who tried to enter the countries of immigration without labor contracts from employers and hoped to find work on the spot. Doty's figures do not include, of course, the many millions of Europeans who migrated somewhat earlier to other countries of Europe and who were naturalized or otherwise became citizens because their spouses or fathers were citizens. Nor do the figures include the more than one million non-Europeans living in the United Kingdom, and the approximately 700,000 non-Europeans living in France. The figures also do not take into account the *frontaliers*, or border-crossers, who earn their living in one country but live in an adjacent one — crossing the border every workday or staying in the "immigrant" country for only a short period each time they migrate.

For all the countries of immigration, the importation has not been only of unskilled labor; skilled labor and highly trained technicians have come too, although in smaller proportions. For example, Yugoslav officials estimated that 15 percent of the Yugoslavs working abroad in 1965 were either specialized skilled workers or professionals, including doctors, engineers, architects, and scientific workers, who were badly needed for the economy of their own country.[29] It was estimated in October 1966 that 5,000 Yugoslavs with university qualifications were living abroad, all recent emigrants.[30] Professionals and technicians from other eastern European countries — notably Poland and Bulgaria — also go to western countries, including Germany which their governments do not officially recognize. The demand for professionals and technicians has been especially great in countries — such as the United Kingdom and the Netherlands — that have lost some of their natively educated people to overseas nations,[31] and in countries — such as Sweden and Germany — that have enjoyed a rapidly rising standard of living. The "underdeveloped" countries of southern Europe, Asia, and Africa, as well as developed but not rapidly expanding countries such as Norway (which has lost technicians to Sweden) and Austria (which has lost technicians to Germany), are the victims of a significant "brain drain."

Not only these, but also many of the labor-importing countries of western Europe which are considered in this book as countries of immigration have been losing professionals and technicians to rich overseas nations (especially the United States, Canada, and Australia). It is estimated that 2,200 scientists and engineers migrated each year during 1956–61 from western Europe to the United States alone. Losses to the United States

Table 7. Origin of Foreign Labor Force in Immigrant Countries (in thousands)

Country of Emigration	Belgium (12/31/64)	France (1962)	Germany (6/30/65)	Luxembourg (1964)	Netherlands (6/30/65)	Sweden (10/1/66)	Switzerland (12/31/65)	United Kingdom[a] 1960	United Kingdom[a] 1966
Greece	6.0	4.4	181.7	[b]	2.2	5.5	7.3	3.4	3.4
Italy	64.9	305.0	335.8	15.0	7.8	5.8	454.7	68.1	24.6
Portugal	0.7	30.1	10.5	0.5	0.9	0.4	[b]	2.3	3.9
Spain	12.9	213.0	180.6	2.5	16.0	3.2	77.3	17.1	26.6
Turkey	5.3	7.5	121.1	[b]	5.8	1.3	4.8	0.8	1.3
Yugoslavia	1.2	10.1	64.1	[b]	1.1	11.9	5.3	8.9	1.4
EEC countries (except Italy)	45.2	68.4	116.9	13.5	29.0	18.7[c]	150.3[d]	[e]	[k]
Special countries	25.0[f]	219.3[g]	59.6[h]		5.2[i]	105.6[j]	39.8[h]		
Stateless or uncertain	1.2	10.9	12.4	1.0	2.9	5.4[l]	12.3[m]		[b]
Other European countries	5.4	117.6	34.0	0.5	4.4	17.0	58.4	239.5	57.4
Non-European countries (except special countries)	5.3	73.4	47.8	0.5	4.4	0.5	[b]	66.6	45.9
Total[n]	172.9	1,065.2	1,164.4	33.5	79.6	175.4	810.2	405.9	164.5

24

SOURCES. For Belgium and France: estimated by OECD from census figures. For Germany and the Netherlands: semiannual tally of work permits. For Luxembourg: estimated on basis of work permits issued and placements registered, but does not include frontier or detached workers. For Sweden: aliens registered as being gainfully employed. For Switzerland and the United Kingdom: census figures; for Switzerland figures do not include workers not under federal control. Since a variety of definitions, categories, and dates are used in calculating the labor force in various countries, the figures in the table are not strictly comparable.

[a] Figures reported are only for those registered with the police; since 1961 aliens are not required to register after four years' residence in the UK. For this reason, the figures as of December 31, 1960, are also offered.

[b] Very small number; included in appropriate other category.

[c] Germans and Netherlanders only.

[d] Germans and French only.

[e] Included in other European countries; 1960 figures include Polish and Hungarian refugees.

[f] Mostly from Belgium's former colonies.

[g] Estimate of 200,000 Algerians and 19,300 Moroccans.

[h] From Austria.

[i] Mostly from the Netherlands' former colonies.

[j] Including 72,811 Finns, 19,379 Danes, 13,377 Norwegians.

[k] Estimate of 500,000–600,000 immigrants from other parts of the Commonwealth plus 350,000 from the Irish Free State, in 1963, but these are considered citizens, not foreigners, and so are not included in the figures.

[l] Including 1,937 Balts and 3,466 Hungarians.

[m] Hungarians only.

[n] Because of rounding, the columns do not add exactly.

were proportionately heaviest from Switzerland (17.0 percent), Norway (16.2 percent), the Netherlands (15.1 percent), Ireland (9.3 percent), Sweden (8.8 percent), Germany (8.2 percent), and the United Kingdom (7.4 percent).[32] Only France (0.9 percent) and Italy (1.3 percent) were not losing many of their scientists and engineers to the United States. The trend was worst for the United Kingdom, whose loss rose from 660 in 1962 to almost 1,000 in 1963. In 1964 the United Kingdom lost to all countries a total of 900 physicians, 3,100 nurses, 2,600 teachers, 2,600 professional and mining engineers and surveyors, 200 physicists, and 100 biologists.[33] A special committee of the United States government, called the Inter-Agency Council on International Educational and Cultural Affairs, reported that in the fiscal year 1963, 27,930 professional and technical workers from all countries migrated to the United States.[34] This figure rose to 30,039 in the fiscal year 1966, when they constituted 9.3 percent of the total number of immigrants. About 40 percent came from Europe, 29 percent from other North American countries, 20 percent from Asia, 8.4 percent from South America, 1.6 percent from Africa, and 1.1 percent from Australia, New Zealand, and the Pacific Islands. While the council acknowledged that the number of professional and technical immigrants had been rising slowly, it did not believe that the situation was critical, and it advised that the main steps to stem the migration should be taken by foreign governments — to improve conditions for their professional and technical workers — rather than by the United States government. It held that the role of the United States government should be limited to (1) aiding foreign governments to "do more to deal with domestic causes of the emigration"; (2) encouraging American businesses and institutions with branches abroad to employ more non-Americans trained or living in the United States and to place them in these branches; (3) asking American universities to encourage their foreign graduates to return to their home countries.[35] This limited role was advised for the United States government because the council felt that the "brain drain" to the United States had been exaggerated. This was in spite of widespread criticism of the "brain drain" from Europe, and the many reports in European newspapers of eminent scientists migrating to the United States because their research budgets had been cut.[36] The British government has responded so far by having the management consultants' Management Selection Group set up an office dubbed "Brain Gain," with a recruiting program operating out of New York, San Francisco, and Toronto, to try to encourage disenchanted British engineers, managers, and scientists to return home.[37]

While several of the European countries of immigration are seeking professional and technical workers from the less developed countries, they do not uniformly create the conditions necessary to attract them. Professional organizations — notably those of physicians, pharmacists, lawyers, and social workers — in some countries of immigration place barriers on the acceptance of foreign-trained professionals,[38] so the latter are sometimes found in lower positions than their training and skills would call for.

In sum, compared with cross-national migration before World War II, migration after 1956 had assumed these characteristics: (1) Migrants came longer distances rather than mostly from bordering countries. (2) There was less emigration to overseas countries. (3) There was more migration than Europe as a whole had experienced before. (4) Migrants were employed more in industrial than agricultural sectors. (5) While migration continued to be thought of initially as temporary, much of it became permanent; some who left went to other countries of immigration rather than home. (6) Particularly in France and the United Kingdom, a large percentage of migrants came from outside Europe. (7) Although most migrants continued to be unskilled, some who came were skilled workers, technicians, and professionals.

FUTURE TRENDS IN MIGRATION

Some aspects of the course of future migration can be predicted on the basis of postwar migration patterns and on the assumption that the present countries of immigration will remain economically prosperous and have continuing needs for more productive resources including skilled manpower.

A prediction concerning the future extent of cross-national migration in Europe must consider sociological, political, and economic factors. The sociological factors to be considered are the extent to which nationals of the countries of immigration favor the immigrants and facilitate their adjustment, the extent to which the migrants themselves find the social climate favorable in the countries of immigration in comparison with that of their native countries, and the extent to which institutional facilities have been set up to aid the process of adjustment to migration (including vocational training, job information, social security, housing location, transportation payments, permission to bring family members). These sociological factors are expressed in political ways — that is, by laws restricting, permitting, or encouraging the inward or outward movement of would-be migrants, and by laws setting up the institutional machinery to facilitate the migration and to aid in the integration or acceptance of the migrants. As already noted, another political factor affecting cross-national migration is the creation of refugees.

But it is the economic factors which are most important in the long run

27

in determining the extent of cross-national migration. The dominant economic factors are those of demand and supply — the demand in the countries of immigration for sources of labor not available within their national boundaries, and the supply in countries of emigration of unemployed or underemployed workers "available" for emigration. Before turning to these, some attention should be given to some minor economic factors which can be subsumed under the rubric of "costs of emigration." From the standpoint of the countries of emigration these costs are the ones of raising and educating young people to the age at which they will be most economically productive only to have their productivity lost to other countries, temporarily or permanently. Their departure may cause labor shortages and hence economic upsets, such as inflation, at home. During economic recessions, as in the winter of 1966–67, the emigrants may be "dumped" back on their home countries, creating great strain on social service funds. The migrants are mostly men, which disturbs the sex ratio and the marriage rate, and sometimes creates family disruption.

In contrast with the pre-World War II emigration — mostly overseas — the countries of emigration now look on their emigrants to other European countries as only temporary, whether or not this will in fact be the case. The philosophy of these countries is that they want these workers back and expect them to come back after a few years of training and working abroad. In the meantime, there are some compensating benefits to the countries of emigration: the migrant workers are getting training and experience in modern techniques of production which many bring back to their native lands; the costs of unemployment payments or social assistance to the unemployed are avoided; there may be less of a housing shortage; the migrants send some of their savings to their relatives in the home country, which provides foreign exchange to the governments of emigrant countries; and the returning migrants bring the rest of their savings home for investment in presumably productive enterprises. In 1963 the total savings of migrant workers remitted in currency to their home countries in Europe was conservatively estimated at between $800 million and a billion dollars.[39] An Italian government agency estimated that Italians alone remitted $522,260,000 in 1963 (this takes into account funds sent by Italians overseas, including those naturalized in their countries of immigration).[40] Yugoslav authorities estimated that remittances during the first ten months of 1966 amounted to $40 million, but that another $100 million had been placed in savings banks abroad by Yugoslav emigrants.[41] In addition, consumer goods were brought home and there were social security transfers. Some Turkish groups in Germany — following a policy encouraged by the Turkish government — were investing in domestic industrial and agricultural enterprises, and the returning nationals of all emigrant countries included some who had saved enough to start individual enterprises (informants say that hotels, taxi companies, and small shops are especially popular among returnees).

The costs to the countries of immigration of using migrant workers, unless they are to give them wages lower than those paid to national workers in order to compensate for these costs, are those involving training the workers to fit the specific requirements of jobs available in their countries; reception, orientation, housing, and sometimes transportation of the migrant workers; loss of experienced and trained workers when these return to their home countries; hiring special supervisory personnel who speak the language of the migrants in order to transmit to them the instructions of their employers; loss of remittances in the balance of international payments. While these costs are over and above those necessary to hire a national, nationals are not available for the jobs; otherwise the employers would rarely prefer hiring foreign labor. This does not always mean that nationals were fully employed. According to one source "half a million British-born workers choose to remain unemployed in the expectation of finding a 'suitable' occupation at a time when at least a million jobs are held by foreign workers." [42] The costs of using foreign labor are more than compensated for by having a cheap source of labor which increases national productivity yet involves low social overhead costs — the country of immigration does not have to bear the cost of raising and educating the workers and, since most workers do not bring their families, it is spared the cost of rearing and educating their children too. The cost to the emigrant country is further offset because "the receiving countries were able — certainly in the earlier stages of the movement — to utilize more fully their productive capacity, overcome the immobility of local labour, engage in profitable expansion, and moderate the rise in their general wage level. Large sectors of the local population gained the benefits of economic and social upgrading and greater social mobility." [43] Supporting this last point is Roger Girod's study in Switzerland which shows that the immigration of unskilled labor pushes up national labor into the higher status occupations, especially when the immigrants are prohibited from obtaining the better jobs. [44] Other side effects of an economic nature involve exports and imports, balance of international payments, contributions to social security and other funds (which may never be paid out if the migrant leaves the country), capital movements, wage levels, and length of working week, to name only several.

Some of the traditionally underdeveloped countries and regions are beginning to develop economically, and their birth rates have fallen; hence they no longer have a surplus of workers to send abroad. This is most apparent in the case of Italy, hitherto the main reservoir for western countries of immigration. As discussed above, Italian emigration is practically at an end since northern Italy has become prosperous and significant amounts of industry are developing in south Italy and its offshore islands. Spain lags behind Italy in industrialization but, beginning in 1964, its emigration rate slowed down as industrial development began to absorb the excess agricultural labor. Yugoslavia has definite plans for modernization, which are already bearing fruit, and its economic planners realistically foresee a radical reduction of emigration in the near future.[45] This leaves Portugal, Ireland, Greece, Turkey, and perhaps Finland as the remaining European countries of emigration. But all of these except Turkey are tiny countries, all have some prospects for economic development, and all expect a drop in their rate of natural increase, so that they are not likely to provide a sufficient supplement to the labor forces of the countries of immigration for many more years. Attilio Oblath of the ILO, after surveying all the relevant influences, concludes: ". . . if estimates of population increments, of economic planning and emigration policies, and of emigration trends are confirmed in a not too distant future, and if manpower reserves diminish, we shall probably see a reduction in the amplitude of migrations inside Europe."[46] In fact, it is likely that some of the present countries of emigration will soon begin to compete for foreign labor with the present countries of immigration — at least to the extent of attracting back their own former emigrants. The movement of Greeks and Spaniards to northern Italy and the return migration of workers to their home countries all over Europe shows that this is already beginning.

With this prospect, Europe can move in three possible ways:[47] (1) expand the search for foreign labor to Asia, Africa, and South America; (2) rationalize the existing labor force further; (3) invest capital abroad, especially in underdeveloped, labor-rich countries. Trends already under way suggest that Europe will get many of its future professionals and technicians from Asia and Africa, if only by retaining a proportion of those it now trains. But if it takes in many unskilled laborers from those continents, it is likely to develop problems of race and caste relations such as have already arisen in the United Kingdom. France is the European country that has so far shown the greatest openness to black-skinned workers, but there seems to be more evidence of discrimination and exclusion than has yet been publicly recognized.[48] Europe has not yet sought many immigrants from South America, perhaps because the direction of migration has traditionally been the other way and because the costs of transportation are high compared to those from European countries with excess labor still available. But much of Latin America is still underdeveloped, and its birth rate is extraordinarily high, so that finding in Latin America a major manpower reservoir for Europe is not beyond the limits of possibility. Dark-skinned Latin Americans will create the same race problems that Africans do, of course, but there are also potential emigrants of light skin color in Latin America. So far, only a very few of them have migrated to Europe, and these have gone mostly to France. It is possible that when Europe later seeks such migrants, particularly technicians and professionals, it will find itself in competition with the United States and Canada.

It is also possible that migration from eastern to western Europe will resume, as it already has significantly from Yugoslavia and to a slight extent from Poland. This will depend not only on an East-West *détente* which may already be developing, but also on the internal policies of the Soviet governments toward free mobility of labor and rationalization of labor. Yugoslavia has adopted both the latter policies, but the Soviet-bloc nations have thus far shown no signs of doing so. Rationalization of the labor force both in long-run and short-run terms is proceeding. The rationalization of agriculture is now going on apace in underdeveloped European countries, and it will produce the labor necessary for the future development of those countries. Only France among the present European countries of immigration has a sizable proportion of agricultural population yet to reduce (see Table 1). The modernization of industry has also been going on steadily in Europe, and only the more extensive use of mechanization and what is called "automation" will release manpower on this account. Sweden and Germany have already proceeded about as far as the United States to rationalize their service occupations, but France and Switzerland have a long way to go. France has many more unskilled laborers than are needed for a modern economy, particularly because it wastes people — that is, keeps them underemployed in service occupations of low productivity — although it has made progress in this respect since 1945. Another way to further rationalization is to find more suitable and more productive employment for those presently regarded as "unemployable." Many European countries have programs to employ these citizens as part of a humanitarian policy, but only Sweden among them has progressed significantly toward developing such programs as a part of a rational economic policy. Insofar as Europe turns increasingly toward rationalization to solve its manpower problems — and one of the predictions made here is that it will be forced to do so if the rate of economic progress continues at the present pace — it will rely less on cross-national migration. Nationalism and xenophobia — which exist in all countries, and in some countries more than in others — will aid this process. So will economic fears, fed on occasional recessions, as was demonstrated by the cutting down of the number of foreign laborers during the business recession in the winter 1966–67.[49] It is even possible to envisage the present heavy rate of cross-national migration in Europe as a brief episode in history.

The exception to all this is that rationalization in the use of unskilled labor will increase the demand for technicians, professionals, and possibly even certain categories of skilled workers. The present countries of immigration may do a better job of training (or retraining) their own technicians, professionals, and skilled workers from within their present population, but they may also seek them from other countries. They will have little problem getting them from Asia and Africa, but it is also possible that they will compete with, and seek to attract them from, the present emigrant countries of Europe. In other words, it is possible that, even though the emigrant countries will have increasing need for their trained workers, the latter will continue to emigrate because of the greater economic attractiveness of the richer countries of immigration.

A third policy for continuing economic development is to invest capital in other countries, particularly in labor-rich countries. Instead of moving labor to where capital is, capital can be moved to where labor is. If this does not create too heavy costs of transportation for raw materials and finished products, it is just as economically productive a process. Of course, a relatively small number of managers, supervisors, technicians, vocational teachers, and sometimes skilled and clerical workers have to be moved along with the capital investment. But the chief problem with this policy is political. Investments abroad almost invariably get both the investors and their governments into trouble with the government and local population of the less developed country. Sometimes this trouble goes so far as to lead to confiscation or nationalization with payment for the investment, and in the past it often led to "imperialistic" war. However, if the investment abroad is politically and economically satisfactory, it will result in a reversal of migration; the heavy movement toward the rich countries will stop, and a smaller movement toward the poorer countries will be substituted. To some extent, this policy is already in operation — a good deal of investment by the rich countries of Europe and North America in South America, Asia, and Africa has been made under the nonimperialistic regimes since World War II — but the political problems keep arising, and rich countries sometimes prefer to make gifts or loans to the poor countries rather than undertake direct investments. Gifts or loans require less migration, "permanent" and temporary, than do direct investments.

3 A THEORY OF ACCEPTANCE OF MIGRANTS

◄──

THE INDEPENDENT VARIABLES: FACTORS FACILITATING OR INHIBITING ACCEPTANCE

In order to consider the extent of the acceptance of foreigners and to ascertain factors associated with that acceptance the theory is proposed here that acceptance and integration of foreigners into a host society is a function of the following: (1) the openness of the host society; (2) the degree of attachment the immigrants feel to their society of origin (that is, the inverse of this should be correlated with measures of acceptance into the host society); (3) the similarity of the cultures of the country of emigration and the country of immigration. This theory thus considers the variables of "acceptance" and "integration" to be a function of the characteristics both of the country of emigration and the country of immigration and of the relationships between them. Before testing this theory with pertinent data, each of the independent variables will be considered in greater detail.

The openness of the host society is largely determined by the policies, programs, and practices (hereafter these three will be subsumed under "policies") of the country of immigration toward immigrants, the relevant policies being those of the government, employers, trade unions, and certain voluntary associations. Most important is the policy of government, since it reflects, to some extent at least, the attitude of the society as a whole toward the immigrants. It is measured by the laws governing conditions of entry, length of stay permitted, controls to which the immigrants are subjected, readiness to grant permission to bring nonworking wives and children, conditions for naturalization and change of name, and other such possibly restrictive stipulations. Openness of policy is further measured by the extent to which the government treats foreigners as equal to its own citizens in the allocation of benefits and the privilege of free movement within the country both geographically and occupationally. Moreover, it is indicated by the creation of special "facilities" for foreigners — such as classes to teach them the language of the country, "remedial" courses to "correct" any deficiency in the education of their children, access to mass media and public meeting places for presentation of information and entertainment of immigrants, and special housing for foreigners.

Just as the government has policies of equal or unequal treatment, and does or does not provide special facilities or opportunities for foreigners, so policies of individual employers, employers' associations, and trade unions affect the degree of openness of a country. The churches and certain voluntary associations may also provide special means to integrate foreigners. There is a minimal extent to which employers must have a positive policy toward immigrants or else there will be no immigration — that is, they must be willing to hire foreign workers and see to it that they have at least the minimum facilities for living (adequate wages and/or housing). Actually the employers in most immigrant countries of Europe have provided much more than a minimum to attract foreign laborers and to aid in their adjustment (major programs of employers will be summarized in Chapter 4). While the trade union movements in the various countries of immigration differ widely in their importance in general and in their policies toward immigrants specifically, there is at least a latent restrictiveness in the policy of trade unions toward immigrants: the unions do not want immigrant workers to enter the country freely when there is a shortage of jobs, and they do not want them to be used by employers to break strikes or otherwise weaken the bargaining strength of the unions.[1] On these matters trade unions can be explicit and make agreements with the government and employers to prevent immigrants from coming into the country to increase unemployment or to participate in strikebreaking. But on another matter — providing equal opportunities for immigrants to rise on the occupational ladder — the trade unions may resist, yet keep their attitude from public expression. (For specific activities of trade unions in relation to foreign workers see Chapter 4.) Native laborers may, however, favor immigration if it permits their own upward mobility and attainment of shorter working hours. Barkin summarizes the European trade unionists' attitude toward foreign workers by stating that it

. . . springs from a restrictionist outlook. Unions in immigrating countries have sought to ensure that the foreign laborer's stay is limited by contract, that he is not invited to areas and occupations where there is surplus manpower, and that he is not given preference over the domestic workers nor engaged on less favorable terms. Although they rarely take the initiative in urging a programme of liberal acceptance of foreign labor they have generally acquiesced to programmes developed by the government, usually inspired by industrial needs. They are likely to insist upon certain safeguards, such as equality of terms of employment, or possibly adequate housing as a condition for acceptance, and urge the foreign worker's participation in the elections for workers' councils. The more far-seeing unions have deliberately cultivated foreign workers to ensure their recruitment.[2]

34

Policies of restriction may exist without being explicitly directed against foreigners. Requirements for access to more desirable occupations, housing, recreational facilities, and welfare benefits may include categorical qualifications which automatically disqualify foreigners, even though nationality is not referred to. For example, graduation from certain national schools and residence in a region for at least ten years are requirements that disqualify foreigners — often intentionally — without being explicitly anti-foreign. Opening the opportunity for occupational mobility is one of the most important evidences of the acceptance of immigrants in a host country, and, with certain exceptions for specific industries or specific nationals with whose government there is a treaty, all occupational mobility is closed to immigrants for at least four years in every country of immigration (except within the EEC, an important exception), and in some countries for as long as thirteen years.[3] Bureaucratic delays when processing foreigners' applications is another means of excluding them. It is difficult to ascertain the full extent of discrimination in a society without detailed study. The social scientists of Europe, with the exception of those in Britain, have not done a great deal of research on discrimination against minority groups.[4]

Thus far only *present* policy has been discussed but *past* policy is also important since it helps to mold the image which the immigrant has of the country of immigration. If a country has had a tradition of openness, it may continue to attract immigrants even though it may have become less open in recent years. Migrants from a given country of emigration or a district of that country are likely to migrate to a country where their compatriots have gone before. The older body of immigrants will probably have developed some privileges in the host country such as achievement of part of the requirements for naturalization, more adequate housing, facility in using the host language, and so on. The early immigrants may have brought the measure of acceptance into the host society up to a fairly high level and thus the image of an open society is created even though in reality the host society has become more closed. This seems to be the situation with Switzerland today and it creates a serious difficulty for the research design of this study, as will be discussed later. The converse proposition is also true. A country may be very open and objectively attractive to immigrants, but if its policy is practically unknown to people in emigrant countries, they do not come.

The openness of a society is reflected not only in deliberate policy and formal practices, but also in attitudes and informal behavior of its citizens. While it is difficult to measure the relative level of prejudice toward outgroups, or xenophobia, this phenomenon exists and plays a role in the acceptance of immigrants. More general than the specific prejudices, or antagonisms toward outgroups, is what might be called the "flexibility of national character," or the ability of a culture to tolerate deviations. Invariably, immigrant cultures differ from native cultures in significant respects, and the ability of a native culture to tolerate deviation in its midst is a significant factor in the acceptance of the immigrants who bear that culture.[5]

The general proposition of the second independent variable is that the stronger the migrant's ties to the country of emigration, the less he will allow himself to be accepted by the host society. The ties that may bind the emigrant to his native country are those of the extended family (which probably rarely migrates as a unit), the church, the local community, and the nation. These ties are different in nature, and they seldom correlate in practice. Further, there may be a selective factor operating among emigrants to stimulate those individuals in the society with the weakest ties to emigrate. In a society where the typical individual is closely linked to the primary social institutions, the deviant individual may feel impelled to emigrate and to tie his fate to an alien society. There is no evidence that this is what is happening in Europe today. What little pertinent evidence there is suggests that most migrants are socially typical and psychologically normal, but the possibility that such a selective factor may be operating should not be overlooked.

Here we must consider the possibilities for maintaining the ties to the country of emigration, which operate independently of the strength of those ties. Most important is the physical distance between the country or region of emigration and the country or region of immigration. If the distance is short between these two, and hence the costs in money and time involved in returning for frequent visits are not great, the individual migrant is likely to retain more home ties. He may even then deliberately leave his wife and children in the home country since he can visit them regularly, and so resist all efforts to become involved in the life of the host society. At the other extreme, the overseas migrant has much more difficulty maintaining ties to the home country, and that immigrant is much more likely to seek and to allow himself to be drawn into social contacts with natives of the host society. Within Europe, there must be a qualitative difference between the Italian emigrant who goes to nearby Switzerland and the one who goes to distant Sweden (although sometimes Switzerland is a stop on the way to Sweden). Geographic closeness of the country of immigration to the country of emigration works *against* facilitation of acceptance for the very reason it works *in favor* of stimulating the migration itself.

Physical distance is not the only barrier to the maintenance of close ties by the emigrant to his native land. Political barriers can be more important where they exist: certain nations have erected barriers against emigration, and thus some of their emigrants are clandestine; this is the case for some of the emigrants from Spain and Portugal today, and it was formerly true of the Yugoslavs. Refugees from the Soviet countries can rarely return without penalty, and they find it difficult to maintain ties to their home countries. Refugees from Germany during the Hitler period very often cut their ties relatively quickly. Finally, there are the penalties which a country of immigration may set for leaving it — such as loss of job, loss of social security and other welfare privileges acquired by longevity, or loss of seniority acquired toward naturalization.

The third independent variable associates the acceptance of immigrants with the similarities, and sometimes the differences, between the country of immigration and the country of emigration. Acceptance of immigrants, and the willingness of migrants to be accepted, is something like a relationship in marriage: often similar and sometimes complementary characteristics contribute to its success. Immigrants' knowledge of the language of the host society may be hypothesized as one of the most important factors leading to mutual adjustment. Immigrants who have as their mother tongue the language of the host country today in Europe include the East German refugees in West Germany, some of the North Africans in France, and the Irish and other English-speaking people from the Commonwealth in the United Kingdom. The Italians migrating to Switzerland do not provide an example because the Italian-speaking area of Switzerland (Ticino) has very few jobs for immigrants, and practically all immigrants go to the German- or French-speaking areas of that country. However, it seems likely that immigrants from Romance-language nations like Italy, Spain, and Portugal have an easier time learning French (in France, Belgium, and *la Suisse romande*) than they do learning one of the Teutonic languages. People with higher education generally can learn a foreign language more readily than can an illiterate, partly because they are familiar with language structure in general and partly because they are more likely to have had contact with foreign languages before they migrate (through school courses, tourism, or reading).

Similarity in religion may be hypothesized to be a significant factor in the acceptance of migrants. Very few of the emigrants in Europe during the mid-1960's were Protestants, so it may be expected that Protestant countries of immigration pose difficulties for all their immigrants. A large proportion of the emigrants were from Roman Catholic countries (particularly Ireland, Italy, Spain, Portugal, and parts of Yugoslavia) and it could be instructive to compare their reception in Catholic and Protestant countries of immigration. The comparison could be even sharper in countries of immigration which have both Protestant and Catholic native regions — such as Germany, the Netherlands, and Switzerland. Some countries of emigration are neither Protestant nor Catholic — Greece and parts of Yugoslavia where the dominant religion is Greek Orthodox, and Turkey, North Africa, and parts of Yugoslavia where the dominant religion is Islam. The latter is a religion wholly alien to the European countries of immigration, and it is said that Muslims have considerable religious difficulties when living in northern Europe because their holy days fall on workdays, they are not sufficient in number to own a place of worship, and restaurants serve taboo food, such as pork.

Cultural and national character traits of other kinds may play a role in immigrants' acceptance in a country of immigration. The quiet and somewhat repressed peoples of northern Europe are sometimes reported to be distressed by the noisiness and boisterousness characteristic of most Mediterranean peoples of the lower classes. On the other hand, many individual Swedes say they enjoy the gaiety of the Italians. Differences in sex customs are frequently reported to be a source of difficulty between immigrants and natives. The equalitarian manners of girls in some countries of immigration are often misunderstood to be sexual invitations by immigrants whose cultures include a double standard of sex behavior. In countries of immigration where premarital sex relations are the norm, immigrant parents of teenage girls castigate the "sexual immorality."

Differences in secondary group institutions often attract immigrants to the culture of the immigrant country just as differences in primary group institutions often repel them. A southern European who has grown up hating his native government — which he believes exploits him and steals from him — is often attracted by the honest and welfare-minded governments he finds in northern Europe. He may also find attractive the numerous voluntary associations of Sweden, Switzerland, and the Netherlands because they permit him to participate in the general society in a way he could never do in most parts of southern Europe. The more highly developed "civic culture" of northern Europe is a difference that can attract. Greater personal freedom and less family dominance are aspects of primary group institutions in northern Europe which also sometimes attract southern Europeans.

One of the most important differences between immigrants and the population into which they move is a rural-urban difference. A considerable proportion of the "excess" population of emigrant countries comes from rural areas. In the post-World War II years, most of the jobs available in countries of immigration have been in manufacturing and construction enterprises located in cities, although the mines of Belgium, Luxembourg, Germany, and France have provided exceptions. Immigrants face problems adjusting not only to the national cultures of the immigrant countries but to the urban culture and to the specific occupations into which they move. Just how extreme this can be is suggested by the fact that many companies in Germany feel compelled to give their Turkish workers a course on traffic signals, because these nationals were found to be so ignorant of traffic safety rules as to be highly accident prone. Studies of internal rural to urban migration, particularly in Italy where the internal migrants are much the same type of people as the ones who make up a good share of the international migrants in Europe, have shown rural migrants have great difficulty adjusting even though there is little national-cultural difference operating.[6]

There is considerable discussion in the literature on the adjustment of immigrants concerning whether physical segregation and the existence of segregating institutions facilitates or retards acceptance and adjustment. On the one hand, it is held that segregation prevents social contact and the informal means of learning the culture of the host society. On the other hand, it is held that the existence of segregated neighborhoods and segregated institutions provides a temporary "shelter" for the culture-shocked immigrant — they provide him with means of entering the alien culture gradually and with knowledge of the social customs of the host society. Probably much of the argument between these two points of view could be dispelled if a distinction were made between voluntary and forced segregation. The evidence from studies of the early problems of immigrants indicates that they need and want a considerable degree of segregation, but that after a time their further acceptance in and adjustment to the host society requires breaking out of the bonds of segregation. If the segregation is voluntary, the latter can occur naturally; if it is forced, the breaking out may be all but impossible.

For the newly arrived immigrant to the United States there are a number of organizations to aid his initial adjustment and accommodation to the "new world": the Hebrew Immigrant Aid Society (HIAS) with its extensive welfare program, the Polish National Alliance (PNA) with its associated insurance offerings, the Japanese-American *tanomoshi* which loaned its members funds in times of personal crisis,[7] the various immigrant newspapers and magazines,[8] and the ethnic fraternal groups such as AHEPA and B'nai B'rith.[9] Milton Gordon states this very well: "The self-contained communal life of the immigrant colonies served . . . as a kind of decompression chamber in which the newcomers could, at their own pace, make a reasonable adjustment to the new forces of a society vastly different from that which they had known in the Old World." He believes the newcomer needs "the comfortable sociological and psychological milieu which the communality of his own group provides."[10] But participation of the immigrant in these ethnic institutions beyond the first

39

few years may have fostered an ethnic identification that inhibited acceptance by the now-native Americans, although in the American setting they offered psychological protection against majority group prejudice and discrimination.[11] Gordon, while opposed to the complete absorption of immigrants, takes a value position against the overly segregating ethnic community after the first few years of immigrant adjustment: "The major problem, then, is to keep ethnic separation in communal life from being so pronounced in itself that it threatens ethnic harmony, good group relations, and the spirit of basic good will which a democratic pluralistic society requires, and to keep it from spilling over into the civic arena of secondary relations to impinge on housing, jobs, politics, education, and other areas of functional activity where universalistic criteria of judgment and assignment are necessary and where the operation of ethnic considerations can only be disruptive and even disastrous."[12] In Europe some of these same kinds of immigrant institutions are growing up in the countries of immigration, although much more frequently some of their functions are provided by government.

THE DEPENDENT VARIABLES: WHAT HAPPENS TO PEOPLE

Thus far in presenting the theory of acceptance of immigrants only the factors *facilitating* their acceptance or *inhibiting* it have been examined. These are the independent variables of this analysis. In considering the dependent variables — that is, what happens to the immigrants and to the people in the country of immigration — some of the literature on "assimilation" and "absorption" must be taken into account. Much of this literature has been written by sociologists and historians of immigrant countries that have sought to retain their immigrants permanently, and hence to absorb them in some way into the dominant social system of the country. Such value premises do not need to be accepted in this study since the dependent variable of acceptance as defined here permits the immigrants to return to their home countries after several years or less. The value premise in the concept of acceptance is that they should return with positive attitudes toward the country of immigration, or at least with recognition of its positive qualities, so that they can utilize these positive qualities in their own lives and in their native countries and so they can look forward with equanimity and even with anticipation to an integration of nations. In the course of the present investigation no systematic studies of such attitudes among returned immigrants were found, nor could it be determined if returnees are representative of migrants generally or merely representative of the unsuccessful or dissatisfied ones among them. For these reasons it would seem suitable to select dependent variables from among the usual "indexes of assimilation," not because assimilation is desirable necessarily, but because assimilation itself is an index of acceptance or of positive attitudes toward the country of immigration.

S. N. Eisenstadt — from the vantage point of the student of Israel — offers a succinct statement of what is meant by assimilation, or "absorption" as he calls it: "The process of absorption, from the point of view of the individual immigrant's behavior, entails the learning of new roles, the transformation of primary group values, and the extension of participation beyond the primary group in the main spheres of the social system. Only in so far as these processes are successfully coped with are the immigrant's concept of himself and his status and his hierarchy of values re-formed into a coherent system, enabling him to become once more a fully-functioning member of society." [13] Following this statement, Eisenstadt refers to three indexes of absorption: (1) acculturation, or the learning of new roles, norms, and customs in the country of immigration; (2) personal adjustment, or the ways in which the new country affects his personality, his satisfaction, and his ability to cope with problems; and (3) institutional dispersion, or integration into the new institutions and structures. [14] Milton Gordon — from the vantage point of the student of immigrants to the United States, and not adopting absorption as a value premise — expands this list to seven assimilation variables: [15]

Subprocess or Condition	*Type or Stage of Assimilation*
1. Change of cultural patterns to those of host society	Acculturation, or cultural and behavioral
2. Large-scale entrance into cliques, clubs, and institutions of host society, on primary group level	Structural
3. Large-scale intermarriage	Amalgamation, or marital
4. Development of sense of peoplehood based exclusively on host society	Identificational
5. Absence of prejudice	Attitude receptional
6. Absence of discrimination	Behavior receptional
7. Absence of value and power conflict	Civic

Gordon's variables, except for the fifth and sixth which have been discussed in the first part of this chapter, will be considered to be dependent variables, for which measurable indexes will be sought.

Acculturation, or cultural assimilation — Gordon's first variable — is difficult to measure, but an effort may be made to do so through two indexes: (1) the proportion of immigrants who *complete* courses in the language of the host country (the proportion who know and use the language

41

may well be greater than this, but there is no way of ascertaining their number except through occasional spot studies); (2) the proportion of immigrants applying for change of name. This is a poor index for the purpose of this study, partly because it is a function of the extent to which the host society considers a "national" name to be important, which is the opposite of the acceptance being sought among the variables, and partly because it indicates an almost irreversible rejection of the native country of the immigrant, which is not part of the concept of "acceptance" used here, however much it may indicate "assimilation." Hence it has been rejected as an index of the dependent variable, but data on it will be reported for independent interest.

Gordon's second variable — structural assimilation — is expanded here to include secondary as well as primary groups and institutions (he discusses structural assimilation into secondary groups and institutions, but then unaccountably leaves them out of his summary list). The proportion of immigrants who become naturalized is not only an index of identificational integration but also an index of structural assimilation, in which the assimilation is into the secondary institution of the state. Because there is a requirement here for a certain period of residence before one becomes eligible for application for citizenship — ranging from five years for France, Germany, the Netherlands, and the United Kingdom, to fifteen years for Luxembourg — the proper measure is the number attaining citizenship in proportion to immigrants *eligible* for citizenship, rather than all immigrants. A larger proportion of Italians, who have been emigrating for a century, are eligible for naturalization than are Turks, who just began to emigrate in significant numbers in 1960.

Other measures of structural assimilation are (1) upward vertical mobility, which it is possible here to measure only crudely as the proportion of immigrants in other than unskilled occupations; (2) proportion of immigrants in nonethnic secondary associations such as trade unions and small businessmen's associations; (3) proportion of immigrants in nonethnic primary associations, such as clubs or cliques. For the last two measures no data have been located except in the form of guesses by persons in a position to make reasoned guesses.

In a most important sense, Gordon's third variable — intermarriage — is a measure of structural assimilation, and data for this will be reported for the various countries of immigration.

The fourth assimilation variable — the identificational one — can be measured by two antithetical indexes: the proportion of immigrants who become naturalized citizens and the proportion of immigrants who leave the immigrant country, either for their native lands or for other countries of immigration. The proportion of immigrants who leave the country for

42

other countries of immigration without first gaining citizenship would be an excellent (negative) measure of assimilation or acceptance, but it is impossible to find data on this.

Gordon's seventh assimilation variable — civic assimilation — could also theoretically best be measured by two antithetical indexes: the proportion of naturalized citizens voting and otherwise participating in the political process and the proportion of immigrants who come in conflict with the host society. No data on the first could be found, but some statistics on the crime rates of immigrant groups can be reported.

A hypothesis has been set up and measurable indexes to test it suggested: acceptance and adjustment of foreigners into a host society is a function of (1) the openness of the host society, (2) the weakness of attachment of the immigrants to their home society, (3) the similarity of the country of immigration to the country of emigration. Now the available data can be examined in order to test the hypothesis to see if it is sufficient to produce indexes for each variable in each of the countries of immigration and the countries of emigration.

An article in an OECD publication summarizes some prominent facets of the problem of cross-national adaptation in Europe today:

Between seven and eight million foreigners are living — and for the most part working — in the countries of Western Europe. A large number of the immigrants come from far afield, but even more significant than geographical distance is the social or cultural distance that separates many of the newcomers from the nationals: only about 15 per cent speak the same language, and more than half speak a tongue which belongs to a completely different linguistic family. An estimated one out of three are completely illiterate, and some two-thirds come from traditional rural societies and thus have no experience of urban or industrial life. Almost a fifth are from Moslem nations, and of the immigrants from other Christian cultures, the large majority are of a different religion from the one predominant in the country to which they migrate.[1]

As suggested in the last chapter, policies, programs, and practices of governments, business firms, trade unions, and voluntary associations concerning cross-national migrants are considered in this study to be the most important factors facilitating the acceptance and adjustment of migrants. In this chapter some data concerning the operation of these policies in the countries of immigration will be examined.

POLICIES GOVERNING ADMISSION OF WORKING IMMIGRANTS

The legal basis for cross-national migration in Europe in the 1960's is a complex of multilateral and bilateral treaties, national statutes, administrative regulations, and informal administrative and police practices.[2] To describe all these systematically, for each country of Europe, would require more than one thick volume; further, these policies are in a continuous process of amendment and other kinds of change. For the purposes of the present study, then, it seems practical and sufficient to present only the main legal bases of cross-national migration, illustrate by selected cases the less important ones, and indicate the trends in their evolution.

Two groups of nations have concluded multilateral treaties establishing free internal labor mobility, with no more required of the migrant than an identity card issued by his country of citizenship. These are the four Scandinavian countries (agreement signed in 1954, called Nordic Labor Zone, later called Scandinavian Common Labor Market) and the three Benelux countries (agreement signed June 7, 1956).

The European Economic Community (EEC) has moved toward free labor mobility by means of a three-stage plan. Articles 48 and 49 of the Treaty of Rome (1957) specified that full freedom of labor mobility was to be achieved by the end of 1969.[3] Apparently it was considered by the authors of the treaty as a necessary aspect of the economic and political integration they envisaged. The treaty looked forward to "the abolition of any discrimination based on nationality between workers of the Member States as regards employment, remuneration, and other working conditions," and stated that the individual rights which it included should be subject to limitations only where justified by reasons of public order, public safety, and public health. The first stage was inaugurated by EEC Council Regulation 15 issued August 16, 1961, which included five main provisions: (1) labor permits are to be given automatically to member-state nationals for occupations in which there is a labor shortage; (2) the domestic labor administration can restrict job opportunities to its own nationals for only three weeks, after which it must make the openings available to other member-state nationals regardless of preexisting restrictive numbers or quotas; (3) foreign workers for whom an employer has called by name will in certain cases be granted a permit without reference to the domestic labor market; (4) member-state nationals are to be given preference over other foreign workers in filling jobs; (5) member-state nationals are granted the right to renew their labor permits for the same occupation after one year of regular employment, for any other occupation for which they are qualified after three years, and for any kind of paid work after four years of regular employment.

The second stage, inaugurated by Regulation 38 issued March 25, 1964, restricted the priorities accorded to the domestic labor market to certain labor-surplus occupations and regions only, extended the rights and privileges of member-state migrant workers, gave them the right to vote in factory elections after three years of employment by the same firm, gave them the right to bring in dependent forebears and descendants — in addition to spouse and minor children — if the worker could offer them satisfactory accommodations, and facilitated clearing offers of and applications for employment within the EEC. There remained a "safeguard clause" which enabled member states to reintroduce priority for national workers for certain occupations and in areas where there is local unemployment. By November 1966 all the member states except France had renounced this opportunity.[4]

The third stage, expected to be inaugurated in 1968, will be devoted to the abolition of the last obstacles standing in the way of free movement, so that workers of all member states will be assured of access to paid employment in each member state on the terms that apply to nationals of that state. They will have equal rights of worker representation in firm organizations, equal tax arrangements and social benefits, and will be able to bring in their families without proving that they have adequate housing. However, if unemployment occurs, member states are to discourage migration. On April 7, 1967, the EEC Commission proposed the institution of a communitywide identity card for all workers to replace the existing work permits given to foreign workers. This card — if adopted by the member states represented in the EEC Council — would eliminate all documentary distinctions among workers, national or foreign, if they are citizens of any of the six nations.[5] Italians have been the main workers affected by all these provisions because, of all the member-state nationals, they have been the most frequent migrants and because they are least likely — due to the geographic position of Italy — to be frontier workers with privileges obtained through earlier binational agreements. During the six years, 1961 through 1966, in which EEC regulations on freedom of movement within the six nations have been operative, an average of 270,600 first work permits a year have been issued to workers of the member states moving from one EEC country to another.[6] Of these, 80 percent have been Italians. If the communitywide identity card should be adopted, all nationals of the six countries would benefit, and a portion of Europe would move a significant distance toward international integration.

On October 30, 1955, and December 20, 1955, the Organization for Economic Cooperation and Development (OECD) — when it was still the OEEC — made recommendations to its member states to liberalize the international movement of workers. OECD does not have the power to require the adoption of its recommendations, and its member states (twenty-one in number by 1960) adopted the recommendations only in part and only gradually over a period of years. The council of OECD does, however, prepare an annual report which notes the progress of each member state on OECD recommendations, which are from time to time expanded by suggestions from its Manpower Liberalization Group. The most important recommendation of OECD, which is adhered to by most European countries, is that work permits must be issued as soon as it is established that no suitable workers are available on the home market, and that this determination should take place within a month. The OECD also has a labor-exchange information system through which each country provides to all other member countries information about its labor market and working conditions, and this information can then be made available to workers.

The OECD recommendations have perhaps been useful in indicating possibilities for employment to member states, but they are too general to cover all the special circumstances involved in the migration from one country to another. For that reason various pairs of immigrant and emigrant countries among the OECD member states have agreed to bilateral treaties. Since each treaty has somewhat different stipulations, but touches on the same general points as all the others only two examples will be given here. To summarize first the treaty signed on September 16, 1966, between Sweden and Yugoslavia:

1. The Swedish Labor Market Board will transmit to the Yugoslav Federal Employment Office detailed offers by Swedish employers for employment of Yugoslav workers.

2. The Federal Employment Office will select from among the interested workers those meeting the requirements, including passing a medical examination (paid for by the Labor Market Board). A joint committee will pass on the suitability of the selectees. Sweden pays for the transportation and provides free residence and labor permits. Spouses, parents, and children of accepted workers may freely accompany or join them in Sweden.

3. From the time the accepted worker arrives until he actually begins work, he is provided free board and lodging by Sweden.

4. Yugoslav workers will be given the same wages and will work under the same conditions as Swedish workers. If an individual employer should discriminate, the Swedish government will provide free board and lodging to the worker until he has been offered other suitable employment.

5. The Yugoslav worker has the same opportunities as the Swedish worker for vocational training, and in case of unemployment he is given the same assistance in finding new employment. Vocational training courses may be arranged in Yugoslavia before migration, with the assistance of Swedish experts, using Swedish standards, and including training in the Swedish language. Sweden will pay for the teachers, materials, and board and lodging for the trainees.

6. Yugoslav workers have the same social insurance as Swedish workers, unless a later special agreement is contracted between Sweden and Yugoslavia.

7. If a Yugoslav worker needs but is not yet eligible for unemployment or other social assistance benefits, he will get the same aid as Swedish workers.

8. Yugoslav workers are allowed to transfer their savings to Yugoslavia in accord with Swedish regulations current at the time of transfer.

47

9. Yugoslav workers may change employment during their stay in Sweden.

10. The contracting parties agree to expedite and simplify the administrative formalities for the worker.

11. Workers may spend their holidays in Yugoslavia without special permits.

12. A joint commission will periodically review problems that may arise and submit recommendations for changes in the treaty.

13. Either party may terminate the agreement with six months' notice.

The generosity of the immigrant country in this treaty toward the migrant workers is exceptional and involves expenses for the immigrant country and its employers which put the costs of immigrant labor well above that for domestic labor. All the benefits are to the Yugoslav worker (and to Yugoslavia if he returns); Sweden gains only a selected labor supply and — it is hoped — good will in Yugoslavia.

A second example of a treaty is that between Switzerland and Spain (both OECD countries) signed March 2, 1961:

1. The Swiss Immigration Office will periodically inform the Spanish Emigrants Institute of the general needs for labor, and the institute will let the Swiss Office know the general extent to which they can be filled. The Spanish Institute can independently circulate a list of workers available for employment, with their characteristics.

2. Any Swiss employer can communicate his needs directly to the Spanish Institute, and the institute will seek workers to meet the requirements.

3. The Spanish Institute will interview the candidates on their occupational characteristics and give them a medical examination. If he wishes, the prospective employer may further examine the candidates. If he hires them, he provides them with a contract and an official Swiss residence permit. The employer may hire a specific Spanish worker by name, but in this case he must pay for the professional and medical examinations, unless he chooses to dispense with them.

4. The Spanish Institute undertakes to deliver a passport to the contracted worker quickly and to notify the employer of the date of the worker's arrival.

5. The employer pays for transportation to Switzerland, unless the worker fails to meet his contract. The worker pays for his return journey to Spain; in the case of seasonal workers, the employer deducts the cost of the return journey from the wages. If the Swiss medical authorities find the worker medically unacceptable after the Spanish medical authorities have passed him, the Spanish Institute must pay for the return journey. If the employer breaks the contract, he must pay for the worker's

return journey up to the Spanish border, unless the worker can find other employment in Switzerland.

6. The Spanish worker, after arrival in Switzerland, must register both with the Swiss police and the Spanish consulate.

7. Spanish workers enjoy the same wages and work conditions as Swiss workers. Spanish workers can appeal to the administrative or judicial authorities in case of alleged violation.

8. Spanish workers are not eligible for Swiss old-age and survivors' benefits until they have paid contributions for at least five years or until they have lived at least ten years in Switzerland (five years without interruption immediately before they claim benefits).[7] Medical insurance is a matter of private agreement between employer and worker, but if there is to be medical insurance the contract is approved by both the Swiss Office and Spanish Institute.

9. The Spanish workers may transfer their savings to Spain, in accord with current Swiss regulations.

10. The Swiss Office will provide information on working conditions to current and prospective Spanish workers through the institute.

11. The Swiss Office will examine, in concert with the Spanish Institute and other interested parties, how Spanish workers can surmount their difficulties in Switzerland.

12. The Spanish authorities will place no barrier in the way of returning migrants. All those who fall to the charge of public assistance in Switzerland will be immediately repatriated.

13. A joint commission from the two countries will reexamine the application of the treaty by both countries and may make recommendations for changes.

14. Either contracting party can cancel the treaty with six months' notice.

This treaty regularizes the conditions for the migrant worker and gives both him and the employer various protections. It gives the worker wages and working conditions equal to those of Swiss workers, but does not give him vocational or language training. In some treaties an age limit — as well as health and skill requirements — may be set for immigrants; for example, in the treaty between the Netherlands and Spain, unskilled immigrants must be between 20 and 35 years old, skilled immigrants between 18 and 45 years old.[8]

There are hundreds of statutes and formal administrative regulations pertaining to immigrant workers in the various countries of immigration. To sample these, the ones reported for 1964 to the OECD are summarized: [9]

France: Workers legitimately brought into France by the Office National d'Immigration no longer need a work permit — their initial contract will suffice to allow them to stay in the country. Algerian immigrants must have a medical examination, and their entry is to be determined on the basis of the labor market situation; accepted Algerians will be given vocational training.

Belgium: Regardless of the labor market situation, the spouse and children of a foreign worker with a work permit can also get work permits.

Netherlands: The act of February 20, 1964, liberalizes immigration. Foreign workers may petition the Ministry of Social Affairs if local authorities seek to take away their work permits or refuse renewals.

Switzerland: The Order of Federal Council of February 21, 1964, provides that residence or renewal permits will not be issued to foreign workers unless the employer undertakes in writing not to increase his total labor force above the number employed on March 1, 1964. With some exemptions, the foreign labor force has to be cut 5 percent during the year by each employer. The major exemptions are in farming and forestry undertakings, domestic service, hospitals, nursing homes and other welfare institutions, and manufacturing establishments where heavy expenditure had been incurred to expand or convert before the order had been adopted and where failure to grant exemption would entail grievous loss to the entrepreneur. In principle Switzerland has for some years admitted workers only as seasonal labor and has required them to leave in less than one year.

United Kingdom: The policy of removing restrictions on the free choice of employment opportunities by foreigners after four years' continuous residence remains in effect.

Austria, the United Kingdom, Sweden, Spain, Belgium, and Luxembourg reported regulations renewing or expanding lists of labor-scarce occupations for which there was automatic granting or abolition of permits. Ireland, France, and the Netherlands reported doing this informally without lists. Sweden added certain nationalities and categories of persons to lists of occupations for which work permits were automatically granted, while Switzerland removed hotel and building workers from its list of such occupations.

Switzerland and the United Kingdom are the two main countries of Europe restricting immigration, and something more must be said about their policies and the reasons for them.[10] Switzerland began to take restrictive measures to reduce the number of foreign workers in early 1963, but the law in effect at the time of writing dates from February 1965 and provides:

1. Only those foreign workers granted a residence permit by the Swiss government — acting in accord with one of its bilateral treaties — are per-

mitted to enter Switzerland. An offer of employment or a labor contract is no longer sufficient. Those who enter as "tourists" will be expelled from the country, even if they have succeeded in finding jobs.

2. By June 1965 all establishments employing more than ten workers had to reduce the number of foreign workers under their control to 95 percent of the number employed on March 1 of the same year.

3. The ceiling established in March 1963 on the total number of workers (foreign and Swiss together) is maintained — no more than 95 percent of what it had been in 1962 (average, or as of December).

4. Changing employment during the first year of residence is prohibited.

5. The maximum number of seasonal workers for the construction industry is fixed at 145,000 (i.e., a 10 percent reduction).

As a result of these measures, the number of foreign workers under control went from 721,000 in August 1964 to 676,000 in August 1965. In March 1966 it was decided that there would be a second 5 percent reduction of foreign workers under control to be completed by January 1, 1967 (see the second point above). Frontier workers and seasonal hotel workers were excluded from this order. On February 10, 1967, the Swiss government ordered a further reduction of 2 percent in the foreign labor force, to take place by the end of July 1967.

Political reasons were more important than economic ones in creating this policy, although it was said that it was developed because the economy was "overheated," causing inflation and an unfavorable balance of international payments (due to excess of imports and to remittances). The percentage of foreign workers in the labor force had risen to 32 percent and the percentage was accelerating; the Swiss feared *Überfremdung* (over-foreignization). By 1960 the majority of foreigners (79 percent) were Catholics and mostly Italian (59 percent); the Swiss feared an imbalance in their traditional religious and linguistic composition. Migrant families had begun to be admitted into Switzerland; some migrants were apparently going to remain permanently and there were demands for more schools, housing, and medical services. Switzerland has probably slowed down her rate of economic development and upward social mobility by restricting foreigners since 1965. Even some partly American-owned businesses have moved out of the country because their top personnel were subjected to limitations in numbers and length of stay (not to speak of housing restrictions).[11] While Swiss workers genuinely fear the economic competition from foreign workers and wonder if the wage level and the rationalization of industry are not being held down because of them, clearly there is also some xenophobia in the national reaction. A right-wing political party centered in Zurich, the Zurich Democratic party, has been demanding that half the foreign workers be expelled,[12] and there

51

is a voluntary association called National Action against Foreign Penetration of the People and the Country. The trade unions have agreed tacitly that they would hold back on wage-increase demands if the new restrictive policy creates an increasing shortage of manpower; this was done to gain the acquiescence of employers to the new policy. Some employers are concentrating on retaining the foreign workers who have been in the country over three years, and hence have some legal rights to remain (employers sometimes provide housing and vocational training for these foreign workers), but the government has not stepped up activities along these lines. Some Swiss employers and intellectuals are opposed on economic and ethical grounds to the restrictive policy.[13]

The United Kingdom is the other country of immigration in Europe which has imposed significant restrictions on worker immigration. The United Kingdom once had a regional multilateral arrangement with Commonwealth nations throughout the world, but the 1962 statute ended that:

This law, the Commonwealth Immigrants Act, does not put Commonwealth citizens in the same position as aliens. It is based on employment, and vouchers can be obtained from the Ministry of Labour for three categories of prospective immigrants: (a) those who have an offer of a specific job from an employer, (b) those who have certain specified skills to offer, and (c) unskilled workers who can apply and wait their turn on a "first come, first served" basis. In addition, the wives (and prospective wives) and children of immigrants resident in the United Kingdom can enter freely. . . .

A particular feature of the situation at present is the drop in the number of West Indians applying for and obtaining vouchers and the considerable rise in the numbers of Indians and Pakistanis. . . . In 1963 a new regulation was instituted under which no one country can have more than 25 per cent of the total vouchers. The present trend for the majority of applications to come from India and Pakistan will probably mean that these countries will each have the full 25 per cent.[14]

Restrictions on workers from Europe seem to stem from economic reasons, while those on workers from Commonwealth countries of Asia and the West Indies seem to be motivated by racist or political reasons. The latter restrictions — beginning July 1, 1962 — set an upper limit of 8,500 Commonwealth immigrants a year, no more than 25 percent of whom can come from any one country (although wives of workers and children under 16 years are exempt from the quota). In effect this immigration is limited to those with special skills and those prepared to work in occupations with a serious shortage of labor (usually those which do not attract white workers).

In 1965 the United Kingdom added further restrictions to its Commonwealth Immigrants Act of 1962.[15] A maximum of 8,500 employment vouchers per year are to be issued for immigrants from the Commonwealth. For the first two years, 1,000 of these were allocated to citizens of Malta. The remaining vouchers were issued in two categories: 2,500 Category A vouchers went to applicants, skilled or unskilled, who had a specific job to come to in Britain, but not more than 15 percent of such vouchers could go to any one Commonwealth country; 5,000 Category B vouchers went to people with special professional or technical qualifications. Separate provisions apply to seasonal workers, students, trainees, tourists, visitors, and others. The wife of an immigrant and his children under 16 may continue to enter the country.

Informally, no restrictions are placed on immigrants from the Irish Free State (allegedly because they cannot be stopped from crossing the border into Northern Ireland, which, of course, is part of the United Kingdom). If immigrants from "white" Commonwealth countries or colonies (Canada, Australia, New Zealand, etc.) want to enter the United Kingdom they come as tourists and hence are not restricted.

"Foreign" immigration — i.e., from countries not in the Commonwealth — is based on a system of permits which are also granted to those with special skills and those prepared to work in occupations with a serious shortage of labor. But there are no quotas for these migrants, as for the Commonwealth immigrants, and each application is judged according to the need for the immigrant's skills or line of work. There is no official recruitment program; permits to hire foreigners are given to employers who can prove they meet the qualifications and who guarantee equal conditions of employment. The permit is usually for twelve months (less for seasonal workers), but it may be renewed for three additional years. After these four years, a foreign worker is eligible to remain indefinitely in the United Kingdom and there are no longer any restrictions on his employment. Families of migrants are admitted for the same period as the worker himself.

Most countries of immigration permit renewal of work and residence permits (Switzerland and, for some occupations, Luxembourg are the exceptions) but do not permit change of place of employment or of occupation until a certain number of years have passed. Within the EEC there is freedom for EEC nationals to change occupation after two years. For non-EEC nationals, Luxembourg and the Netherlands require five years' employment; Germany permits one change after five years but complete occupational mobility requires ten years' residence; the French require ten years for Greeks and Spaniards but thirteen years for all others. The Swiss require five years for the French, Belgians, and Dutch, ten years for Germans, Austrians, and Italians, and leave it up to local authorities to decide how much more for those of other nationalities.[16] Belgium requires four years' residence for immigrants from seven countries, six years for others, three years for political refugees — with one year less for all workers if they bring their families with them.[17] These are the laws; exceptions are sometimes made when the foreigner seeks permission to move into another occupation for which there is a labor shortage.

Countries of emigration have diverse policies toward the out-migration of their nationals. Several countries try to control emigration by having it all administered under regulations of treaties with certain countries of immigration: when Japan sent a group of miners to Germany in 1965–66, there were strict provisions in the agreement for their training and return after a stipulated time; Senegal, Mali, Mauretania, and Morocco also have arrangements with France for the training and return of their workers, but these arrangements are more flexible in allowing the workers to stay in France for longer periods of time if the workers want to and if France is willing to let them stay.[18] Most of the treaties signed by Greece, Yugoslavia, and Turkey are similarly flexible, but at least the former two countries have long-range plans for attracting back their emigrants when economic conditions warrant their return.

Portugal is the most restrictive country in Europe today in allowing emigration. According to its laws emigrant passports are provided only in those cases where employment in the immigration country has been guaranteed, family maintenance in Portugal has been assured, military obligations have been satisfied, paternal authorization has been given for minors, the migrant has had the required education (at least the third year of secondary school), not more than a certain quota has already gone to the proposed country of immigration, and not more than a certain quota has already left the region of the would-be emigrant's home and his occupation. This last matter seems to disturb the Portuguese authorities most: some regions and occupations of Portugal have been depleted to the point where it is difficult to carry on local economic activity, and this results in wage rises and in protests from Portuguese employers. The Portuguese government is also concerned about maintaining the demographic and military strength of its population and about keeping a certain flow of emigration to its colonies. Because of the restrictions on emigration, there is a clandestine movement out of the country. Informed sources have estimated this to be about 70,000 persons from 1956 to 1965, and the trend is upward. Some migrants use a tourist passport, but others just cross the border — often aided by illegal agents to whom the emigrant pays a sum of money. "Against a payment of 2,500 or 3,000 French francs ($500–600), these workers were taken charge of by the 'passers' organisation, which crowded them together under the false floor of lorries which regularly transport sheep or pigs. They were taken to the woods at Seine-

Port (France) and sometimes lived there for some time in a barn, guarded by a post-office employee. Then a discreet message would be sent to taxi-drivers in the Paris district, and they were driven into Paris in small groups." [19] These clandestine emigrants often become dependent on unscrupulous agents, take the poorest jobs in the country of immigration, and fear to return to Portugal because they have committed a crime in emigrating. In 1965, in an effort to curb the agents, Portugal made it a criminal offense to encourage any national to emigrate, but made it possible for Portuguese who had already migrated to legalize their position. [20] Portugal, like Spain, has long had some emigration to Latin America, but this has been declining in recent years in favor of emigration to other European countries.

Spain has also attempted to discourage emigration from certain regions and occupations, but not so repressively as has Portugal. Rather, the Spanish government has sought to channel emigration from the unskilled occupations and from the population-surplus regions, not only for international emigration but also for internal movement. Spain has also assisted, oriented, and trained emigrants before their departure, during their stay abroad, and after their return, thereby trying to cut down on the number of expensive repatriations caused by immediate rejection from the receiving countries. Spain's rapid economic development is now reducing the number of emigrants, especially since many of the new enterprises have been deliberately located in regions of unemployment. The Spanish government exhibits continuing concern for the status of its nationals working abroad and urges other nations to adhere to the ILO convention on equal labor standards.

Turkey, before 1950, had a policy against emigration, except for its Armenian, Greek, and Bulgarian refugees; since 1961 Turkey has encouraged emigration — except of skilled workers — because of its high unemployment and rate of natural increase (3 percent per year). The Greek authorities are not favorable to emigration, but have not found it practical to take any steps to restrict it and have concluded treaties with countries of immigration to promote it. [21] Both Turkey and Greece have sought agreements which would provide training for their emigrating nationals, and both countries look forward to the return of their nationals in some indefinite future. Turkey and Greece have facilitated remittances by creating favorable exchange rates and investment opportunities for their nationals abroad.

While the countries of emigration use economic arguments when they seek to discourage their citizens from emigrating, the main issue is political and nationalistic. Kindleberger summarizes the Greek government's position: "Greece would rather accept a lower [economic] return for its citizens and have them remain at home. The Greek government objects that emigration takes the most energetic, the healthiest, the politically most reliable, and leaves behind the young, the old, the shiftless, the sick, and the Communists. A lesser and more directly political point is that it objects to emigration from the border provinces, which weakens the country's power to resist Communist aggression or infiltration from Yugoslavia, Albania, and Bulgaria. Recently, to counteract this manpower drain, the government has undertaken a program of overseas recruitment of emigrated nationals." [22]

Italy has long had the largest number of emigrants, has never tried to restrict emigration (except briefly during the Mussolini era), and has had the greatest success in attracting its emigrants to return (both earlier from overseas and recently from northern Europe).[23] Because of rapid economic development in the 1960's, reduction in the birth rate, and depletion of population through emigration from some of the areas of greatest unemployment and underemployment, Italy's rate of emigration has rapidly decreased. It is now repatriating emigrants almost as rapidly as it is losing new emigrants, and some immigrants (especially from Greece) have begun to appear in northern Italy. Since the 1950's Italy has sought to aid its emigrants with information, training, language instruction, and social services, so that the returnees may be better qualified vocationally.

Thus it can be seen there are a great variety of laws — multilateral, bilateral, and unilateral — governing admission of foreign workers. The organizations of nations — Scandinavian Common Labor Market, Benelux, Common Market, OECD — are all working to liberalize the movement of the labor force. In general, until the end of 1966 at least, most of the countries of immigration, with the major exceptions of Switzerland and the United Kingdom, were working in the same direction.

SOCIAL WELFARE POLICY TOWARD MIGRANTS

Since the mid-1950's, what might be called a "social welfare policy" has developed in Europe toward cross-national migrant workers and their families. This includes social security provisions, requirements for equal pay and working conditions, orientation to the country of immigration, vocational training, language training, and special programs for the wives and children of immigrants. Social welfare policies have been encouraged or directed by both bilateral and multilateral treaties and have been frequently implemented by national legislation.[24] The bilateral treaties — between a specific country of immigration and a specific country of emigration — have been illustrated in the previous section. In this section multilateral treaties and unilateral national legislation, especially on social welfare policies, will be examined.

The multilateral agreements among the Scandinavian countries and among the Benelux countries providing for the free flow of workers within these regions give to the workers from the other signatory countries all the economic and social rights and privileges granted to nationals of the countries of immigration. These immigrants might just as well be citizens in the country as far as their economic and social rights are concerned, but of course they do not have the right to vote in political elections or to hold political office. Language similarities often prevailing within each regional group make the "equal access" to information and training meaningful — which is seldom true for foreigners from outside the region who have different native languages. Each of these countries also has for foreigners some kind of programs in vocational training, language training, and social orientation. Since these programs do not distinguish between workers from the regional-pact countries and other immigrant workers, these provisions can best be considered as part of the social policy of each immigrant country.

The Common Market countries, like the regional-pact nations, have made consistent progress in securing social equality for migrant workers. This is because the Treaty of Rome authorized the EEC Commission to equalize social security benefits and laws concerning working conditions in the EEC nations — requirements which no doubt fit into the economic trends within the six nations making up the Common Market. Even during the years 1963–66 when occasionally there was some pessimism about the future of the Common Market, steady progress was being made to extend and equalize the social policies of the member states in regard to workers from other member states. Of course, it should be recalled that Italy was the only major country of emigration among the six in the Common Market, and its rate of emigration was declining. Other cross-national migrants within the six EEC countries were largely frontier or seasonal workers who created few difficulties for the countries to which they migrated. Still, the application of the social security programs of member states for the benefit of workers from other member states covered about two million people and involved about $80 million of expenditures in 1964.[25] By July 1966 the EEC Commission had sent two recommendations to member states: one on improving social services for community nationals working in another community country and the other on providing housing for these workers and their families (although there is little evidence that the member states have acted because of these recommendations). By the end of December 1965 the European Social Fund — set up by the 1957 Treaty of Rome, and one of the few examples of independent administrative activities of EEC on a supranational basis — had allocated \$31.7 million for the retraining and resettlement of 454,000 workers (275,000 of whom were Italians).[26] The Social Fund spent another \$8.7 million for the benefit of 53,632 workers in 1966.[27] In 1967 plans were being formulated by the commission for more independent and developmental use of the Social Fund, for a European-wide system of industrial health and safety (including protection of young people and working women), and for harmonization of certain social security provisions — but no action had been taken on these at the time of writing.

The EEC has made considerable progress in encouraging the improvement of working and living conditions, usually in ways specifically mentioned in the Treaty of Rome: the treaty set the end of 1964 as the date by which there should be equal pay for men and women, and this recommendation has been implemented although some loopholes remain; the aforementioned steps toward free movement of workers and the training of workers have been taken; social security for migrant workers has been established under existing national laws. The EEC Commission lacks both legal powers and funds to go much further, however, and future developments will depend on authorization and funds that may be granted by member states acting through the council.[28] Thus far the member states have agreed to practically nothing beyond that which was specified in the Treaty of Rome, even regarding such matters as standardizing statistics collection and terminology. In sum, considerable progress in expanding social welfare policies — particularly as they affect migrating workers — has been achieved, mainly because of far-reaching commitments of the member states when they signed the Treaty of Rome. But this progress cannot be continued beyond 1969 unless the member states make further commitments. The major exception may be the commitment to the Social Fund, since the commission governing it is allowed flexibility in its use — such as setting rules for granting aid — if one or more of the member states do not actively oppose extended uses for the fund. The exchanges of information, through conferences and commission studies, are also likely to have a continuing influence on member states, even though no powers are involved in them.[29] The best example of achievement through exchange of information has been some movement toward an alignment of national social security programs. Some alignment may also have come about as a result of opening the economies of the six to each other — a kind of "rub off" effect. It is hard to know whether the trend toward equalization of wages, hours of work, paid holidays, and other conditions of work actually has been influenced by a Common Market program; equalization here might simply be a result of overcoming the economic backwardness in the relatively backward countries of the Common Market.

Independent Variables: Openness of Policy

Coordination among the six in regard to migrant labor could be improved in many ways, although it would require more political authority than now exists in the community.[30] There is practically no coordination among the six nations of manpower recruiting policies in non-EEC countries, and each country of immigration is in competition with every other one. Vocational guidance and training to meet the special needs of migrants is still in its infancy except for notable spot achievements by the Germans and the retraining program in Italy under the European Social Fund. Since 1963 migrants from one EEC country to another can use the educational facilities of the country of immigration on the same terms as its own nationals. Reduction of differentials in social security, social assistance, and other welfare programs has a way to go. There is scope for much more imagination in the use of the Social Fund. Whether these things will or will not develop depends on the general political direction of the EEC.

The European Coal and Steel Community (ECSC) also created a Social Fund when it was established by the same six nations of the EEC in 1952.[31] That fund was created to provide aids for the readaptation of workers whose employment was reduced or suspended as a result of the elimination of all barriers to the free flow of trade in coal and steel. Specifically, it offered assistance for occupational retraining, allowances for resettlement in the same country or any of the other five countries, and compensatory payments up to 90 percent of previous annual wages for one year for workers whose employment was temporarily or wholly terminated as a result of closure or conversion of their enterprise to other production. Over 10 percent of the coal mines have received some form of readaptation assistance from the inauguration of the program in 1954 through 1964. In the fiscal year ending June 30, 1967, a record $13.6 million was spent for this purpose, and the probability was that it would increase in the following year.[32] But few have used the aid for cross-national relocation, partly because the coal miners have been reluctant to leave their home region and partly because the economic boom in their home countries allowed them to find other employment nearby. Two-thirds of the miners who benefited were in West Germany (the nation with the most rapid economic expansion during 1954–64) and only 3.5 percent were in Italy (the only nation of emigration among the six). The reason for this, of course, is that Germany has many more mines than Italy, but the differential benefits to these two countries show that not all the Social Fund activities are equalizing.

A multilateral agreement concluded by the Council of Europe supports free movement of workers, subject only to restrictions based on cogent

59

economic and social reasons, and the right of migrant workers to protection and assistance for themselves and their families in the territory of any other contracting nation. This agreement, called the European Social Charter, affects migrants in a large framework concerned with the rights of citizens to get various social benefits from their states without discrimination on grounds of race, color, sex, religion, political opinion, *national extraction*, or social origin. Most European countries signed the charter after it was drawn up in 1961, but it did not come into force until February 26, 1965, when the required five nations had ratified it. By January 1, 1966, it was presumably in operation in the United Kingdom, Norway, Sweden, Ireland, Germany (FR), and Denmark. These countries "have undertaken to accept a number of broad aims of social policy, to observe a large proportion of the detailed provisions of the charter and to notify [*sic*] those they cannot immediately undertake to implement." [33] The difficulty with this charter is that it leaves a number of loopholes and is not detailed; it is almost an expression of high ideals rather than a concrete agreement. However, it is an important step in that it indicates that the two major non-EEC countries of immigration which are among the ratifying powers — the United Kingdom and Sweden — have the intention of granting to all foreign workers the same kind of rights and privileges which the EEC nations grant to each other's nationals.

Another significant development of the same type — worked out jointly by the Council of Europe and the International Labor Organization — is the European Social Security Code, which was opened for signature on April 16, 1965. It sets a series of standards (higher than those in the 1949 ILO Convention) which member countries should apply to their national health schemes and social security provisions. It also provides for equal treatment of migrants and nationals, but by 1967, its suggested policies, too, were far from adoption.

The ILO Convention, ratified by France, Germany (FR), Italy, the Netherlands, and Norway as of June 1, 1964, recommended to its signatory states that they facilitate the departure, journey, and reception of migrant workers by providing information, accommodations, food and clothing to be given on arrival, vocational training and other access to schools, recreation and welfare facilities, and equal employment conditions. [34] This recommendation is also unenforceable, but it indicates the intention of the ratifying immigrant countries of France, Germany, and the Netherlands to do what they can to aid immigrant workers. Since northern Italy is in the process of becoming an immigrant territory — especially for Greek and Spanish workers — Italy's signature to the ILO Convention is also important.

SOCIAL SECURITY AND SOCIAL ASSISTANCE

The extensive cross-national migration of labor in post-World War II Europe necessitated international agreements regarding social security.[35] A convention of the Scandinavian countries in 1955 resulted in a unified program. One of the first actions of the Common Market — taken in 1958 and put into force January 1, 1959 — was to coordinate national systems among the six member nations, replacing the eighty bilateral agreements (and several multilateral agreements) that had been worked out between 1946 and 1958. The EEC agreement was based on three principles: (1) equality of entitlement to social security — including family allowances, health care, old age and unemployment benefits, and compensation in case of employment injury or occupational disease — for all nationals of the six countries under the laws prevailing in the country of residence, except that family members domiciled in countries other than that of the insured workers receive medical and family allowance benefits at the level prevailing in their country of domicile (usually their country of birth); (2) aggregation of periods of insurance and employment in more than one country, both for entitlement to benefit and for calculation of its amount; (3) payment of most benefits in any EEC country.

The implementation of the detailed regulations based on these principles presents many problems of interpretation, and a committee — composed of the directors of the six social security bodies along with representatives of the EEC and the ECSC — meets monthly to settle these questions. Sometimes the committee calls in representatives of workers', employers', and farmers' organizations. Special regulations for seasonal workers and frontier commuters were adopted in 1963 and came into force on February 1, 1964. Special regulations are also being developed for seamen and for self-employed persons. The interest of the EEC in "harmonization" or "leveling upward" the diverse social security systems has involved an enormous amount of study, discussion, and differences of opinion, but by July 1963 an agreement was reached on general guidelines and on a short-term program which goes only partway toward harmonization. The latter, in revised form, is now being implemented, but full harmonization had not been achieved by 1967.

Social security coverage for workers and their families who migrate from one country to another, at least one of which is not in the Common Market, is determined by bilateral treaties and national statutes. The diversity and complexity of these agreements prohibits doing more than drawing a few general observations and citing a few examples here.[36] Some nations, either by unilateral statute or by bilateral treaty, give foreign workers the same social security benefits that they give their own nationals. Other nations provide such benefits except for family allowances and medical benefits to family members who reside outside of their national borders (e.g., United Kingdom). Even those nations that do not give foreign workers all the social security benefits they give to their own nationals usually do give some benefits, as provided by treaty or by national statutes. On the other hand, "At present in some countries, several categories of migrants are not insured or are most inadequately insured against major risks or, because of the absence of bilateral arrangements, cannot benefit from certain rights, for instance dependency allowances for their families which have remained in the country of origin." [37] Many treaties permit the migrant worker to accumulate his rights to social security benefits across national lines. Unemployment insurance benefits are nearly always complicated by the power of the country of immigration to eject a foreigner when he becomes unemployed, especially if he came into the country as a "tourist" rather than under a contract established by treaty. Usually a worker must have been employed for a certain length of time in the country of immigration before he becomes eligible for unemployment and sickness benefits. In Belgium, for example, six months' employment is needed to be eligible for sickness benefits, and a varying length of time for unemployment benefits, depending on the treaty with the country of emigration. Many countries of immigration have set up special offices to deal with the welfare problems of immigrants, but in some countries (for example, Belgium and Switzerland) the offices are organized by regional authorities and not all regions have set them up. Some countries of emigration (notably Italy) have set up offices to help their emigrants.[38] In addition there are state-aided or semipublic agencies and services, and private agencies and services (business firms, trade unions, voluntary associations, churches, migrants' associations) which provide some kinds of temporary social assistance. Some of the private organizations, in both immigrant and emigrant countries, have a longer history of helping migrants than do the state agencies, but generally they do not have as large resources. Some of the private associations were set up to aid especially those among the migrants with whom they had affinities — for example, Catholic organizations in receiving countries to aid Catholic immigrants. Retired foreign workers who reside in the country of immigration usually receive old-age pensions, but for several countries (Belgium, for one) these are not normally paid if the retired person leaves the country, unless a specific treaty provides for it.

Descloîtres makes a valuable distinction among three types of social assistance in countries of immigration, depending on the relationship of the state to it: [39]

1. The first type of policy is followed by the Netherlands and Switzer-

land where the main responsibility is left to the individual employers, who perform mainly in proportion to their size. The state reserves the right to define a policy, issue regulations about standards, encourage local initiative, support the training of social workers, and assemble documentation.

2. Germany provides the leading example of the second type, where employers still are responsible for the bulk of the effort on behalf of foreign workers, but both the federal and provincial (*Land*) governments lend financial and expert aid. Belgium may perhaps also be put in this category. Social assistance in these countries is more complete than in the first category, and is supplemented by the strong trade union movements which have set up assistance centers for foreign workers.

3. France and Sweden follow a third pattern, in which the central government directly sets up a number of aids and does a more extensive and systematic job.

Descloîtres summarizes the activities of the French government:

In 1964, a senior official, direct representative of the Prime Minister, was made responsible for promoting social welfare on behalf of foreign workers through the Fonds d'Action Sociale pour les Travailleurs Etrangers (FASTE), a national public service endowed with separate legal personality; and for mobilising financial resources for the execution of the social programmes drawn up (*cf.* action concerning training and housing under Section IV). In the course of 1966, this responsibility was transferred to the Ministry of Social Affairs, in which a Populations and Migration Department was set up, in particular to prepare and co-ordinate social programmes for the benefit of all migrant workers.

The FASTE, which became the Fonds d'Action Sociale pour les Travailleurs Migrants, was attached to the Ministry for Social Affairs, and its field of action has been extended to all migrant workers (French and foreign).

In addition, the Service de Liaison et de Promotion des Migrants, responsible, to the Ministry of the Interior, prepares and promotes action in the matter of reception proper and training, by allocating officials to Départements of France with a high proportion of migrants in the population.

For the reception and assistance of foreign workers and families, a somewhat original French solution is worth mentioning here: this concerns a form of very close co-operation between the public services and a private association. The "Service Social d'Aide aux Emigrants" (SSAE) an association founded in 1921 for the purpose of helping emigrants to adapt themselves, was made responsible by the Ministry of Labour in 1939 for organising and directing the work of the "Service Social de la Main-d'Oeuvre Etrangère" (SSMOE). Whilst retaining the flexibility in its work which only a private body can enjoy, the SSAE, thanks to the official mission entrusted to it, can handle all the administrative procedures on which the success of social welfare in an industrial society often depends. In addition to its headquarters in Paris, this service has 41 offices in the Départements and a supervisory staff of over 80 full-time welfare officers, most of whom speak at least one foreign language. Liaison with the social services of the emigration country is easily established through the Inter-

63

national Social Service of which the SSAE is the French branch. The field of its action is very varied, ranging from reception on arrival to repatriation and including contacts with employers, assistance with health services or family welfare services, etc. It is considered that on an average 10 per cent of emigrants make use of SSAE.[40]

Sweden has a type of social assistance which is unique: it provides migration aid to another location within the country where more appropriate and better jobs are available.[41] This includes travel allowance, starting assistance, fitting-out grants, and family grants. Unemployed persons can also receive retraining grants. Available to all citizens of Nordic countries and refugees domiciled in Sweden, it is also available to other foreign workers who have been employed in Sweden for six to twelve months. Vocational guidance and placement are provided free to everyone by the State Employment Service. Regardless of any mutual agreements with other states, foreign citizens in Sweden are fully or partly equated with Swedish citizens in regard to the usual social benefits — children's allowances, study assistance, general supplementary pension, sickness and accident insurance, unemployment insurance and assistance, social assistance, and housing grants.

INTEGRATION INTO WORKING LIFE

Immigrant workers, especially those who are poorly educated or who come from cultures (especially peasant cultures) considerably different from the ones where they come to work, need orientation when (or before) they arrive in the country of immigration.[42] Social workers and other experts report that much needless misunderstanding and friction with employers and supervisors develop that could be avoided with a good orientation program for both workers and supervisors.[43] The numerous provisions in statutes, administrative regulations, and treaties dealing with recruiting, industrial regulations, working conditions, taxation, social legislation, and rights and opportunities need to be summarized in simple language and made available to employers. An example of source material for employers is the 1,500-page loose-leaf collection prepared by the Federal Union of German Employers' Associations (Bundesvereinigung der Deutschen Arbeitgeberverbände). Migrants need to be given the opportunity to learn technical vocabularies and to receive rudimentary language training if they are to be able to function adequately in factory and town. Notices and signs — especially those dealing with safety — have to be in the several native languages of the workers. In Germany the Research Center for the Prevention of Industrial Accidents has produced documentary films on safety for Italian, Spanish, Greek, and Turkish workers, and it has also translated signboards and pamphlets on safety. Either some

64

supervisors must learn the native language of the immigrant workers or special interpreters must be hired; some medical personnel who speak the workers' language must also be available. German industry has probably made the most systematic efforts in these directions.

Since 1961 the EEC countries have granted to each other's nationals equality of voting rights for representatives on industrial committees.[44] Germany, Luxembourg, and the Netherlands are equally generous in this regard toward nationals of non-EEC countries, but Belgium requires that the worker have held a work permit in the country for two years, and France requires five years. Except within the EEC, few foreign workers have the right to stand for election as representatives to these committees, which makes it much more likely that they will be discriminated against in their places of work. Unions in modern industrialized countries have now accepted cross-national labor mobility and recognize that it facilitates economic growth which benefits all.[45] Unions generally open their membership to foreign workers [46] and insist on equality of employment conditions. In Germany, where immigrants are seldom allowed to stay longer than a year, the unions have made an outstanding effort to foster occupational adaptation and ensure that foreign workers enjoy a certain measure of comfort in their living conditions. Union assistance to foreign workers is also considerable in the Netherlands and Sweden, although the unions there feel little need to work out long-range programs. In Belgium, France, and Luxembourg the unions have done much less in the way of short-run assistance to foreign workers, but have done more to work out long-run work policies for their protection. The unions in Luxembourg have come out against seasonal contracts,[47] and the French unions have campaigned to have their foreign members sit on works committees. Swiss unions also have open membership and favor social adaptation policies for foreign workers. The British unions favor adequate provisions in welfare departments for immigrants, but otherwise there are no separate arrangements or rules that would segregate foreign workers, give them special work privileges, or prevent them from participation in British labor-union practices.[48] In general, however, the trade unions have adapted their structures and their policies to open membership to foreign workers, but they have not yet given them any considerable share in union activity. Many migrants of rural origin see little value in unions; some migrants distrust unions as political organizations or hesitate to join since they don't want to appear to be dissidents in a host country. Some fail to join because they move around so much. Estimates of the proportion of foreign workers who have joined trade unions vary greatly: in the Netherlands, for example, one estimate is as low as "1–2 percent," while another is "30 percent," which is practically as high as for Dutch nationals. Therefore, no reliable figures can be offered on the union membership of foreign workers. It would seem there is a latent hostility between unions and foreign workers, but it is gradually being covered over by rational economic and humanitarian interests.

VOCATIONAL TRAINING

Vocational training can be obtained in a variety of ways — before or after immigrating, in courses routinely offered by a country for all citizens, or in special courses designed for immigrants. Both governments and private firms offer training. Italy and Spain offer vocational training courses in major trades to prospective emigrants.[49] The courses last for a period of three to eight months during which the workers receive a living allowance and sometimes a bonus at the time of emigrating. The individual countries of immigration have vocational training programs sponsored both by government and by private industry. The government programs are generally for both nationals and foreigners, sometimes with quotas for foreigners or with standards of admission which many foreigners cannot meet. The private enterprise programs are sometimes for foreigners only, and then are often taught in the native language of the workers. Margaret Gordon describes the best government-sponsored programs for foreigners — those of France, West Germany, the Netherlands, the United Kingdom, and Sweden (the preliminary training program the Swedes set up in Yugoslavia, by treaty, for prospective Yugoslav migrants to Sweden was discussed above):

[In France] the number of aliens admitted to Government training centers varies according to the labor market situation and the availability of French applicants for admission to training for various occupations. The total number of aliens being trained at any given time may not exceed 10 per cent of all trainees in the center. Aliens are subject to the same selection standards as French applicants and also must have an adequate knowledge of the French language. Preference is given to young aliens residing in France or having family ties with French nationals. Moreover the French Government has entered into arrangements with underdeveloped countries, particularly former French colonies in Africa, under which nationals of those countries are brought to France for training in the Government centers.

In 1952 it was estimated that there were about 230,000 of these North Africans in the country, of whom 130,000 were unemployed. . . . Numerous steps were taken by public and private agencies in France to meet this situation. From 1949 on, Government responsibility toward the North African immigrants was centered in the Ministry of Interior, which developed reception centers, vocational guidance services, provisions for the repatriation of unsuitable applicants for work, and vocational training centers. These centers, so far as I have been able to determine, were administered separately from those under the auspices of the Ministry of Labor and Social Security. In 1952, 76 centers offered 146 courses, and attendance was increasing rapidly.

The Governments of West Germany and the Netherlands have been involved in agreements with the Italian Government in the last few years under which Italian workers recruited for emigration to these two countries are given an initial period of training in Italy followed by employer-sponsored training in the country of immigration. This type of arrangement is partially financed by the Common Market Social Fund.

In Sweden there are no restrictions on the immigration of workers from other Scandinavian countries, and such workers are eligible for Government retraining programs if they reside in Sweden. Other aliens may be admitted to vocational training courses for adults if they have had steady employment in Sweden for at least 6 months and otherwise meet the usual eligibility conditions.

Unemployed Negroes are admitted to Government training centers in Britain, provided they are accepted by the advisory committees for their trades and meet other selection standards. I observed a number of Negroes among the trainees at the training center in Perivale on the outskirts of London but, interestingly, nearly all of them were in a single class which was being trained for wood machinery work. I was told that the admission standards for this class would require some knowledge of mathematics but were considerably easier to meet than for certain other types of training, such as instrument making or radio and television repair. The concentration of Negroes in this class may have been explained by these easier admission standards but a more liberal policy toward admission to training on the part of the advisory committee concerned may also have played a role. The manager of the center informed me that the Negroes in the class were likely to be placed eventually but that it would take longer than in the case of Caucasian trainees and that some employers discriminated against Negroes.[50]

France has signed binational agreements with Spain, Portugal, Yugoslavia, and with the African states which were its former colonies to give their migrants the same rights to adult vocational training that Frenchmen have, although there is a legal upper limit of 10 percent for foreigners' participation in the regular vocational training programs.[51] Participation in this program requires knowledge of the French language. France gives training to certain Spanish and Yugoslav workers before they emigrate, and it has recently created an elementary vocational and language training program particularly for Africans.[52] Germany, Sweden, and some Swiss firms also provide training in the country of emigration. Sweden, Belgium, and Luxembourg give the foreign worker equal access to training courses available in those countries.[53] Belgium, Sweden, and some German firms pay the workers an allowance while they are getting vocational training.[54] In 1967 a vocational training center for 130 Italians was opened in Berne, Switzerland, under the auspices of the Italian consulate and with support from local authorities, Swiss industrialists, and trade unions.[55] Germany provides much vocational training for migrant workers through private firms rather than through the government, but by bilateral treaty it offers special training to Japanese miners in the Ruhr when the latter come to work there for limited periods, and it pays one-fourth of the costs to train Italian semiskilled workers before they emigrate. Simply offering vocational training to migrants on the same basis as to nationals does not usually attract many foreign workers because they do not wish to sacrifice hours when they might be earning more money, and sometimes they cannot understand a course designed for native citizens. For this reason, the special programs for migrants — often with pay for subsistence — offered by France, Germany, and Sweden are the only ones that reach any large numbers of migrant workers. Because of a lack of standardization of training requirements across national lines, sometimes a migrant is required to attend unnecessary training courses in a receiving country in order to obtain formal recognition of a skill he already has.

Note must also be taken of the fact that universities in countries of immigration provide professional and technical training for foreign students who — after completing their courses — decide to stay in the country and use their professional and technical knowledge there rather than return to their home countries. In the United Kingdom, Leicester University has a six-month refresher course for immigrant teachers who have not been able to find jobs in Britain because of an inadequate knowledge of the English language or of British teaching methods.[56]

ORIENTATION BEFORE MIGRATION [57]

The uprooting of an individual or family from a familiar society and replacement in an alien one is an extremely difficult and sometimes traumatic process, especially if at the time that the migrant is crossing a national and cultural border he is also moving from a rural social system to an urban one. Most would-be migrants concentrate only on the work aspects and are not aware of the other problems involved in migrating. Emigrant countries — with the exception of Italy and Spain — usually do little to prepare their emigrants before departing because (1) they lack the means to do the orienting; (2) they see little reason for encouraging migration; (3) they do not know how to reach the would-be emigrants and the emigrants do not know where to apply; (4) some of the emigrants see no need for orientation — they migrate just to "see" if they like it better in another country; (5) some of the emigrants do not want to attract attention (because they are clandestine emigrants from Spain or Portugal or because they are entering the countries of immigration as pseudo-tourists). Some informal orientation — partially based on misinformation — occurs through letters from and direct contacts with relatives or friends who migrated earlier. Perhaps the best orientation before departure occurs in the country of emigration when officials of the country of immigration work with those of the country of emigration, as provided for in some of the binational treaties.[58] There is some risk to the country of immigration when it invests money for this purpose, especially in the expensive vocational training programs, in that the prospective migrants may change their minds about migrating or about their destination. This occurred in the large-scale German-Italian training program — cosponsored by the European Social Fund — when many of the trained and oriented southern Italians decided to take up work in northern Italy rather than in Germany.

The Spanish Emigrants Institute, sponsored by the government, circulates information on the characteristics of the receiving country (cost of living, climate, housing, conditions of work, admission of families) in the form of small brochures. This same institute has officials scattered around Spain to transmit such information orally. In 1967 the institute opened a large center in Irun at the French border to aid migrants in transit.[59] In Italy there are private associations, usually church groups, encouraged by the authorities, that provide the same kind of information. Spain offers courses on language, labor law, and living conditions. Italy offers more courses, including some vocational training.

Outside these two, countries of emigration have only the information provided by the countries of immigration, which does not reach all would-be migrants. Bilateral treaties provide for recruiting centers, run by the immigrant countries in selected cities of emigrant countries, to be set up to dispense information as well as to select migrant workers. Trade union channels sometimes are used to transmit information, but this reaches only those already in industrial employment in their own country. The French government distributes phrase books and information guides informing would-be migrants of their rights and obligations if they go to France.[60] The German government distributes a brochure on living and working conditions in Germany. The EEC has a guide to social security regulations among its six member countries. Certain German firms and the Swedish government offer vocational training and general orientation courses for workers already selected to migrate to their respective countries.

RECRUITMENT

The various countries of immigration have different procedures for recruiting foreign workers abroad. Belgium and Switzerland give the responsibility to the employers, subject to national regulations regarding health and the form of the work contract. Ordinarily the Swiss authorities are not informed of a migration until the work contract has already been signed and the employer requests — sometimes after the migrant is already in Switzerland — a residence permit. Very rarely is there rejection of a residence permit on grounds of insufficient skill.[61] The United Kingdom has only temporary recruiting missions, although it has a general migration program. France and Germany give a legal monopoly to a public body to handle recruiting of foreign manpower abroad, and Sweden does likewise when there is a treaty with the country of emigration.[62] Germany has set up recruiting missions in Spain, Greece, Italy, Portugal, Morocco, and Turkey; and France has done so in Spain, Italy, Morocco, Portugal, and Yugoslavia. There are requirements of skill and health. Sometimes age limits are imposed: the French have upper age limits of 35 and 40 for unskilled and skilled workers; the Germans theoretically have no age limits, but in fact do. Firms in Germany and France specify their needs to the recruiting missions, which make the selection and transport the workers to the firms. In France if a candidate does not suit the employer, another worker is proposed; the failed migrant is offered other jobs or repatriated. In Germany the recruited worker usually comes with a contract for one year, which is binding both on himself and on the employer (but certain exemptions are permitted). The German employer guarantees transportation and housing, and the foreigner is on the same footing as nationals regarding wages and working conditions. However, foreigners are generally placed in low-level jobs so that the actual wages for aliens are lower than for nationals. Work permits must be renewed each year and may be broken by the worker only with proper notice. If the worker fails to give proper notice, he is blacklisted from further employment in Germany. Only after five years does he have the right to change occupations and employers, but in practice, unofficial procedures permit him to change before that if he has given due notice to his old employer.

The large number of would-be migrants rejected by the French and German recruiting offices (for France in 1958, 50 percent were rejected on grounds of skill and 10 percent on grounds of health) suggests that problems of some magnitude confront countries of immigration that do not have such selection procedures. Of course, a very large percentage of immigrant workers evade official recruitment and enter the country of immigration as "tourists" (even to France and Germany the percentage is more than half and increasing every year). These "tourists" usually find a job, and then apply for residence and work permits. They are unselected, they miss most orientation, and they are subject to the hazards of the market and to exploitation by labor agents and by some unscrupulous employers.

LANGUAGE INSTRUCTION [63]

Ignorance of the language of the country of immigration is a tremendous barrier to effective relations with others both on the job and in the community. For understanding work orders, following safety rules, expressing oneself to the employer and to fellow workers, knowledge of language is essential; so is it for talking to neighbors, making acquaintances, claiming rights from the authorities, and taking advantage of recreational opportunities (including radio and TV).

As noted earlier, Italy and Spain are the only two emigrant countries which attempt systematically to offer their emigrants foreign language courses. Italian missions also offer language courses in France, Belgium, Switzerland, Germany, and the Netherlands, and Spanish Catholic missions do so in Germany, Belgium, and Switzerland. Some firms in all countries of immigration offer their foreign workers language courses, usually during off-hours but sometimes during company hours for a few lessons dealing with the language of safety or of the occupation. The German trade unions have an extensive program of language teaching; the Luxembourgian trade unions have organized French courses for Italian workers; the Swiss trade unions in Lucerne have instituted French courses for Spanish workers. Private associations — especially in Germany, France, and Belgium — teach the local language to foreign workers, sometimes coupling it with elementary training in literacy for the illiterate immigrant.[64]

Local or provincial government authorities offer language courses for foreigners in France, the United Kingdom, Luxembourg, and some provinces of Belgium. For many of these courses workers are required to pay a nominal fee. In Sweden, France, Belgium, and the United Kingdom the national authorities have set up or subsidized free language courses in some localities, sometimes offered in schools or workers' hostels. In Sweden numerous cultural associations, trade unions, and employers offer programs to teach Swedish to foreigners and to facilitate the integration of migrants generally.[65] In 1963 the British Ministry of Education issued a booklet titled *English for Immigrants*. In some English towns, organizations run by Indian immigrants themselves provide classes in English.[66] A television station in Bavaria began in 1967 to broadcast once a week a half-hour German lesson intended for Italian workers.[67] Most of the commentators on language teaching say that it is inadequate (although some experiments with promising new techniques of instruction are going on), and that workers evince little interest in it.[68]

France undoubtedly has the best program of language teaching for foreigners. The French National Education Ministry has a section to or-

71

ganize courses in the French language.[69] These are offered free, after work hours, for six hours a week. A great deal of attention has been given to the methods of teaching. Courses can be offered wherever there are at least ten people wanting to take them. For adult women there are daytime courses (four hours a week) giving practical and general information about France as well as teaching the French language. The French government has now associated itself with the Alliance Française, which offers all levels of language instruction in day and night courses, for a fee; at its high levels the Alliance Française is tied to the universities. As noted above, private groups — such as firms or churches — also offer French language courses. A Comité de Coordination pour l'Alphabetisation coordinates all private groups who give *cours d'alphabetisation* (literacy courses), primarily to Algerians and other Africans who cannot read. While the main goal of this committee is to teach literacy, it also serves to teach the French language. There are about eighty such courses in the Paris region, with from twenty to eighty "students" in each. For many years the French schools have been offering after-school classes in French for foreign children (given at five P.M., three times a week, for one and one-half hours). Since October 1966 the elementary schools have been trying intensive *cours d'initiation* in which all foreign children in an *arrondissement* (ward) are grouped together for all-day classes conducted in French. It is hoped that after a year or so, they will have caught up. The remedial courses for adolescents (14–18 years) include three-month sessions of intensive French (three hours a day; another three hours for general education, sports, manual training). These classes are intended to prepare youngsters for regular technical schools (the younger ones) or for regular adult vocational training (the older ones). While these courses are given only in Paris, parents elsewhere in France may send their children if they can afford to pay for lodging (financial aid is available from the Fonds d'Action Sociales pour les Travailleurs Etrangers). Actually, the demand for such courses is greater than the supply, so that only a portion of the needs are being met. According to the bilateral treaties France has with Spain and Yugoslavia, French authorities pay for language and vocational training for the expected emigrants in their home country before they leave.[70]

ORIENTATION AFTER MIGRATION

Initial reception information — regarding administrative formalities, local social services, and temporary housing — and sometimes small financial aid are best provided by POA-ONARMO, an Italian private association operating by an agreement with the Italian Ministry of Labor. It has centers in Verona, Genoa, Rome, and Naples, cooperating with fifty centers in various parts of Germany and five in Belgium. Frequently an Italian social worker accompanies a group of Italian emigrants and stays with them for a period of time.[71] Some of the Italian consulates abroad have permanent social attachés or welfare assistants to aid their emigrants, and nonexperts in the consulates of other emigrant countries perform like services on a less well organized basis. Catholic and other private societies in Switzerland aid in the reception of young female migrants. The Swiss and Luxembourgian authorities distribute guidebooks containing practical information to immigrants at principal points of entry into Switzerland. Most countries provide little reception aid to "tourist" arrivals, but do have a procedure for meeting and aiding the migrant workers who have gone through the regular selection procedures. Migrants are often exploited by unscrupulous persons of their own nationality who pretend to be helping them.

The United Kingdom has more than four hundred Citizens' Advice Bureaus, scattered over the country, to aid all residents — nationals and foreigners — with domestic, financial, personal, and legal difficulties. This is a private organization financed by both the local governments and voluntary contributions. Local governments and the governments of the Commonwealth countries employ experts, who are themselves nationals of the emigrant countries, to provide information and orientation to the immigrants directly, as well as to specialized government agencies and to private agencies and individuals who have to deal with immigrants (e.g., social workers, landlords, the police, and trade unions).

An inquiry by the German Federal Employers' Associations (Bundesvereinigung der Deutschen Arbeitgeberverbände) in 1964 showed that of sixty firms employing foreign workers, eight regularly published supplementary periodicals in the different languages of the workers, thirteen had once published a brochure for their foreign workers, four published welcome leaflets, and fifteen distributed information on factory regulations and safety rules.[72] The German union federation (DGB) in 1964 started a monthly newsletter for Turkish workers to educate them about political developments, legal matters, and the activities of the trade unions. Several radio and TV stations in Germany, Belgium, Switzerland, Italy, and Spain broadcast special programs for migrant workers which provide information, sometimes along with entertainment.[73] Since 1966 the French radio has devoted ten minutes a day to orientation information in Spanish and Portuguese. A bulletin jointly published by the Belgian Ministry of Labor and the Turkish Embassy in Brussels provides advice about food, recreational facilities, and so on.[74]

In most of the immigration countries of Europe, various Roman Catholic organizations run immigrant orientation and aid programs. In France the private association CIMADE, sponsored by Protestant and Orthodox church groups, runs a number of centers and provides other programs for the orientation of migrant workers and refugees. The center for Portuguese working in the Paris region concentrates on basic literacy (in French) but is also concerned with teaching about the French way of life, and it has a cultural program for more advanced migrants.[75] In Belgium the coal industry has an extensive social service and orientation program for its foreign workers — providing home-making courses, infant-care and school information, hospitals, maternity facilities, nurseries for small children, and social clubs for workers.

HOUSING PROGRAMS

It need not be stressed how important adequate housing is for the worker's health, mental balance, protection, social integration, status, and sometimes opportunities (e.g., for education of his children). Thus, inadequacy of housing has been a chief obstacle to migration at times and in places where job opportunities have been readily available. Dormitories and private sleeping rooms in rundown buildings, with many sleeping in one room and sometimes several sleeping in one bed (the so-called "hot bed" when workers on different work shifts take turns sleeping in the same bed), have not infrequently been the major accommodations available to single men.[76] The absence of sufficient family housing is the major obstacle preventing the married worker from bringing his family to live with him in countries which permit immigrant families when housing is available. With the partial exception of Sweden, Belgium, and Luxembourg, immigrant countries have severe housing shortages, particularly in the major industrial cities. Where there is a housing shortage, the worker can obtain adequate accommodations at a moderate rental usually only by proving the presence of dependents; but the immigration laws of several countries prohibit the entry of families until the worker can prove he has adequate housing accommodation for them. Thus a peculiar vicious circle is created which prevents the worker from obtaining family housing.[77] Even when the worker is eligible to apply for family housing, he may lack information and may not speak the language of the host country, which makes it difficult for him to initiate the required administrative procedures.

The recruited single migrant who goes through the regular selection procedure is usually given a clean, if very modest and sometimes makeshift, room by his employer, but the "tourist" migrants have to forage to find even the worst kind of housing — often at very high rents considering what they are getting. The majority of migrants in the mid-1960's were in the latter category. In no country are there laws requiring segregation of nationals and foreign workers, but the housing shortage — combined with the migrant worker's desire to get the cheapest accommodations and to live with his conationals — tends to segregate them. Some landlords refuse to rent to foreigners, and subtle segregationist practices can even get around the few nondiscrimination laws which exist.[78] Many countries — either through EEC rules, binational treaties, or national regulations — can legally claim there is no discrimination in housing, but the absence of specific and enforced minimum housing standards in a situation of extreme housing shortage, as well as the prejudice of and exploitation by some landlords, puts the migrant workers in housing much inferior to that of nationals at the same wage levels. The effective segregation of foreigners prevents many social contacts with the people of the host country and thus reduces acceptance and mutually positive attitudes.

France encourages families of foreign workers to immigrate, and makes credit for private home ownership and low-rent housing equally available to foreigners and nationals, but the considerable capital outlay required and the general rules for obtaining low-rent housing — especially the one giving priority to those on the list longest — eliminate most foreigners. Exceptions occur where additional funds supplied by employers or by the Caisses d'Allocations Familiales provide additional accommodation units for foreigners' families.[79] The French Office National d'Immigration (ONI) recruits foreign workers under two forms of contract: under a *contrat anonyme*, the ONI is responsible for finding accommodation for the worker, while under a *contrat nominatif* this is the employer's responsibility. An order of November 2, 1945, stipulates that an employer may bring a foreign worker into France only if he can ensure that he has accommodation. It should, however, be remembered that immigration organized by the ONI accounts for less than 50 percent of total immigrant workers and only 10 percent of all immigrant family members, the remainder being represented by independent "tourist" immigration.[80]

Belgium has subsidized-housing societies, to which foreigners may apply for housing on an equal basis with nationals. Foreign coal miners share with Belgian miners preferential treatment in renting or buying. On the other hand, Switzerland puts certain barriers on family living for foreigners: they must have three years of continuous residence in Switzerland to rent an unfurnished apartment (this excludes seasonal workers unless they have been working in Switzerland for many years), their personal behavior must not have given rise to criticism during the three years, and they may not rent any accommodation belonging to the city of Geneva.[81] By a treaty with Italy ratified in 1965, Switzerland permits nonseasonal

75

Italian workers to bring their families after eighteen months rather than after three years as required of all others. The Luxembourgian government has given a good deal of attention to the housing of foreign workers and their families,[82] but it does discriminate both for and against foreign workers in regard to subsidy (contrary to EEC rules).[83] The German government and employers have provided adequate housing for single workers in most cases, but have done very little for families.[84] In the Netherlands there is no discrimination against foreigners by the government, but the shortage of housing is so severe that the government has asked employers to hire only single workers.[85] The Dutch government partly subsidizes nonprofit private associations to build housing for poor persons, but the supply does not keep up with the demand for housing. In Britain, where families may emigrate without proving they have accommodations in advance, there is no discrimination as such, but there is a waiting period for public housing which in effect excludes newcomers.[86] The British government is providing more adequate housing for foreigners, however, since it is anxious to reduce intergroup tensions.

In building new accommodations for single foreign workers by private employers, Germany has made the greatest effort among countries of immigration in recent years. France has also made some notable progress.[87] In France, Germany, and Luxembourg the governments lend money to manufacturing firms, building companies, and private associations that will build new accommodations for single workers, and sometimes the governments partially subsidize this. Germany gives restricted loans to foreign workers who have two years' residence in the country to purchase a family accommodation. In France the government has made itself directly responsible for building dwellings for foreigners, both for single and family migrants. Specific steps have been taken to discourage segregation of foreign workers in housing owned by the governments, trade unions, and many employers in France, Germany, and Sweden.

LEISURE-TIME PROGRAMS

Free time presents a special problem for foreign workers, especially single ones, because they are not accustomed to the local and urban ways of utilizing it and they do not like to spend money for commercial recreation. Leisure time can generate feelings of solitude, isolation, and frustration which are not experienced to the same degree during work hours. The migrants are somewhat in the position of the traveler who is passing through a town on a public holiday and kills time either sitting in his hotel or wandering aimlessly along the main streets. Foreign workers try to "pass the time" in the company of their fellow countrymen, but where no leisure centers have been specially organized for them they very soon find themselves sharing nothing more than their common idleness and collective disillusion. Free time is thus very often more harmful than beneficial and gives the workers no opportunity for throwing off their cares or improving themselves culturally.[88]

Ideally, leisure-time pursuits can help provide the "decompression chamber" [89] which aids in the ultimate adjustment of migrant workers to the country of immigration, and for this reason are often best organized along national lines. But foreigners should not arbitrarily be cut off from the public recreational activities of their current communities. Business firms and unions in Sweden, Germany, and Luxembourg offer such things as leisure clubs, recreation rooms in hostels, libraries, and film shows organized along national lines. A survey by the International Catholic Migration Commission [90] in the EEC countries (not including Italy) and Switzerland suggests that Germany is the country in which leisure activities are best organized, especially in Italian and Spanish centers. In Germany by the end of 1962, 215 leisure centers for foreign workers were operating, equipped with radios, television, film projectors, records, books, and sometimes hired sports grounds. "The Italian 'Centri' are particularly active (there were about 120 in 1964). They are generally run by an Italian welfare officer and offer their members all kinds of entertainment and cultural facilities. They also run a bar and, in big cities, a restaurant which serves national dishes." [91] Religious organizations (both Catholic and Protestant) often promote the establishment of leisure centers and look after them. Italian and Spanish Catholic missions are particularly active in Belgium, France, Germany, and Switzerland. Other private organizations, sometimes with financial aid from government or business, also run leisure centers. The Dutch firms hiring foreigners have set up recreational centers for them in the large cities where they can listen to radio and TV, read foreign publications, play table games, and so forth.[92]

Germany, France, and Belgium have special radio programs for certain groups of foreign workers in their own language (but the Netherlands does not).[93] The active Service Provincial d'Immigration et d'Accueil of Liège, Belgium, has sponsored a remarkable series of cultural and hobby programs for foreign workers, to which the public is invited.[94] The emigration countries often circulate national newspapers and popular books to their nationals abroad. Switzerland has a lending-library service for foreign workers. Italian Catholic and other private organizations have a daily newspaper and two periodicals, specially prepared for emigrants abroad. Trade unions, employers, religious organizations, and other groups in the country of immigration sometimes sponsor small "newspapers" for foreign workers in their own languages.[95] Sometimes the regular union or

77

firm newspaper will have a column or two in Italian, Spanish, or some other language of foreign workers. Many local groups of foreign workers, if they are present in sufficient numbers, publish their own newspapers in their native languages.[96] In France there are over two hundred foreign-language newspapers and magazines to serve the needs of immigrants and visitors.[97] The immigrants sometimes organize their own voluntary associations and social centers. In Belgium, for example, the Greeks and Italians have done this, but the Portuguese have not.[98]

The British have experimented with a type of program which is otherwise found extensively only in the United States, Australia, and Canada.[99] The program aims to orient British nationals to the problems and needs of foreigners, with a view to diminishing prejudice against them.[100] In 1964 about twenty-five local committees were formed, sponsored by local governments or private associations, to educate the public in the various cities of the United Kingdom where migrants had settled. The membership comprised a great variety of knowledgeable people (including leading members of migrant communities) who organized talks, presented films, offered specialized conferences and discussions (where citizens were urged to air their prejudices), served as investigating bodies for complaints, sponsored intergroup activities, encouraged migrants to participate in local civic events, interpreted migrants to the local press to discourage sensational or unsympathetic reporting, and produced leaflets designed to help migrants know what services were available to them. In a mixed ethnic neighborhood in Birmingham, a voluntary neighborhood association has been operating for some years to cope with neighborhood problems, and to prevent any conflict from developing along ethnic lines.[101] The British Broadcasting Corporation has special programs to promote good group relationships and it guards against prejudice being reflected in any of its programs. While the British government has adopted a policy of severe restriction on immigration, especially from the colored Commonwealth nations, it has also adopted a policy of equality and integration toward those already in the country. The government has ruled that employers who discriminate against foreigners or nonwhites are not to be helped to fill vacancies by the Government Employment Exchanges, and a nondiscrimination clause for government contracts was under discussion in 1967.[102] Immigrant associations have long existed in Britain, but in 1965 a combined association comprising West Indians, Indians, Pakistanis, and Africans was formed following a visit from the American Negro leader Martin Luther King. The new organization is called Campaign Against Racial Discrimination (CARD).[103]

In 1965 the United Kingdom adopted a Race Relations Act to restrict the practice or advocacy of racial discrimination in public places (in the

United States this would be called a "civil rights law" or "public accommodations law") and to punish incitement to racial or ethnic hatred. The government established a Race Relations Board to enforce this law by procedures of public hearings, persuasion, and ultimate coercion — similar to procedures used in the United States by fair employment practices commissions — and it also established a National Committee for Commonwealth Immigrants to aid the public education campaign against discrimination. The Race Relations Board inaugurated a professional study of discrimination in Britain against ethnic minorities and the study, completed in early 1967, revealed significant discrimination in employment and housing.[104] The board then proposed to the government a new law that would work against discrimination in these areas, and it suggested stronger procedures of implementation. A *Sunday Times* poll showed that, while the British people were deeply divided concerning such a projected statute, the majority were in favor of it.[105] The answers to the question "Would you be for or against laws to ensure equal treatment for everyone in housing and jobs regardless of their race and colour?" were distributed as follows: for, 59 percent; against, 31 percent; don't know, 10 percent. When "tougher" questions were asked, the answers were not as favorable to a stronger law: "Do you think it should be illegal to refuse a job to someone because of his race or colour?" — yes, 48 percent; no, 44 percent; don't know, 8 percent. "Do you think it should be illegal to refuse to sell or rent someone a house because of his race or colour?" — yes, 44 percent; no, 45 percent; don't know, 10 percent. On the last two questions, upper-middle-class respondents were significantly more opposed to legislation than were those in the lower occupational classes. The outcome of the effort to pass a greatly expanded and stronger law against discrimination is not known at the time of writing, but the extensive discussions of the proposed legislation in the press and in groups throughout the country show that the United Kingdom is facing the problem much more openly than are other countries of Europe, where the situation is often just as serious.[106]

In Belgium the Service Provincial d'Immigration et d'Accueil of Liège performs some of the tasks of informing the local citizenry about migrants and their culture, but it is basically a small group of paid experts rather than a high-level voluntary citizens committee. At the time of writing (spring 1967), the Belgian government was contemplating a bill similar to the British Race Relations Act. The German trade union federation (DGB) was urging its members not to isolate themselves from foreign workers but to welcome them, and this admonition was occasionally found in other union newspapers throughout northern Europe. In April 1967 the French radio put on a series of short programs designed to inform the French people about immigrants and their problems. It was surprising to an American that so little was being done to counteract prejudice on the European continent, for such work has become a major citizen activity and a profession for paid employees in the United States.

POLICIES AND PROGRAMS TOWARD MIGRANT WORKERS' FAMILIES

Certainly one of the most important factors in the successful integration or acceptance of migrants is their living in family units rather than as single persons. Forced celibacy can lead to both personal and social disorganization: many men will have recourse to prostitutes or to homosexual practices, some men who have left their families in their native countries will develop extramarital relationships that may lead to the abandonment of their families. Single migrants are more likely than others to have an inadequate diet as well as an unfamiliar one; the single migrant usually does little to improve his housing condition whereas the migrant with a family usually does much. The family is one of the most important parts of the "decompression chamber" which provides the early psychological nurturance for ultimate adjustment to the country of immigration, and its absence creates various psychological problems. The intellectual horizons of the family members who stay in the home country are not expanded along with those of its migrant member (usually the father and husband), which may make for marital conflict when the migrant returns to his native country. The cost of maintaining two housing units per family is greater than maintaining one. The absence of wife and children eliminates two of the most effective ties that a migrant can develop with the country of reception. The migrant deprived of family life will often feel bitterness toward the depriving authorities and their country. There are benefits to the country of immigration if it permits the migrant worker to bring his family: he will send much less of his savings to his native country — thus reducing the strain on the receiving country's foreign exchange — and he is likely to be a more permanent and stable worker.[107]

As noted earlier, since 1964 the EEC countries have agreed not to exclude any family members who accompany or who later wish to join the migrant, if they come from another EEC country. Table 8 summarizes the facts regarding receptiveness of countries of immigration to family living for migrant workers. France, Luxembourg, Sweden, the United Kingdom, and Belgium are favorable or open to it.[108] The United Kingdom permits it if the worker has a skill in short supply or if he works in an occupation which has a labor shortage; France and Belgium encourage the migration of families, but their shortage of housing makes it difficult. Germany permits the entry of families but makes it very difficult in practice by requir-

Table 8. Sex Ratio of Foreign Population and Policies toward Admitting
Families of Foreign Workers in Countries of Immigration

Country	No. of Men per 100 Women for 1960–62[a]	Policy toward Admitting Families
Belgium	133	Treaties with Turkey, Spain, Greece authorize admission of families if workers have accommodations for them. Belgian government pays 50% of travel expense if 3 children or more.
France	133	Treaties with Spain, Portugal, Morocco, Algeria, Tunisia specifically admit families, but workers must provide suitable housing. Allowance given for travel and for initial expense of settlement. Encourages family living. Permits families to enter as tourists. Families must have medical exam.
Germany (FR)	222	Treaties with Spain, Greece, Portugal allow workers to bring families if workers find suitable housing, but standards are strict. Does not permit families to enter as tourists. Tries to find work contracts for wives, but provides no help to children of working mothers. Only about 10% of married workers brought families.
Luxembourg	105	No barriers to bringing families. Workers must have jobs and housing, but housing is easily available.
Netherlands	182	Until recently opposed entry of families. In 1964 began to admit wives but not children. Employment preference given unmarried workers. Non-EEC nationals may bring families after 2 years if adequate housing is available.
Sweden	104	No barriers to bringing families.
Switzerland	130	Does not generally admit families. Grants permission only for (1) Workers in skilled or managerial positions for which there is a scarcity of nationals. (2) Workers in country for 3 years (since 1965 Italians need only 18 months' residence), with unexceptional conduct, and if housing available (but difficult to get residence permit for more than a year). (3) Seasonal workers in country for 5 consecutive seasons (45 months or more).
United Kingdom	106	No barriers to bringing families. Workers must have jobs and housing, but housing is easily available.

SOURCES. G. de Rochcau, "L'Etat actuel de l'immigration familiale en Europe," *Migration News*, 1:2 (March–April 1963), pp. 1–3; OECD, *Joint International Seminar on Adaptation of Rural and Foreign Workers to Industry, Supplement to the Final Report Annex by Swedish Joint Team to Germany* (Paris, 1965), p. 176; United Nations, Office of Social Affairs of the European Office, *European Seminar on Social Welfare Programmes for Migrant Workers, Madrid, April 2–10, 1964* (Geneva, 1965), p. 50; Robert Descloitres, "Adaptation of Foreign Workers to Industrial Work and Urban Life," MSS/66.167 (OECD, June 1966), pp. 157–159; Interviews with government officials.

[a] Sex ratios calculated from most recent census data from each country. The United Kingdom sex ratio is for those born outside the British Isles with nationality or citizenship in a European country.

ing that the worker secure housing which is almost unobtainable at moderate rates; the Netherlands and Switzerland are quite negative to family migration. For the latter three countries, and for some of the former ones as well,

The reluctance to admit families goes beyond the housing shortage and is a result of basic policy towards the permanent admission of foreigners. So long as the workers concerned are single or live like single men it may be considered that they will sooner or later return to their own countries. But as soon as families are reunited with the head of household it is obvious that the chances of permanent settlement are increased. . . . There is no prima facie case for concluding that most of the families which rejoin the head of household wish to settle definitely in the receiving country. The progress of transport facilities, the resultant increase in mobility, the speed-up in the development of certain regions from which the migrants originate, etc., suggest that a large number of families after several years residence abroad return to their original countries.[109]

By 1967 Switzerland had made family migration for new foreign workers all but impossible, although according to the 1965 treaty with Italy the Swiss authorities can permit the entry of the Italian worker's wife and minor children when his employment is considered sufficiently stable and durable and when he has found suitable housing for them. The Netherlands requires the non-EEC immigrant to work two years, have a labor contract for the third year, and find suitable living quarters before he can bring his family.

Data on the migration of workers' families are very sparse. Only France among the countries of immigration collects data on the admission of workers' families. During the period 1947 through 1963, only 12 percent of the immigrant workers registered in France brought their families or had their presence regularized. A study of Sicilian migrants to Germany in 1965 indicated that only 5.5 percent brought their families.[110]

A cruder but more available index of the presence of families among migrants is the sex ratio. Table 8 shows the sex ratios of foreign nationals (number of men per 100 women) in the census years 1960–62, and these reflect somewhat the policies toward admitting families of foreign workers. The sex ratios for Germany and the Netherlands were abnormally high. The sex ratio for Switzerland in later years would perhaps be as abnormal but the figure in the table reflects the older, more liberal policy. Sweden, Luxembourg, and the United Kingdom have almost balanced sex ratios among their foreigners, reflecting their liberal policies toward admitting families.

Trade unions and employers in some countries — notably Belgium, Luxembourg, and the Netherlands — make holiday homes available to families of workers on vacation, so the family may then visit the worker and the country of immigration.[111] Germany has a generous "leave" policy to permit foreign workers to visit their families in their home countries during vacation periods, but in 1966 German employers seemed to favor a change of policy to permit families to join the workers so as to encourage them to reduce their turnover.[112]

There is a close relationship between assistance to families and a country's admission policy.[113] Italy has a significant welfare and orientation program for its emigrant families, and many church organizations in most countries have provided this service regularly. In France certain official services and charitable associations financed by the state give assistance to foreign families. France subsidizes educational institutions to give courses in general education, French language, and domestic economy for wives. In the Paris area there is even a *Camion Ecole* (mobile school) which provides language and domestic-economy training for wives as well as a nursery for children. France and Italy are almost unique among the governments in providing special aids for migrant families, although other governments permit wives to enter foreign language classes. Sweden has a comprehensive adult education program subsidized in large part by the government, and both migrants and their wives can take advantage of this on an equal basis with Swedish nationals. The special educational needs of foreign children (language training, remedial teaching, orientation) are given attention in a number of regions in Belgium, the United Kingdom, France, Germany, and Switzerland.[114] In Sweden foreign children are given one year of special instruction in the Swedish language; if eight or more children apply they can get language training in any foreign language.[115] Germany has provided some special schools for foreign children, in which they are taught the language and history of their own country; [116] some classes are sponsored by the Belgian Ministry of National Education in Polish culture and language for Polish children, and in Italian civilization and language for Italian children, for the purpose of preventing a rupture between parents and children.[117] A number of schools in the German-speaking parts of Switzerland offer regular classes in Italian for immigrant children.[118] Italian and Spanish consulates and church organizations in Switzerland operate a number of schools, from the nursery level to adult vocational and cultural classes. (There is a danger that these special classes to aid immigrant children will result in educational segregation, and in the United Kingdom the Commonwealth Immigrants Advisory Council drew up a report to the government on the means of avoiding this. The British Department of Education advised local authorities that they should not allow the proportion of immigrants in any one school to exceed 30 percent.)[119] Maladapted adolescent children of foreign workers, believed to be vulnerable to juvenile delinquency, are given a year of special training in a boarding school in Marseilles (one hundred boys a year since 1966) to bring them up to grade level educationally, and follow-through attention is given to them after the year is over. In Marseilles also there is a three-year course for two hundred undereducated adolescent girls, to give them general elementary education, courses in domestic economy, hygiene, care of young children, and other practical education. As of 1967 the number of special programs — all mentioned in this paragraph — was sparse indeed.

Family allowances, when provided by countries or sections of countries to their own nationals, are also provided to foreign workers' families *if* the latter are domiciled in the country of immigration (except for one Swiss canton which provides no family allowances for foreigners under any circumstances).[120] But not all families domiciled abroad in non-EEC countries are paid these allowances. Where they are paid, it is usually at a lower rate and for a limited time only. There is a special problem in the case of Moslem workers — from North Africa and Turkey — who sometimes have more than one wife and a large number of children, or claim to have them when seeking family allowances. Another restriction applying to non-EEC workers is that allowances are not paid to the families of seasonal workers (except for France where by treaty agreement they are paid to Spanish seasonal workers). Since Switzerland now regards all new immigrants as seasonal workers, none of their nonagricultural workers' families get allowances. Agricultural workers are included in family-allowance schemes in Switzerland (except for one canton) and the Netherlands, but Portuguese agricultural workers in France are not (because family allowances do not exist in Portugal).

France gives foreign workers special rights to loans for housing and household equipment so they may bring their families.[121] Since 1965 Belgium has paid half the travel expense of the wife and children when they join a foreign worker, provided there are at least three minor children in the family. Belgium is also more likely to extend a work permit indefinitely if the worker has brought his family. In Sweden and Belgium work permits are automatically granted to wives and are extended on the same basis as the husbands'. In other countries there are the same difficulties in getting work permits for foreign wives as for their husbands, except for domestic-service jobs.

REQUIREMENTS FOR NATURALIZATION AND CHANGE OF NAME

The policies toward migration thus far examined deal directly with the adaptation of immigrants to the problems of migration; they are concerned with "aids to adjustment." In this section two policies will be considered that are more relevant to the controversial issue of assimilation than to adjustment: the legal requirements for naturalization (that is, conferring citizenship on foreigners) and for changing one's name (presumably to one more typical of the country of immigration). Ease of naturalization and name changing are not necessarily advocated here as policies that facilitate assimilation, but rather are used as further indexes of the acceptance of immigrants by the countries of immigration. For reasons that will be considered shortly, national policies toward name change turn out to have little relevance to the context of this study. The topic is included here to explain why the expectation one might have that easy facilitation of name change would be an index of acceptance is not borne out.

The major requirements of the countries of immigration for naturalization are summarized in Table 9. Special circumstances, such as service in the armed forces, are not included nor is the universal requirement that the applicant for naturalization must have attained the age of adulthood. Blanks in the table under "knowledge of language" and "moral behavior" do not mean that these are not requirements, but merely that they are not specified formally in the statutes: the citizenship-conferring authority (court of law or administrative agency) usually takes them into account when deciding whether or not to grant citizenship. The critical items are the required length of time in the country and the readiness (routineness) of the citizenship-conferring authority to grant citizenship when the statutory requirements have been met. The table shows that Luxembourg and Switzerland set up the highest barriers to naturalization; the most accepting countries are France, Germany, the Netherlands, and the United Kingdom.

Table 10 is a summary of the requirements for changing one's name. In general this is very difficult in Europe; requests are not encouraged and most requests are refused. The exceptions are France and the United Kingdom. In France it is expected that one would want to "francisize" one's name; it is encouraged at the time of naturalization, and the request is granted unless someone objects during a six-month waiting period. In the United Kingdom name changes are even easier: a person can change his name "by custom" (although he could get into legal difficulties this way), but there is also a simple procedure of advertising the name change in the newspapers and registering it in court. Only in these two countries is a foreigner encouraged to change his name to fit better into the society. The Dutch consider that having an "unpronounceable" name is a reason for changing it; the Swedes permit changing to a "Swedish-like" name if someone else does not already have the name. Only the United Kingdom permits a noncitizen to request authorities to grant a change of name.

85

Table 9. Requirements for Naturalization in Countries of Immigration

Country	No. of Years of Residence	Reduction of Residence Requirement	Knowledge of Language	Moral Behavior	Fee
Belgium	6 or 10[a]	Reduced to 3 or 5 years, if EEC national, married to Belgian, living in Belgium before age 14			2,000–16,000 FB ($40–$320), according to income
France	5	Waived, if wife or child of citizen (inc. naturalized); 2 years, if married to French woman, born in France, French university diplomate	French		Very low
Germany (FR)[b]	Not fixed; usually 5	Waived for spouse of citizen	German; some knowledge of German life	No criminal record	
Luxembourg[c]	15, inc. last 5				
Netherlands	5, just prior to application	Waived for wife of Dutch man		Investigation of character	200–1,000 florins ($56–$280), according to income, but exceptions made if low income
Sweden[d]	7	Reduced to 5 years, if Norwegian or Finn	Swedish	Good repute	
Switzerland[e]	12, inc. 3 of last 5	Length of time married to a Swiss woman, or between ages of 10–20 counts double. Waived for wife of Swiss man			
United Kingdom	5		English; elementary knowledge of British history	No criminal record	Very low

[a] 6 years: ordinary naturalization (without certain rights); 10 years: "grande" naturalization (with all political rights).
[b] The *Länder* (states) grant citizenship, and hence requirements vary somewhat. In addition to the requirements listed, a would-be citizen must show ability to support himself and must have adequate housing.
[c] Citizenship voted by Chamber of Deputies in closed session.
[d] Would-be citizen must also be able to support self and family.
[e] Cantonal and communal requirements may exist, in addition to federal requirements, e.g., length of residence in canton; certain religious confession.

86

Country	Reason for Changing Name	Procedural Delays	Difficulty (likelihood of granting change)	Restrictions
Belgium	None specified	1 year, for others to pose objections	Very difficult; new law planned to make it easier	No change of first name; very costly
France	None specified; especially "francisation"	6 months, for others to pose objections	Usually easy	
Germany	Want some other name in family		Very difficult	Very costly (up to 2,500 DM, depending on income); new name should be similar to old one
Luxembourg	None specified; especially if old name has bad connotation	4–5 months; granted by permission of civil court (first name) or act of parliament (last name)	Very difficult	Expensive ($400)
Netherlands	None specified; especially if old name unpronounceable or has bad connotation	Through courts; "permitted by the Queen"	Very difficult	
Sweden	Want some other name in family; old name has bad connotation		Fairly difficult	Cannot take some other existing family name unless name is in own family
Switzerland	Extremely bad connotation; "moral prejudice"		Very difficult	No change of first name
United Kingdom	None specified; to make more like English name	Advertise in newspaper; granted by court or by custom	Very easy	

Not much weight should be given these requirements as an index of facilitation of adjustment of immigrants since the policy of most countries is a traditional one, concerned with protection of family names rather than with policies toward immigrants. Whether or not a negative policy toward permitting name changes "hurts" a foreigner is very much a matter of the meaning or significance of foreign names in the culture of the country, and on this matter no information is available.

GENERAL LEGAL LIMITATIONS ON ALIENS

Citizens in the countries of immigration have certain rights which aliens do not have. Since these are not too different in all the countries, only the ones for Sweden [122] will be listed, and some of the variations in other countries will be noted:

1. Theoretically, aliens can be refused a work permit, which means that they can stay in the country only as tourists, without permission to take employment. Actually, all countries of immigration considered here (except the United Kingdom and Switzerland) permitted "tourists" to find jobs and then get a work permit, until the winter of 1966–67 when Germany, Belgium, the Netherlands, and Luxembourg at least temporarily prohibited this practice because of the economic recession.

2. Aliens can be deported for criminality or serious "asociality." This is usually decided by a court on an individual basis.

3. Nonnationals cannot be employed in government service, with certain exceptions (service and university jobs, mainly).

4. Special permission must be granted for aliens to conduct a business or acquire real estate (in the matter of real estate, the Swedes are somewhat stricter than other countries of immigration). Since April 1961 foreigners wishing to buy land in Switzerland have had to get cantonal permission, which is usually not forthcoming in the crowded cantons. In Geneva, for example, none of the many international civil servants have been able to purchase a home, nor have any of the heads of the famous international private associations centered there.

5. No aliens may vote or otherwise participate in government, but they may engage in other political activities (Sweden is more liberal about this than other countries).

6. Residence permits must be renewed periodically. In Sweden the first permit is given for six months, the second for a year, then for two years, then for longer periods up to five years. In considering applications for residence permits, attention is paid to the applicant's ability to support himself, his good behavior in Sweden, and his circumstances generally. Sweden also has a permanent residence permit, renewable every five years,

which allows an alien to stay in Sweden without visa, passport, or labor permit. Most other countries do not grant permanent residence permits, or grant them only after, say, twelve years of residence.

7. Exemptions are made to the requirement for a work permit. In Sweden such exemptions are granted for citizens of the other Scandinavian countries (including Finland and Iceland), the former Baltic countries, holders of service and technical positions for short periods of time (e.g., tourist-bus drivers, artists, assembly personnel, technical instructors in use of foreign equipment), and students during the summer months. As noted, nationals of EEC countries automatically get work permits in other EEC countries.

8. Work permits are given for a specific occupation and for specific employers, although these sometimes can be changed with a new application. Sweden is more liberal about this than other countries: work permits are granted for a definite time and occupation, but are not tied to any particular employer, and — by special permission — an alien can freely change his occupation.

CONCLUSION

This chapter on policies toward immigrants as indexes of "acceptance" and of facilitation of adjustment, while lengthy, has not covered all the varied details for each country. It is supplemented by Appendix B, a synoptic table prepared by T. Stark for the International Institute for Labour Studies.[123]

Table 11 is offered here as a way of summarizing the material in this chapter. Not included in this table are the very important policies toward admission of foreign workers, since such policies are a function of the economic needs of a country, the proportion of foreign workers already present, and the concern for "balance" (of religious categories, linguistic groups, or political parties, for example), rather than an index of acceptance or of facilitation of adjustment for immigrants already admitted. The only way policies of admission could be justified as the latter is in a psychological sense: if a country is open to further immigration, it probably gives the present immigrants the feeling they are wanted; conversely, when a country (like Switzerland) has a policy of forcing some of its present immigrants to leave, they can't help but have a definite feeling of being rejected. It is only necessary here to restate the finding that France seems to be the country of immigration most open to new immigration, while Switzerland and the United Kingdom are the countries most closed to further immigration. Included in Table 11, however, are the policies toward admission of the foreign worker's wife and children, since this is

Table 11. Aspects of Policies of Countries of Immigration
Favorable or Unfavorable to Immigrants [a]

Item	Bel-gium	France	Germany (FR)	Luxem-bourg	Nether-lands	Sweden	Switzer-land	United King-dom
Vocational training programs ..	2	1	1	2	2	1	2	2
Language training programs for adults	3	1	3	3	3	2	3	2
Orientation to work ...	2	2	1	1	1	1	2	2
Orientation to country..	1	1	1	2	2	1	2	1
Social assis-tance pro-grams	2	1	1	2	2	1	3	2
Educational programs for immigrant wives and children ...	2	1	2	2	3	2	2	1
Housing for single workers ...	2	1	1	1	2	2	2	2
Housing for families ...	1	1	2	1	2	1	3	2
Free-time programs ..	1	2	1	2	2	2	2	1
Openness to immigration of workers' families ...	1	1	2	1	3	1	3	1
Discourage-ment of seg-regation of immigrants .	1	2	3	1	2	1	2	1
Openness to naturaliza-tion	2	1	1	3	1	2	3	1
Total ...	20	15	19	21	25	17	29	18

[a] The number 1 is used to characterize the most favorable policies toward immi-grants; 3, the least favorable.

90

clearly an index of acceptance and of facilitation of the adjustment of immigrant workers.

Twelve policies are evaluated for each country in terms of a three-point scale. For six of the policies — openness to immigration of workers' families, avoidance of segregation, social assistance programs, special educational programs for immigrant wives and children, making housing available for families, and openness to naturalization — there seemed to be enough information available about different policies and enough differences to use all three points in differentiating countries. For the other six policies — vocational training programs, language training programs, orientation to work, orientation to country, making housing available for single workers, and assisting free-time programs — there seemed to be smaller differences between countries or merely enough information available about different policies to justify using only two of the three possible points. In the table, 1 is used to characterize the relatively most favorable policy toward immigrants, 3 to characterize the relatively most unfavorable policy toward immigrants. Thus, the lower the total score, the more favorable is the country's policy toward immigrants.

The weaknesses in such a table are obvious: (1) The policies chosen and the number of points used in evaluating each policy are arbitrary, although arguments could be made in support of choosing them. (2) For many of the policies there is insufficient information, and in all cases reliance has been on published and unpublished reports and on arbitrarily chosen informants rather than on direct observation and measurement. As noted, where information was sparse, only two points were used, rather than three, to differentiate countries. Thus, the judgments are inevitably partly subjective, possibly even biased, although they do not always conform to what the author anticipated when he began the study. The judgment of the degree of segregation encouraged by the country's policies is especially subjective. Because of these weaknesses the table is offered only tentatively, and it should be considered as open to criticism and revision.

The advantages of Table 11 are that it permits a summary view of the many pages of description of policies that have gone before, and it permits a correlation — to be made later in this report — of policy with certain indexes of adjustment or integration of immigrants. Of course the table also permits an invidious distinction to be made among countries. If it is incorrect, an unfair slur has been made on certain countries; if it is correct, it evaluates fairly what was going on in Europe during the 1960's. Many of those who have written reports which have been used as source material are officials of international agencies and their positions prevent them from making any invidious distinctions publicly. This limitation should not apply to an independent scholar. The evaluation, crude as it is, may

91

be said to indicate the importance which the receiving country puts on facilitating adjustment of foreigners.

The following major conclusions are drawn from the data presented in this section:

1. There are gaps in the organized activities of each immigrant country to aid in the acceptance and integration of its immigrants. A country may have an excellent program in several respects, but have little activity or a negative policy in other respects.

2. Nevertheless, it is possible to discern different central tendencies among countries in the intensiveness and extensiveness of their programs. France, Sweden, and the United Kingdom lead the immigrant countries of Europe in the variety and completeness of the organized efforts (by government, business, labor unions, and voluntary associations) and in the favorableness of their policies toward foreign workers. At the other end, Switzerland does the least for its immigrant workers, and in some respects has official policies of discrimination (for example, in prohibiting most immigrants from renting or buying family-type housing during their first three years, and in excluding nonagricultural immigrants from family allowances). Part of the problem for Switzerland is that it has a federal type of government structure and it follows a political philosophy of leaving many social efforts to private initiative (which then does not rise to the challenge). But Germany also has a federal structure and leaves much to the private employer; there much more is done to aid the migrant worker and there is no official discrimination against foreign workers except insofar as families are discouraged from accompanying immigrant workers. Switzerland has the highest proportion of foreigners in its working force, and is — probably wisely — trying to reduce this. But Luxembourg also has a very high proportion of foreigners in its working force, and yet has one of the more generous programs for aiding foreigners. The program of Switzerland to reduce immigration and to cut back on its foreign labor force can be justified, but it does not explain or justify the open discrimination and little aid extended toward the new immigrant (although immigrants who have been in the country more than three or five years are not officially treated quite so differently from native-born workers). Still, it should be understood that only 5 percent of the non-seasonal foreign workers are still in Switzerland after four years, and only 2 percent remain to get their permanent residence permit after ten years.[124] Switzerland gets a large proportion of its trained professionals from these foreigners with permanent residence permits. According to Girod, the 1960 census of Switzerland showed that 45 percent of the physicians, 19 percent of the chemists, 19 percent of the university professors, and 26 percent of the mechanical engineers of Switzerland were foreigners.[125]

It would be presumptuous to make distinctions among the remaining immigrant countries, for their differences are not so great. If the Netherlands is relatively low in the help it gives to the immigrant worker, it must also be recognized as the poorest of those considered here as immigrant countries and the one with the smallest proportion of foreign workers in its labor force. Also, from the meager public opinion information available (see later section on public opinion), most of the Dutch were not hostile to immigrant workers.

3. The international agreements — especially those of the EEC, the Council of Europe, and the Scandinavian Free Labor Market — have done a great deal to upgrade the programs and activities of their ratifying countries. While the benefits are specifically for the nationals of the member states, some of them tend to "spill over" and are applied to other migrants.

On the other hand, the elimination of distinctions between nationals and workers from other member states within the EEC has *created* distinctions between workers from member states and those from nonmember states. In practice, since 80 percent of internal EEC "permanent" migration is Italian, Italian immigrants get many privileges that, say, Spanish and Greek immigrants do not get. This becomes "discrimination" only with regard to entry and expulsion policies: because Italians can enter freely into Germany and Belgium, for instance, those countries feel obliged to place higher restrictions on the entry of workers from non-EEC countries so as not to endanger the employment of their own nationals. And when a recession leads these immigration countries to expel foreign workers, they expel more from non-EEC countries because they cannot legally expel Italians. Although there has been no public discussion of the matter, it is likely that the "freedom of movement" provisions of the EEC, expected to be complete in 1968, will militate against the entry of additional nations into the Common Market. It seems impossible to imagine that Germany, Belgium, Luxembourg, the Netherlands, or even France will permit the accession of, say, Greece or Spain to the EEC if this means — as it did in 1967 under the regulations — free movement of workers from these countries. If anyone were to have raised it as an issue, it might be a barrier to the accession of the United Kingdom to the EEC, for Britain has over one million dark-skinned citizens and "unlimited" Irish, who could — if Britain were to be permitted to enter the EEC — freely migrate to the existing EEC countries. It would seem that this could become an explosive political issue at least in Germany, where racism has by no means disappeared.[126]

4. Italy and Spain are the only emigrant countries to have programs to aid significantly in the adjustment of their nationals going abroad. Italy

93

has benefited as a nation from this since many of its emigrants — trained for industry — are returning and a number of would-be emigrants from southern Italy — after getting German-sponsored orientation and vocational training to go abroad — prefer to move to northern Italy instead.

5. Private employers are supplementing the activities of government in aiding the reception, training, and adjustment of foreigners, especially in Germany. The trade union movement has usually shown itself aware of the problem, but active union programs are outstanding only in Germany, Luxembourg, and Switzerland. The unions are realistically concerned about the possibility that the inflow of foreign workers may threaten established national labor standards. When they acquiesce in liberal immigration programs, they urge the government to work for good employment and living conditions. Among emigrant countries, Italy is the one with a trade union movement which has had the most active program for both emigrating workers and returnees.

6. Various voluntary associations — especially ones with connections to the Roman Catholic and Protestant churches — have been organized to aid immigrants or have turned their attention to helping immigrants after having been organized for other purposes. While their activities have been considered as parts of the special programs for immigrants — e.g., orientation, language training, free-time activity — there is not sufficient systematic information on them to offer a reliable index that would differentiate the various countries of immigration. Probably the activities of voluntary associations in behalf of immigrants correlate closely with the strength of voluntary associations generally in the countries under consideration: among the immigrant countries, Sweden, the United Kingdom, and possibly the Netherlands and Switzerland have strong traditions of voluntary associations, while the other countries have had traditions not as strong. France has had perhaps the weakest tradition of voluntary associations, but there is evidence today that that is changing.[127]

7. At various points throughout this chapter mention has been made of various "decompression chamber" institutions of immigrants — ethnic voluntary associations, foreign-language newspapers, ethnic churches, and the creation of self-segregating community life, for example. This information does not properly belong in a section on policies of immigrant countries, but since information on this is so scattered and sparse it has been included here as illustrative of what a country's policies encourage, rather than being offered as an independent nonpolicy variable in the next section where it more logically belongs. Furthermore, even if systematic information on these "decompression chamber" institutions of immigrants had been obtained, undoubtedly they would have been found to differ less by country of immigration than by country of emigration (which will be

considered in the following section). Insofar as they do differ by country of immigration, they are probably highly correlated with the percentage of immigrant workers who have their families with them, and this is a function of the country's policy of permitting foreign workers to bring their families with them.

8. While progress was made in the 1960's, the inadequacies of the programs to aid cross-national migrants make an adjustment — in the light of their initial handicaps of cultural limitations, rural background, low educational level, poor vocational preparation — suggest that, by and large, the life of the cross-national migrant is not a pleasant one.[128] The inadequacies of housing and the exclusion of the family of the worker are probably the most unpleasant features. A large proportion of the immigrant workers have been exploited economically without compensatory social advantages — or, because of insufficient orientation, they have thought they were being exploited.

Despite progress, and despite the efforts of several countries and many groups throughout western and northern Europe, policies, programs, and practices toward migrant workers cannot be considered as generally a favorable force toward the future integration of Europe.[129]

Nonpolicy Factors Affecting Acceptance and Adjustment

In this chapter an attempt is made to describe, and if possible measure, those characteristics of the cultures of the countries of immigration and emigration which have been hypothesized to influence the acceptance and adjustment of migrants, but which are usually not subject to deliberate control. Of course, the boundary line between what is and what is not subject to control or policy is somewhat arbitrary, but it does not make any appreciable difference to the research design of this study if a factor is placed in this chapter or in the previous one on policy — both include independent variables that are being considered as ones that facilitate adjustment.

ECONOMIC FACTORS

As noted earlier, economic factors affect immigrants both by stimulating them to migrate in the first place and by facilitating or retarding their adjustment once they arrive in the immigrant country. While it has been mentioned previously that the average income level is higher in all countries of immigration than in all countries of emigration, there are some differences among the countries of immigration that should be considered here. Sweden stands out among the countries of immigration as having the highest average wage level in Europe, followed by Germany (see Table 12). It is difficult to make distinctions among the other countries since there are variations in the practice of deducting sums for social insurance and direct taxes. Comparable wage figures for Switzerland could not be obtained because of cantonal variations in social insurance requirements. France pays the lowest direct wages among the countries of immigration, but it's social insurance contributions from employers are very large (making its social security benefits very generous). France has very low direct taxes (income and withholding taxes) but its indirect taxes (mainly excise and value-added taxes) are very high — making the price level for consumer goods seem very high. It is impossible to get comparable cost-of-living figures for the various nations of Europe, but for the average worker it is likely consumer goods prices are relatively high in Sweden and France. On the other hand, it should be noted that Sweden and France probably give the average worker more "free income" — by way of housing subsidies and recreational opportunities, for instance — than do most other European countries of immigration.

Because of all these complications, it is very difficult to compare these countries in the financial rewards they offer the immigrant worker. If he is anxious to send money home, he can probably do a little better in Sweden and Germany, and a little less well in France, than in the remaining countries. But if he decides to bring his family and settle down, France offers about as many financial attractions as do most of the others. As previously noted, Germany and the Netherlands have a severe housing shortage, and many workers live in makeshift slums (*bidonvilles*) in France. For the average immigrant worker, probably only Sweden would have a noticeably higher standard of living than the other immigrant countries of Europe.

Opportunity to rise on the occupational ladder is another very important factor in the acceptance of immigrants and it considerably affects their adjustment if they remain in the country of immigration for longer than a year. It must be recognized that most foreign workers get only the lowest level jobs and have little opportunity to move into better positions, partly because they are mostly unskilled and partly because employers' prejudices and the migrants' own handicaps with language and customs make it difficult for them to compete with nationals for the more desirable jobs. It is true that some foreigners are deliberately recruited for skilled and even technical or professional jobs, but there are educated and skilled foreigners working as unskilled laborers in certain countries of immigration because this was the only type of work they could find (probably they entered the country as "tourists" rather than under treaty controls).

The availability of vocational training programs influences the degree of occupational mobility, and these programs were found to be most available in France, Germany, Sweden, and the United Kingdom (see Chapter 4). Opportunity for upward occupational mobility is also affected by government policy toward permitting foreign workers to change their occupations. Some facts on this were presented in the preceding chapter, and they are summarized in Table 12: In general, it seems that Sweden and the United Kingdom are most generous in this regard, with the Benelux countries following them. However, the policy does not mean too much in most countries in times of full employment, for if a foreign worker finds a better job for which he is qualified, and the employer wants him, he can usually go to the authorities and get a new labor permit. The policy is applied rigorously, to prevent change of occupation, only when there are

97

Table 12. Economic and Policy Factors in Countries of Immigration
Which Affect Adjustment of Immigrants

Country	Direct Wages per Working Hour in Manufacturing (1965 U.S. $)[a]	Total Wages per Working Hour in Manufacturing (1965 U.S. $)[a]	Percentage of Foreign Workers in Professional or Managerial Occupations	No. of Years Residence Required for Free Choice of Occupation for Non-EEC Nationals
Belgium	0.91	1.36	5.8[b]	5
France	0.77	1.34	8.1[c]	13; 10 for Greeks and Spaniards
Germany ...	1.06	1.58	[d]	10, but after 5 may change once
Luxembourg .	[d]	[d]	16.7[e]	5
Netherlands .	0.93	1.37	3.0[f]	5
Sweden	1.61	2.02	5.7[g]	None, but annual work permit must be renewed indefinitely
Switzerland .		1.09	8.4[h]	10 for Italians, Germans, Austrians; 5 for French, Belgians, Dutch; more than 10 for others (decided by authorities)
United Kingdom ...	1.09	1.24	37.2[i]	4

[a] Swedish Employers' Confederation, Bureau of Statistics, *Direct and Total Wage Costs for Workers, International Survey 1957–1965* (Stockholm, 1966), pp. 58–59. Direct wages are those paid directly to the worker; total wages includes the social security and other tax and benefit payments, incentives and gratuities, pay for nonworking days, recruiting and training costs, and payments in kind (*ibid.*, p. 4). Figure for Switzerland calculated from *Annuaire statistique de la Suisse, 1966* (Berne, Bureau Fédéral de Statistique, 1966), p. 377. Figures for Luxembourg not available, but they are likely to be not very different from those for Belgium.

[b] Institute National de Statistique, *Recensement de la population du 31 décembre 1961* (Brussels, 1963).

[c] Institute National de la Statistique et des Etudes Economiques, *Recensement général de la population de 1962, population active, resultats du sondage un 1/20 pour la France entière* (Paris, 1963), pp. 174–177.

[d] An exhaustive effort to locate comparable data proved unsuccessful.

[e] Service Central de la Statistique et des Etudes Economiques, *Recensement de la population du 31 décembre 1960* (Luxembourg, 1961), Table 331.

[f] *Statistical Yearbook of the Netherlands, 1963–64* (The Hague, 1965), p. 31.

[g] Statistiska Centralbyrån, *Sverige Officiella Statistisk Folkräkningen, den 1 November 1960*, Vol. X (Stockholm, 1964), pp. 118–119. Figure is solely percentage of foreign-born who are employers and own-account workers; salaried professionals and managers are not included.

[h] E. Duc, "Programmes for Preparing Immigrants to Return to the Home Country: Switzerland," in *Supplement to the Final Report, Emigrant Workers Returning to Their Home Country, International Management Seminar, Athens, October 18–21, 1966* (Paris: OECD, 1967), p. 3. Data are for 1965. If frontier

nationals available to take the better job (especially in periods of unemployment) and when the foreign worker seeks to start his own business or otherwise become self-employed.

Table 12 shows the extent to which foreigners are in "middle-class occupations" in countries of immigration, and this should be considered a key index to the country's "acceptance" of foreign workers. The figures are not exactly comparable because each country has slightly different classification schemes, but in general "middle-class occupations" are taken to include the self-employed free professions, managerial and administrative posts, and sometimes the employed professions. Table 12 shows that the United Kingdom stands out in having a large proportion of its foreigners in these occupations. The main reason for this is that the United Kingdom will *admit* foreign workers only if they are highly trained or skilled or if they can engage in occupations for which there is a shortage of personnel in Britain (these are mostly the skilled occupations). Thus, it is mainly selection rather than mobility which puts the United Kingdom at the head of this list. Then, too, the figures for the United Kingdom are for 1964 — the earlier migration, mostly from the Commonwealth countries (and from Ireland at all times), is not included. The second country in order of high percentage in the better occupations is Luxembourg, and the main reason probably is that Luxembourg has not been attracting (or needing) so many foreign workers in recent years, and its older population of foreigners has risen somewhat in occupational status. To some extent this is true for Switzerland also. Among the countries which continue to have mass immigration on a practically free basis, France seems to be the one with the highest proportion of its foreign workers in middle-class occupations. (It should be noted that the figure for Sweden is not exactly comparable, since it excludes professionals and managers on a salary.) The lowest country on this index is the Netherlands, and this is undoubtedly because the Netherlands is the poorest country on the list, with the greatest amount of competition among nationals and foreigners for the

workers are dropped, leaving only seasonal and nonseasonal foreign workers, the percentage in the liberal professions, commerce, and administration is 8.2.

[1] General Register Office, *Births, Deaths, and Marriages, Quarter Ended 30 September 1964* (London: Her Majesty's Stationery Office, 1965), pp. 22–23. Figure is percentage of administrators, managers, professionals, and technical workers among all those indicating an occupation (i.e., excluding students, housewives, children, not specified) among those immigrants in 1963 intending to stay for at least one year, arriving by routes other than from Ireland. A comparable figure for the September quarter 1966, also derived from the International Passenger Survey, shows that among all immigrants indicating an occupation (i.e., excluding children, housewives, students, armed forces personnel, and those without occupation), those with "professional and managerial" occupations were 42 percent.

better occupations, and because immigration into the Netherlands is mostly recent.

In trying to assess the proportion of foreign workers in middle-class occupations as an index of "acceptance," or as a facilitating variable in the adjustment of the foreigners, it could probably be said that *if* one succeeds in getting into the United Kingdom he is likely to be well off in this regard, but that opportunities for upward mobility into these occupations are best for the immigrant to France (and perhaps Sweden).

PUBLIC OPINION TOWARD IMMIGRANTS AS MEASURED BY POLLS

Public opinion is very difficult to assess. Theoretically, it is extremely important, for it is in itself the "acceptance" which is being measured in this study; the other variables thus far recorded are merely indirect indexes. But a "true opinion" expressed in behavior toward immigrants must be distinguished from the opinion expressed in public opinion polls. There are several reasons for the discrepancy between these two:

1. There are technical difficulties in measuring opinion through polling techniques — including wording questions properly, getting respondents to answer honestly, and selecting a representative sample.

2. There is a distinction between an abstract attitude toward migration or migrants in general — which, at best, is what is measured by public opinion polls — and the concrete attitude expressed when one is confronted with flesh-and-blood migrants or when one has to decide seriously and with effect what national policy toward migration should be.

The distinction between attitudes and behavior occurs in most areas of life, and not least in the public attitude toward minority groups. This is the distinction Myrdal, Sterner, and Rose found between opinion and behavior of white Americans toward Negroes.[1] Girard and Stoetzel state it very well for French attitudes toward foreigners. They point out that through most of modern history, France has opened its doors (and even its opportunities) for economic and demographic reasons, but there has always been an emotional reserve and even a latent hostility.[2]

The polls reported here are all those relating to cross-national migration and migrants in Europe which could be located for the years 1957–66. This span of time was selected because opinions change with changing conditions, and excellent studies made before the mid-1950's — such as those by Girard and Stoetzel for France, Zubrzycki for the United Kingdom, and Clémens, Minon, and Vosse-Smal [3] for Belgium — perhaps have little applicability to the mid-1960's. It might even be said that polls taken before 1961 or 1962 should be regarded mainly as historical because a new situation for migration in Europe has come about since then. Borrie summarized the relevant studies made between 1945 and 1956 — for Belgium, France, and the United Kingdom only — and came to the following conclusion: "The general public looks upon the foreign workers as a necessary evil, a productive asset in time of economic need, a liability otherwise." [4] But to some degree in some countries, a more positive attitude toward immigrants arose during the 1960's.

Public opinion polls on attitudes toward immigrants are sparse, and those that have been undertaken are rarely comparable across national lines. Attitudes toward other nations are not considered here because this involves images and stereotypes of people in their own countries rather than attitudes about the immigrant living in the country whose nationals are being polled. The polls reported on in this section were obtained from the various individual polling agencies of Europe, since most of them had not published their results or had published them in nonscholarly sources.

One cross-national study of attitudes toward free movement of labor was conducted for the *Reader's Digest* in 1963 as part of a general survey of opinions concerning Common Market developments. [5] This context created several biases: the question dealt only with freedom of movement *within* the Common Market area; it was one of a series of questions on other Common Market developments toward which there was a generally favorable response; the United Kingdom was not a part of the Common Market, so its sample's responses are not strictly comparable with those from the other six nations. Nevertheless, for the time at which the poll was taken (1963), the results, shown in Table 13, indicate a generally positive attitude toward the free movement of labor. The Benelux nations had the highest proportion of positive attitudes, but Germany and Italy could not be said to be much different since they had the lowest proportion of negative attitudes (they also had the highest proportion of "don't know" responses). The positiveness of the Germans is interesting in view of the development, three years after the poll was taken, of a minority party in Germany — the National Democratic party (NDP) — one of whose planks was the exclusion of foreign workers from that country. (Switzerland and the Netherlands also have small political parties hostile to the further admission of foreign workers.) The Common Market nation whose people showed the relatively greatest hostility toward the free movement of labor was France, and this was the nation whose government had demonstrated in legislation and other actions the most favorable policy toward foreign workers. The British people polled showed even more unfavorable attitudes.

Another survey permits a more detailed analysis of French opinion on the same subject; this is an unpublished survey in 1962 by the Service des Sondages et Statistiques of Paris, also in the context of a survey of opinion toward Common Market objectives. [6] This poll (see Table 14) confirms

101

that of the *Reader's Digest,* showing that 58 percent of the French were unequivocally favorable to the free movement of labor. It shows, however, that some of the opponents were ambivalent, while only 15 percent were definitely against free movement of labor. Contrary to what is generally believed, young people were not more positive toward this Common Market objective than people in other age categories. In fact, no significant age differences appear. In the occupational breakdown, blue-collar workers were slightly more hostile than others, while white-collar workers (including the *fonctionnaires*) were slightly less likely to be hostile.

The same survey provides information about French attitudes toward cross-national marriage, which is considered in this study as a major index of acceptance of foreigners (see Table 15). The results seem to indicate that most Frenchmen were not opposed to intermarriage between their children and foreigners. Attitudes were more favorable among the young than the old, and more favorable among men than women.

Table 13. Percentage Responding Favorably or Unfavorably on Free Movement of Labor within the Common Market, as Reported by the *Reader's Digest* Poll of 1963

Country	For	Against	Don't Know
Netherlands	76%	13%	11%
Belgium	69	14	17
Luxembourg	69	14	17
Germany (FR)	64	8	28
Italy	62	8	30
France	57	24	19
United Kingdom	51	33	13

Table 14. Percentage Responding on Degree of Acceptance of Free Movement of Labor within the Common Market, as Reported by SSS[a] Poll in France, 1962

Category	No. of Respondents	Good Thing	Yes and No	Not a Good Thing	No Opinion
Total sample	1,844	58%	17%	15%	10%
By age:					
18–29	425	58	17	17	8
30–44	533	58	18	15	9
45–59	481	57	14	17	12
60 and over	405	57	20	14	9
By occupation:					
Employers	464	57	17	17	9
White-collar workers (inc. civil servants)	383	63	20	10	7
Blue-collar workers	380	55	17	19	9
No occupation	617	57	16	15	12

[a] Service des Sondages et Statistiques.

Table 15. Percentage Responding on Degree of Acceptance of Cross-National Marriages, as Reported by SSS[a] Poll in France, 1962

Category	No. of Respondents	Fully Approve	Depends on Nationality	Would Be Disturbed	Would Be Grieved	Would Not Approve
Total sample	1,844	52%	12%	16%	7%	14%
By age:						
18–29	425	61	13	13	5	9
30–44	533	56	9	20	5	11
45–59	481	47	14	15	9	16
60 and over ...	405	44	12	15	10	19
By sex:						
Men	883	55	13	13	6	13
Women	961	49	11	18	8	15

[a] Service des Sondages et Statistiques. The persons polled were asked to answer the question "If you had a daughter of marriageable age and if you knew that someone who wanted to marry her was a foreigner what would be your feeling?" by choosing one of these answers: A — I would not see it as a drawback, if the boy was good and had adequate employment; B — It would depend on the nationality of the boy; C — I would agree, but it would disturb me; D — I would agree, but it would grieve me; E — I would not be in agreement.

Table 16. Percentage Reporting Disapproval of Number of Foreigners in France, as Reported by IFOP[a] Poll in 1966

Category	Too Many Foreigners in General	Too Many North Africans	Too Many Spaniards	Too Many Black Africans
Total sample	51%	62%	27%	18%
By age:				
20–34	51	65	25	18
35–49	51	57	27	18
50–64	57	66	30	18
65 and over	44	56	26	15
By occupation (of head of household):				
Farmers	60	62	22	20
Industrialists or businessmen	43	61	28	16
Professionals or managers .	26	52	22	16
White-collar workers	48	64	28	16
Blue-collar workers	63	68	33	21
No occupation	45	59	24	14

[a] Institut Français d'Opinion Publique. Reported here are the percentages of those who answered "yes" when directed to say if they found each group of foreigners listed in the table too numerous in France.

A survey by the Institut Français d'Opinion Publique in 1966 (see Table 16) indicates that over half the French adult population believed that there were too many foreigners in France, especially too many North Africans.[7] There are no consistent differences by age, except that slightly more of those between 50 and 64 years believed there were too many foreigners than did those who were either younger or older than they (this is the generation that were children during World War I and in the prime working age during World War II). There are great differences by occupational groups: more than any other group, workers and farmers believed there were too many foreigners; professionals and managers were least likely to believe so.

A British poll conducted in May 1961 by Social Surveys Limited (Gallup Poll) provided some surprising evidence that colored immigrants from Asia and the West Indies were generally more accepted than white immigrants from Cyprus and Italy. This study was based on a national cross section of 1,000 Britons age 16 years and over. The questions for this poll were stated: "There are people of many different nationalities living and working in this country now. I expect you have come across some of them. Are there any of these that you particularly like? Are there any of these that you particularly dislike?" The answers and the percentage for each are shown in the accompanying tabulation:

Like		*Dislike*	
West Indians	12%	Cypriots	13%
Indians (from India)	10	Italians	7
Poles	10	Pakistanis	6
Nigerians	10	Poles	6
Italians	9	Indians (from India)	5
Pakistanis	8	West Indians	4
Cypriots	2	Nigerians	3
Like them all	23	Dislike them all	6
Those mentioning one or more	49	Those mentioning one or more	29
"Don't know; none of them"	51	"Don't know; none of them"	71

A few years after this poll, the British population was still concerned about immigration. A Gallup Poll conducted July 29–August 3, 1965, asked: "Which of these things would you like to see Mr. Heath concentrate Conservative policy on?" The third most frequently listed item, after old-age pensions and full employment, was "keep strict controls on immigration," which was mentioned by 39 percent of the sample population. Another Gallup Poll, conducted March 18–23, 1965, asked about a list of possible problems, "Do you regard any of these as raising very serious problems in Britain today?" The fifth most frequent item — after crimes of violence, bad housing, juvenile delinquency, and drug taking — was "immigrants; coloured persons," which elicited the response of 55 percent of the adult sample population.

Dutch attitudes toward immigrant workers are the topics of two student theses as well as one public opinion poll. One thesis involved interviewing twenty-five community leaders in three large Dutch cities, and asking their opinions about Italian and Spanish workers.[8] The opinions about Italians were mainly negative: they were said to be lazy, extravagant, not punctual, and they bothered the Dutch girls. The opinions about the Spaniards were mainly positive: they were said to be hard-working, serious, honest, respectful toward women, punctual, anxious to improve. The second thesis involved interviewing fifty-three Portuguese workers and their employers in three large cities of the Netherlands.[9] The employers were generally favorable to the Portuguese workers, considering them to be hard-working and serious, but self-segregating. The Portuguese workers themselves thought the Dutch favorable to the Portuguese, but also said the Dutch were cold and unapproachable, although several of the workers lived with Dutch families and 45 percent said they had Dutch friends.

The public opinion poll conducted by the Netherlands Institute for Public Opinion (NIPO) was based on a cross-sectional survey of the Dutch population in 1961.[10] As is shown in the tabulation, considerably more people were opposed to the employment of foreign workers than favored their employment in the Netherlands:

	Total	*Women*	*Men*
For	33%	28%	38%
Against	45	43	45
Don't know, no reply	22	29	22

The replies given by those in favor of the employment of foreigners and the percentage citing each were as follows:

We have a lack of manpower; our country needs workers; it is in the interest of our country; there is enough work 12%

It favors international relations; it is good for European unity; within the framework of the EEC, exchanges are to be approved; one learns by getting to know others; it is good for learning languages 3

If foreigners come, they must also eat; it is good for production; it is necessary for our economy; I am in favor of this now, but not when there is unemployment here; I am not opposed as long as Dutch workers are not thrown out of work 8

Various other replies 7

No special reply 3

Below are the replies given by those against the employment of foreign workers and the percentage citing each (the 52 percent total results from some persons giving more than one reply):

They cause trouble here 11%
The Netherlands has enough manpower; it has enough good workers; it is already overpopulated 10
Foreigners increase unemployment; we will find ourselves without employment; there is already enough unemployment; here there are still people without jobs; the authorities must undertake professional retraining for our unemployed 10
The authorities chase away our people and welcome the foreigner; if they didn't force the Dutch people to leave there would be no need for foreigners; they shouldn't encourage our own people to emigrate 8
A person should stay where he is; foreigners should stay in their own countries and our people should stay here to work; the husband should stay with his family 6
Various other replies 5
No reason given 2

As these lists show, the most frequently given reason for both opinions was economic, but 3 percent of those who favored foreign workers mentioned the improvement of international relations, and 6 percent of those who opposed foreign workers thought they should stay in their own countries.

It was pointed out earlier that the Netherlands had many emigrants as recently as the 1950's and its immigrants came only recently — in the 1960's. NIPO polled citizens on their answers to the question, "Are you for or against the fact that Dutch citizens go to work in other countries (Belgium, West Germany)?" As the results show, an even greater proportion of the sample were opposed to emigration than had opposed immigration:

	Total	Women	Men
For	28%	21%	35%
Against	50	49	52
Don't know, no reply	22	30	13

The reasons given by those for emigration and the percentage citing each were the following (the total, 30 percent, is greater than 28 percent because some people gave more than one reply):

Because they earn more; salaries are higher there; foreign countries pay better 13%
A person must be free to work where he wants; each person must know for himself; we live in a free country 7
Various other replies 8
No special reply 2

The replies of those against emigration are given below (the total is higher than 50 percent because some people gave more than one reply):

106

There is enough work here, even too much; they can just as well find work
here 15%

There is already a lack of manpower here; Dutch industry cannot get along
without our workers 10

It is not good for the family when the husband is absent; the man must stay
with his family, otherwise the women are alone; it is bad for married
life 5

If the employers would give them better salaries, they would stay 4

Dutchmen should stay in the Netherlands and foreigners in their own countries; each person belongs in his own country 4

It is only a question of earning more; they can very well earn more here if they
just work hard 3

If the authorities would build more houses here, the lodging crisis would be
helped 3

Salaries may be higher abroad, but there are risks; there are not the same social provisions; social provisions may be worse 2

The best people are the ones who leave 1

Various other replies 6

No special reply 1

In giving reasons for their favorable or unfavorable answers, the largest
single number mentioned economic factors again. But 7 percent of those
who favored emigration mentioned the right of the individual to free
movement. Of those who opposed emigration, 4 percent gave as their reason the opinion that each person belongs in his own country.

The Swedish (Gallup) polling agency SIFO (Svenska Institutet för
Opinionsunder sökningar) asked questions about the liberal Swedish immigration policy on several occasions during the years 1957–66. The results from national cross-sectional surveys of persons over 16 years of
age [11] are given here:

	September 1957	October 1958	December 1965
Mostly favorable	16%	20%	26%
Mostly unfavorable	28	40	29
As much favorable as unfavorable	42	27	33
No opinion	14	13	12

A larger percentage were unfavorable to the liberal immigration policy
than favorable at all three times the question was asked, but the proportion of favorable replies increased each time, and in 1965 the largest proportion was of those who said they were as much favorable as unfavorable.

The poll taken in December 1965 included a question about attitudes
of the Swedish population toward the *number* of foreigners. The percentage responding to each reply by socioeconomic class is shown in the tabulation:

	Total	Upper socio-economic class (8%)	Middle socio-economic class (48%)	Lower socio-economic class (44%)
We have too many foreigners now	31%	14%	29%	37%
About enough	46	51	47	43
We ought to have more foreigners	6	18	6	3
Cannot say	17	17	18	17

In the same poll another question was asked, this one about policy toward foreigners already in Sweden. Of those answering, 74 percent said foreigners should have the same rights and opportunities as nationals; 21 percent thought that Swedes should have preference; 1 percent thought foreigners should have preference; and 4 percent had no opinion. The lower socioeconomic class was only slightly more negative than the middle and upper socioeconomic classes. Opinions expressed about the impact of the presence of foreign workers on wages showed only 6 percent thought they reduced wages significantly; 31 percent said they had not much impact on wages; 43 percent thought they had no impact on wages at all; and 19 percent had no opinion.

The social psychologist Hardi Fischer made an opinion survey of Swiss workers in 1961 on their attitudes toward foreign workers.[12] The questions asked and the percentage responding positively to each were as follows:

Do you see a threat to the Swiss way of life in the percentage increase in foreign workers? 75%

Should we encourage the assimilation of foreign workers into Switzerland? 51

Do you agree that foreign workers should be able to bring their families into Switzerland as soon as they begin working? 36

Should the children of foreign workers be allotted their own schools with their own teachers? 14

Would you permit foreign workers in Switzerland to take part in politics?   9

Are you, in principle, for admitting foreign workers into Switzerland? 84

Would you raise the quota for foreign workers if the need arose? 42

Are you for making it easier for foreign workers to settle down? 19

Would you be for giving foreign workers citizenship automatically after 5 years as in the United States? 11

Would you be for giving foreign workers, who had been resident in Switzerland for at least three years, a voice in communal affairs? 10

Would you be willing to invite a foreign worker in Switzerland to your home once or twice a year in order to promote mutual understanding? 75

Would you personally accept a foreigner as a boss? 70

Would you entrust the undertaking of the management of a business to a foreign worker? 54

In your opinion should foreign workers be guaranteed the same social welfare benefits as Swiss workers? 90
In your opinion should the money which foreign workers earn in Switzerland stay in Switzerland? 55
Do you, in principle, support governmental subsidies for the social construction of housing for foreign workers? 38
Would you welcome the paying of expenses for a trip to the home country and back once a year for foreign workers if it is possible? 37

The results reveal very mixed attitudes, although it must be understood that the sample is not representative of all of Switzerland and that opinions may have changed since the study was completed in 1961.

The Gallup Institute of Switzerland (ISOP), in spring 1965, asked a cross section of 749 employed adults (exclusive of farm workers and high officials): [13] "You surely know that there have been attempts for some months now to diminish the number of foreigners working in Switzerland. For business to do well in the future it would be necessary that some Swiss blue- and white-collar workers work a few hours more during the week. Personally, would *you* agree to work a few hours more per week at your present job — of course these hours would be added to your pay?" The answers were distributed this way: yes, without restriction, 36 percent; yes, with overtime pay (of 25 percent), 11 percent; no, decidedly opposed to overtime work, 28 percent; no clear opinion, 25 percent. The proportion willing to work overtime for the sake of doing away with foreign workers was especially large in smaller towns and among men. Of those willing to work overtime, 68 percent thought 3–6 hours more per week would be all right; 15 percent, less than 3 hours; 14 percent, more than 6 hours; 3 percent had no opinion.

For Germany there are a number of public opinion polls relevant to immigrants. Minta cites one which arrived at the finding that 36 percent of the Germans polled were of the opinion that "all goes well with the guest workers," while 32 percent said "the foreigners are quite a problem." [14] In June 1966 a survey of the same subject was conducted by the Institut für angewandte Sozialwissenschaft (IFAS) using a representative cross section of the West German population (564 cases). [15] The percentage responding positively to each statement or question is reported below:

They worry much about their families 75%
Wherever they appear there is lots of noise 70
They are after our women and girls 53
They don't know what to do with their leisure time 43
Gastarbeiter start fights and knifings whenever there is an opportunity 41
Do you think *Gastarbeiter* are hard-working or not so hard-working? .... 46, hard-working
Are the foreign workers reliable or not so reliable? .... 25, reliable

109

Are *Gastarbeiter* a problem for us in Germany? 67
Are *Gastarbeiter* thrifty or not so thrifty? .... 68, thrifty
Much of the public fears today that the increasing employment of *Gastarbeiter*
will bring difficulties for the German economy. Do you personally also hold
this opinion? 57
Occasionally one hears that these difficulties can best be solved by firing all
Gastarbeiter. Do you personally think that this is a good suggestion
or not? .... 35, good
Others believe that at least no further foreign workers should be admitted into
this country. Do you think this is a good idea? 73
Do you think that *Gastarbeiter* change their place of work often or not so
often? .... 21, often
Do *Gastarbeiter* take many sick-days off or not so many? .... 24, many
Would you personally be willing to work an hour more a week — of course for
regular pay — if the hiring of *Gastarbeiter* could be avoided by such an
action? 51

It is, of course, difficult to generalize from the many questions on the
IFAS poll, but the answers to the general questions, such as whether the
foreign workers are a problem, suggest that there was a good deal of concern and hostility. The hostility seemed to be related to the foreign workers' alleged behavior in the community rather than at work. The last question — asking whether the respondent would be willing to work an extra
hour a week to eliminate the need to hire foreign workers — is perhaps especially important since it links behavior with attitude: slightly over half
of the German respondents said they would be willing to take such action.
The same type of question asked in Switzerland elicited almost the same
proportion of answers hostile to foreign workers.

In 1965 the ENMID Institute for opinion research asked a cross section
of the German population a series of questions about the German policy
of hiring foreign workers.[16] The main question was "How do you consider
the fact that the Federal Republic calls foreign workers to Germany? Are
you rather in favor of it or rather against it?" The distribution of responses
was as follows: "rather for," 27 percent; "rather against," 51 percent; no
opinion, 22 percent. The responses were similar to those reported for the
IFAS poll of 1966: young people were slightly more in favor of the policy
than older people, but there was no difference by sex. A great difference in
response was shown by size of community: whereas only 17 percent living
in communities with a population under 2,000 were in favor of the open
policy, 35 percent of those living in cities of 100,000 or more were in favor of it. In other words, those who actually came in contact with foreign
workers — those in large cities — were more in favor of the policy of bringing in foreign workers than were others. By occupation, farmers were
most opposed, and white-collar workers most favorable (although even a
plurality of the latter, 45 percent, were opposed). The free-answer rea-

sons advanced in favor of the *Gastarbeiter* policy were these: "in need of workers," 45 percent; "for the sake of our economy," 34 percent; "humanitarian reasons," 9 percent; "they are good workers," 4 percent; other reasons, 7 percent. The major reasons given for opposing the *Gastarbeiter* policy were as follows:

Employment-based fears ("take jobs away from our men") 30%
National economic fears ("take money out of the country") 17
Moral fears ("they bother our women," "many criminals among them") 17
Rationalized racism ("they have a different mentality," "alien blood is a danger") 9
Open racism ("I don't like foreigners") 5
Resentment of privileges given *Gastarbeiter* 5
Other economic reasons ("they work for less," "they want money but work less") 6
Housing shortage 2
Other reasons 7
No opinion 9

An earlier poll conducted by ENMID in 1961 asked a similar question about German policy toward hiring foreign workers, and at that time answers were more favorable to that policy. It asked: "Here I have a number of different opinions regarding employment of foreign workers. Would you please tell me which opinion comes closest to your own?" The answers:

"In Germany there are not enough workers; the German economy needs them in order to fill the open positions" 48%
"One should not employ foreign workers because they pull down the wages of our own workers" 15
"Foreign workers cannot adjust to German conditions; there will always be quarreling" 15
"By importing foreign labor there will arise no advantages or disadvantages" 20
No opinion 2

In Spain a nationwide poll (3,535 persons 18 years and over) taken by the Gallup Poll agency (IOP) in October–November 1965 asked: "In general, what is your opinion about the Spanish workers' migration to foreign countries?" [17] The results were as follows:

	Total	*Men*	*Women*
It is a solution for a national problem	4%	6%	2%
It is the result of a low standard of living	41	41	42
It is the government's fault	2	2	1
It is bad for Spain	4	5	3
It should not exist	24	22	26
If they worked here as hard, they would be just as well off	8	8	9

111

Other answers	10	11	9
No answer	7	5	8

The largest single number of respondents attributed emigration to a low standard of living in Spain. This answer is not really an attitude, but it suggests that those who gave it were agreeing with those who gave the next most frequent answer, "It should not exist." Small groups of respondents answered outright "It is bad for Spain" and "It is the government's fault." Only 4 percent took the fatalistic attitude that emigration is a solution for a national problem, and 8 percent blamed the laziness of the emigrants while they were in Spain.

The Reverend Sanchez Lopez asked a sample of 333 Spaniards reached by Catholic missions in several countries of immigration what their opinion was of the manner in which they were treated by nationals.[18] Fifty percent said "with harshness or egoism"; 37 percent said "with politeness only"; and 13 percent said "with sympathy." Asked about their relations with nationals, 60 percent said "work relations only"; 24 percent reported "superficial relations"; 15 percent said "friendly relations"; and 1 percent said "family relations." These Spanish emigrants were also asked what cultural values they had assimilated in the countries of immigration: 53 percent said "nothing significant"; 29 percent said "equality of classes"; 6 percent said "freedom of political opinions"; 7 percent said "independence"; 3 percent said "a lively consciousness of religion"; and 2 percent mentioned other values. The intensity of the influence of foreign cultural values on the mentality of the immigrants was asked of them: 81 percent said "none"; 11 percent said "moderate"; 8 percent said "intense."

Nermin Abadan's study of Turks in Germany showed that 77 percent of them had no social contacts with Germans.[19] A third of the Turkish workers believed the equalitarian family structure of the Germans was superior to the Muslim seclusion of women; another third found it decadent and absolutely condemnable.

The Greek Institute of Research and Communication polls public opinion in Athens, using samples of 400–500 persons (homes selected at random, and youngest person over 18 years in household interviewed, alternating male and female). In September 1963 the question posed was: "People have said emigration is God's blessing. Do you agree?" The largest percentage of respondents answered negatively, as is shown below:

I agree	16%
I agree under certain conditions	12
I don't agree	37
"God's curse"	4
It's bad for the country ("we lose workers, young people")	18

Sentimental opposition ("people separated from relatives") 4
Other negative 2
Don't know 7

In March 1965 the sample was asked if they would like to emigrate (on a long-term basis) if they were given the chance. Positive answers were given by 29 percent ("at once," 17 percent; "perhaps," 4 percent; "under certain circumstances," 8 percent) and negative answers were received for 71 percent ("no," 42 percent; "never," 29 percent). Those answering positively were asked to which country they would emigrate, and the answers were distributed as follows:

USA	10%	France	2%
Australia	4	Africa	1
Canada	4	Other	4
Germany	4		

A poll conducted in 1962 gave results similar to this 1965 one. The conclusions that may be drawn from the polls in Greece are that, while a majority were opposed to emigration, 28–29 percent were in favor of it and had themselves entertained the thought of emigrating. The largest proportion of those favoring emigration would prefer to go overseas; in Europe, Germany and France were the favored countries.

Two more extensive studies of the attitudes of foreign workers themselves were being conducted in 1967 in Germany and Sweden (by the ENMID and SIFO organizations, respectively), but the results of these were not yet available at the time of writing.

IDEOLOGY AND SOCIAL STRUCTURE

The variables to be examined in this section are ones for which it is not possible to get "hard" data, and the indexes for them will be highly subjective and probably unreliable. The indexes in Table 17 are therefore presented with a great deal of hesitancy and doubt, but with recognition that they are important independent variables and cannot be ignored. As in the other tables of this type, a low score in Table 17 is the most favorable one.

The first index is the existence among the nationals in the country of immigration of an ideology favoring the integration of immigrants. While this is theoretically very close to the "public opinion" examined in the preceding section, in fact it is quite distinct. The distinction can be made clear by noting the existence in the United States of an ideology of the "melting pot" at the same time that Americans had strong prejudices against immigrants and resisted practical forms of integration with them. It seems there is a similar ideology in France: it is a French tradition to take in foreign-

113

Table 17. Differences between Countries of Emigration and Immigration Which Relate to Adjustment of Immigrants[a]

	Belgium	France	Germany	Luxembourg	Netherlands	Sweden	Switzerland	UK
Ideology favoring integration of immigrants	2	1	3	2	2	2	3	2
Flexibility of social structure	2	2	2	2	3	1	2	2
Religion	1	1	2	1	2	3	2	3
Language	2	1	3	2	3	3	2	3
Geographical distance of migration	2	2	2	2	2	1	3	1
Attractiveness of climate	2	1	2	2	2	3	2	3
Total	11	8	14	11	14	13	14	14

[a] The number 1 is used to characterize differences that are most favorable to adjustment; 3, the least favorable. For religion, 1 is used to characterize a predominantly Catholic country; 2, a mixed Catholic-Protestant country; 3, a predominantly Protestant country. For language, 1 is assigned to a country where a Romance language predominates; 2, a multilingual country where one of the languages is a Romance one; 3, a country in which the predominant language is not a Romance one. For distance of migration, 1 is assigned to the countries of immigration that are farthest away from the countries of emigration; 2, most other countries; 3, the one country (Switzerland) that is close to its sources of foreign labor (Italy and Spain).

ers of all cultures and races and to make Frenchmen out of them. The term "francisation" is well known in France, and hardly has an equivalent in any other country of Europe (but it *is* comparable to "Americanization"). Like Americans, many Frenchmen may despise the immigrants to their country, but they seem to have little doubt that they should and can make Frenchmen out of them. It is partly a pride in culture, like bringing Christianity to the heathen. The British, and possibly some of the other old imperialistic peoples like the Dutch and the Belgians, had something similar to this ideology when they went out to govern Africa and Asia, but they never dreamed of applying it in their home countries, as the French did. Menie Gregoire, describing the relationship between French culture and the immigrants, says:

Sure of our own nationality, which has resisted all kinds of attacks and has so valiantly digested all kinds of bastardization, we have developed as one of our national characteristics a sort of tolerant, individualistic and chauvinistic, indifference toward foreigners, which will persist in this thoroughly bourgeois era because it is essentially based on self assurance. . . . We assimilate the children. We naturalize with great generosity . . . the principle is that we do not refuse naturalization without a reason. . . . The social policy of today, insofar as it is possible to draw general laws out of facts, seems to concentrate strongly on two points: 1) assimilate the young, 2) provide for the others housing and the "tools for work," that is, the minimum equipment in terms of language and skills.[20]

The British — and probably the Dutch, Belgians, Luxembourgers, and Swedes — also have a certain tolerance of integration of foreigners, as already suggested by the public-opinion poll data. Rex and Moore, after a systematic study of race and ethnic relations in Birmingham, conclude that "many of the English displayed an underlying reasonableness which showed itself actively when they felt there were legitimate and effective channels of protest and action open to them." [21] These authors show how this reasonableness works in a neighborhood voluntary association; for the country as a whole the existence of the Race Relations Act and the Race Relations Board reflects the same phenomenon. Tonna, in a cross-national study of the integration of Italian families, found that they integrated more rapidly in England than they did in Belgium, mainly because there were more complete families of Italians in England and the society is more open and less traditional.[22]

The Germans, with their tradition of racism dating back to the post-Napoleonic era, have had almost the antithesis of this ideology. Other countries of Europe (except Italy and possibly Spain, which of course are not countries of immigration) have had traditions of xenophobia, but none so powerful as that of Germany. The very word that contemporary Germany uses to refer to a foreign worker — *Gastarbeiter* — reflects the compromise the Germans have made by inviting foreigners to work in their country while rejecting any idea that they might become Germans. In 1966 directors of many large German firms expressed the belief that it would be economically desirable to have a lower turnover rate among foreign workers, but it is doubtful that many Germans will subscribe to the idea that foreign workers should be allowed to stay permanently and become Germans. (This is not contradicted by the fact that contemporary Germany has a fairly liberal naturalization law, for Germany does not allow its foreign workers to stay long enough to meet the requirements for naturalization.) The xenophobia that prevails through central and northern Europe has, of course, aided in the maintenance of ethnic distinctions — like that between Walloons and Flemish in Belgium; English, Scottish, and Welsh in the United Kingdom; and Bohemians, Slovaks, and Moravians in Czechoslovakia, to name a few. In countries like these, how could it ever become possible for a Turkish worker to become a national in the true sense? The suggestion is made here that this could happen in countries such as France, Italy, and the United States, where there is an ideology favoring the integration of immigrants.

It is difficult to characterize this ideology for Switzerland: nineteenth-century Switzerland made sharp distinctions among its cantons according to what language was spoken, but a person who lived permanently in any canton was expected adopt the language of that canton; he was not, however, expected to change his religion to that dominant in the canton. Although Switzerland has had a long tradition of welcoming immigrants and assimilating them into the "federation," that tradition seems to have been broken since about 1960, and today many Swiss exhibit more than the average European xenophobia.[23] It is probably true that the Swiss make a distinction between the foreigners who have lived among them for a number of years (mostly north Italians) and those who arrived during the early 1960's (mostly south Italians and Spaniards). The Swiss express their hostility mainly toward the latter group of arrivals, but those who advocate a drastic reduction in the number of foreigners are not always explicit about this distinction. Many Swiss have almost made an ideology of their opposition to *Überfremdung*, which is a very popular word in Switzerland today.

The second subjective variable, flexibility of the social structure, is as elusive as are attitudes and opinions of individuals. Can the institutions and systems of the society absorb the influx of immigrants and adjust to the social changes which they create? In its physical aspects, this is easy to measure: the Swiss, who have suddenly become hostile to immigrants, complain very strongly that the influx of immigrants creates shortages in housing, hospitals, schools, public vehicles, and so on; the social institutions intended to provide these facilities have not been able to do so. It is much more difficult to determine the flexibility of the class system to absorb not only the immigrants but also the nationals who are being pushed upward because of the influx of immigrants at the lower levels. A passable measure of both the observable and the elusive aspects of flexibility of social structure is provided by the level of economic development achieved: to the extent that the society has been able to absorb economic growth in general, it could probably absorb the increase in the labor force through immigration, which is but one small aspect of economic growth. Indexes of level of economic development placed Sweden at the top, and the Netherlands at the bottom (see Table 1).

OTHER FACTORS

Migrants from Italy, Ireland, Spain, and Portugal, and some from Yugoslavia, are mostly of Roman Catholic background, and it has been hypothesized that they can most easily adjust to those countries of immigration that are primarily Roman Catholic. Migrants from Greece, Turkey, and other parts of Yugoslavia inevitably move to a new religious-cultural setting no matter where they migrate in northern and western Europe, but these are a minority of the total European migrants. The countries of immigration are predominantly Roman Catholic (France, Belgium, Luxembourg), predominantly Protestant (Sweden, United Kingdom), or about equally Roman Catholic and Protestant (Germany, the Netherlands, Switzerland).

Similarly, the majority of migrants speak a language which is Latin in origin, and it has been hypothesized that they can most easily learn another Romance language and hence adjust most easily to a country of immigration where a Romance language is spoken. Migrants from Italy, Spain, and Portugal speak a Romance language (and the migrants from Ireland speak a language — English — which is the same as that of the country to which they migrate). Only France among the countries of immigration is entirely Romance-speaking, although the portions of Belgium, to which most migrants from these countries go, are also Romance-speaking. Luxembourg and Switzerland are also partly Romance-speaking, although most of the migrants to Switzerland go to the non-Romance-speaking part of that country. The remaining countries of immigration — Germany, the Netherlands, Sweden, and the United Kingdom — are definitely not Romance-speaking.

Distance of migration also has been hypothesized as a factor in adjustment: the supposition is that a greater distance requires a more definite commitment, and hence a greater motivation to adjust on the part of the migrants. It seems probable that those who migrate a greater distance return to their home countries for visits less frequently and thus are more likely to loosen the ties that bind them to their homelands, which makes them more amenable to adjustment in their new homes. While there is a considerable difference in location among the countries of emigration (especially in the case of the Turks), the index of distance of migration used here is crudely based on the location of the country of immigration: in general, those who migrate to Sweden and the United Kingdom (again with the exception of the Irish) have to go the longest distance; those who migrate to Switzerland have to go the shortest distance (these are mostly Italians and Spaniards).

The attractiveness of the climate has been hypothesized as another factor in adjustment, especially since practically all the cross-national migrants (with the exception of the Irish) come from Mediterranean countries where the climate is very mild. It seems reasonable to hold that France has the most attractive climate (because the mildest) among the countries of immigration, and that Sweden and the United Kingdom have the least attractive climates.

These last four independent variables — religion, language, distance of migration, and attractiveness of climate — are not factors affecting acceptance, but are factors affecting adjustment. Up to this point, it has been assumed that acceptance and adjustment are perfectly correlated, but there is no correlation when *differences* between the countries of immigration and emigration are being considered. Also, acceptance ceases to be a factor when considering climate and distance since they are beyond any possible control of either the country of immigration or the country of emigration.

A sum of the evaluations listed in Table 17 would have little meaning in itself, but in regard to the factors listed in the table, France is in a most favorable position for the adjustment of migrants, among the countries of immigration.

CHARACTERISTICS OF COUNTRIES OF EMIGRATION

It is difficult to obtain data on the basic culture and social structure of the countries of emigration as they relate to adjustment of migrants. What systematic sociological studies have been undertaken of the countries of emigration do not concentrate on the question of how to prepare emigrants for life in another society. Yet such studies do incidentally provide much relevant information, and they have been utilized in the preparation of this section. Also from three to several dozen social scientists in each country of emigration have been interviewed in order to get the information summarized in Table 18. The technique of classifying each country on a three-point scale is a crude way of measuring the variables under consideration but it probably ensures a high degree of reliability for the data in the table, despite the incompleteness and subjectivity of the underlying information. In Table 18, the low scores indicate what is most facilitating to adjustment.

Table 18. Characteristics of the Culture of Emigrant Countries
Which Relate to Adjustment of Immigrants

	Greece	Ire-land	Italy	Por-tugal	Spain	Turkey	Yugo-slavia
Tradition of emigration[a] .	2	1	1	1	1	3	2
Strength of national ties ..	2	3	2	1	1	3	2
Strength of local ties (vs. alienation)	2	2	2	2	2	3	3
Strength of family ties ...	3	2	2	3	2	3	2
Strength of religious ties ..	2	3	2	3	3	2	1
Flexibility of national character	2	1	1	2	2	2	2
Proportion of the population of peasant background ...	3	2	2	3	3	2	2
Proportion of the population illiterate	2	1	1	3	2	3	2
Total	18	15	13	18	16	21	16

[a] The number 1 is used to characterize countries which have a dominant tradition of emigration (Ireland, Italy) or which were former imperial powers that colonized the lands they dominated or formerly dominated (Spain, Portugal); 2 is used to characterize countries which have had many emigrants for a long time, but which do not meet the other criteria for 1; 3 is assigned to countries which never had many emigrants until the mid-1950's (Turkey).

"Tradition of emigration" as used here characterizes a country of emigration in which the prevailing opinion holds that emigration is a normal process to which people can adjust. If their country has a long history of emigration, today's emigrants probably feel they can survive and adjust to the hardships of emigration better than can those who find themselves to be pioneers in emigration and for whom the unpleasant experiences associated with life in a new country turn out to be unexpected and possibly traumatic. In Table 18 the countries of emigration have been classified into three types: (1) those with traditions of heavy emigration that have continued over at least a century (Spain, Portugal, Ireland, and Italy); (2) those with weaker traditions of emigration that have continued over many decades (Greece and Yugoslavia); (3) those which have begun emigration in the 1950's (Turkey). In some countries the tradition of emigration was interrupted during World War II and the immediate postwar years, but a general knowledge of it must have carried through to the

119

1950's and 1960's. The public opinion polls on attitudes toward emigration in Spain and Greece reported on earlier showed a substantially greater acceptance of emigration in Spain than in Greece, which corresponds to the distinction made here between those two countries concerning tradition of emigration.

Strength of national ties (which could also be called "love of country," or "national pride") is often associated with some kind of recent national crisis in relation to other countries. The long-drawn-out revolution against England, culminating in independence in 1922, gave the Irish a strong love of country. The traumatic transformation of the huge Turkish empire into a smaller republic — accompanied by continuing friction with some of the former subject people — created a like nationalistic sentiment among the Turks. One might have expected something similar in Yugoslavia, because it achieved nationhood only after World War I, but that country remains a federation of six states often at odds with each other — which reduces both national and provincial pride. In countries like Yugoslavia, Greece, and especially Italy, there is love of the geographic country and the people, but not much attachment to the state or the government [24] which controls it. In Spain and Portugal there is still less national pride: many of the ordinary citizens of these countries think of their nations as once great but now worn out. The hypothesis set forth here is that the stronger the attachment to one's "homeland" the less the propensity to adjust to the country of immigration.

Local ties are much less definable than national ties because they cover a range from region to community to friendship group. All the emigrant groups considered here have significant local ties in one form or another, and one hesitates to make sharp distinctions among them. The existence of a significant proportion of emigrants "alienated" from their home communities would indicate weak local ties, but this was not found to be true for any of the groups. Informants in Turkey and Yugoslavia have emphasized the strength of local ties, and so these countries have been distinguished somewhat from the others in Table 18. One hears of *campanilismo* in Italy, but the Italians have moved enough toward cosmopolitanism for local attachments to be superficial.

There are two special types of local ties in the emigrant countries that need to be given independent attention: that of the extended family and that of the church. Both of these tend to be strong in traditionalistic, peasant societies, which is the home background for most of Europe's emigrants. The opinion of informants used in this study is that the extended family is partly broken down in Ireland, Italy, and Yugoslavia, although there is some variation among all the countries under consideration. Religious ties seem to be strongest in the traditionalistic Roman Catholic countries — Spain and Portugal — and in Ireland where nationalism seems to have fortified religion. The Catholic Church in Spain does not so much inhibit emigration as carry its attachments to the worker into the country of immigration. In Yugoslavia religion has been deliberately weakened by the state over the past quarter of a century. In Greece and Italy there is a traditionalistic attachment to religion, especially in the rural areas from which most emigrants come, but the church has become rather formalized. In Turkey there are strong attachments to religion, but the Muslim church has become secularized in the past forty years under the republic. The Spanish informants consulted for this study felt that family ties were not important as a source of attachment to the homeland since a large proportion of wives emigrate with their husbands — either because jobs are available for them too (as maids, particularly in Switzerland) or because the immigration countries (France and Belgium) encourage family living. Of all Spanish male emigrants, 29 percent are accompanied by their families.[25] In some cases, leaving the wife in Spain is a form of abandonment, since it is a country where legal divorce or separation is extremely difficult. On the other hand, the extended family is still a viable institution in Spain, although this is partly because of the housing shortage. It is assumed here that the stronger these ties to the home society and its institutions, the more they inhibit adjustment to the new society of the country of immigration.

An individual's ability to adjust to new situations is dependent on some personality characteristics that might be called flexibility of national character. Recognition of this concept implies that the national culture includes a trait which tends to make its participants adjustable to new situations generally — to bend to vicissitudes rather than crack under their weight, to take advantage of new opportunities rather than ignore all but the tried and true. Among the social scientists interviewed, the opinion was that Irish and Italians were the emigrant nationalities that had this trait of flexibility in abundance. Italians might complain a great deal and exaggerate their hardships, but they adjusted. Irish were quick to take advantage of opportunities. While in America or Australia many other ethnic groups showed remarkable flexibility of national character, in Europe there did not seem to be enough differentiation among the others to warrant making any further distinctions.

Table 1 showed the large percentage of the population still engaged in agriculture in the countries of emigration — particularly in Turkey, Greece, and Yugoslavia. In Europe, especially in these three emigrant countries, farming is generally not merely an occupation, it is also a traditional way of life that has deep roots in the social structure of the Middle Ages: in south Europe most farmers are still peasants, which means that

121

they are poorly educated, provincial in outlook, seldom ambitious but accepting of their low social status (even when they occasionally became financially well-off), and conservative in their personal habits and opinions (even when they vote for radical political parties in protest against the urban elite whom they believe exploit them). Since modern technology and economic growth are now radically reducing the need for farmers, many of them join the ranks of emigrants. However, the proportion of rural people in a population should not be assumed to correlate directly with the proportion of peasants among the emigrants. Nermin Abadan's study of 494 Turkish workers in Germany shows that 51 percent came from cities of 100,000 population or more (of course, some may have lived in these cities for only a short while).[26] Also, the Yugoslav Statistical Office estimates that 50 percent of the emigrants from Yugoslavia — with the second highest proportion of the labor force in agriculture among the emigrant countries — were urban. Spain and Portugal, which are much more urbanized countries, seem to have a higher proportion of rural people among their emigrants, although no exact figures were available to support this. Until better data might contradict it, the conclusion seems to be that the more urbanized (economically developed) the emigrant country, the larger proportion of rural people there will be among its emigrants, with the qualification that many of the urban emigrants from less urbanized countries may have lived for only a short time in the city. The rationale for this is that economic development pushes people out of agriculture, while in a more static society peasants are too tradition-bound to emigrate until they have had some experience with city life. Urbanism, however, involves more than mere residence in a city: an urban person can also be defined as one who is influenced by a city regularly through visits and communications. In this sense, many of the Italian country-dwellers are more urban than the Turkish city-dwellers who inhabit barracks in Ankara and Istanbul. Since no data exist to measure this difference it cannot be taken up in further detail. Thus, in Table 18 "peasant background" is assessed in terms only of measured or estimated proportions of emigrants who come from rural areas.

Figures on illiteracy, which are given separately in Table 19, have been incorporated into Table 18 as a measure of sophistication and hence adjustability. That is, the proportion of illiterates in the population of emigrant countries is considered here as another factor in the adjustment of their emigrants, on the ground that illiteracy is a bar to communication, and communication is a necessity for adjustment.

The sum of the evaluations contained in Table 18 represents an attempt to measure the adjustability of emigrants from the countries under study. It is probably a fairly valid measure, even though the data for some of the

Table 19. Percentage of Illiterates in the Population of
Countries of Emigration

Country	Percentage of Illiterates	Date of Census	Age Group
Greece	19.6%	1961	15+
Italy	8.4	1961	6+
Portugal	38.1	1960	15+
Spain	17.6	1950	15+
Turkey	61.9	1960	15+
Yugoslavia[a]	23.5	1961	15+

SOURCE. *Statistical Yearbook, 1965* (Paris: UNESCO, 1966),
Table 4, p. 42.
[a] Based on a 5 percent sample survey.

components are not highly reliable. The prospects for the Italians are best, followed by the Irish, while prospects for the Turks are worst, with the Greeks and the Portuguese having only slightly better prospects. This finding has parallels in certain descriptive studies: Elspeth Huxley, for example, in her observations on the ethnic minorities in England, holds that Italians are much more integrated into British life than are Greeks or Poles.[27] Abadan's excellent study of the Turks in Germany finds that three-fourths of them have absolutely no contacts with Germans outside of work.[28] A distinction should probably be made between general adjustability, which is measured here, and adjustability to work. It is commonly said that the Turks are excellent workers, although their score on the general adjustability index in Table 18 is low, which means that they tend to stay aloof from the society to which they have migrated.

If the countries to which these various groups have gone are considered, we can get an idea of which countries are likely to have the least difficulty in integration of emigrants. Table 7 showed the distribution of the foreign labor force, by country of emigration, for each of the countries of immigration. In terms of the adjustability measure, then, Switzerland is probably the best off among all the countries of immigration since it has the highest proportions of Italians and other EEC nationals among its immigrants; most of its other foreign workers are Spaniards and Austrians, who also have favorable adjustability measures. Sweden too is in a favorable position; most of its immigrants consist of fellow-Nordics and EEC nationals, with Yugoslavs providing the largest proportion of the south European immigrants. The Netherlands is also favored by the high proportion of EEC nationals in its immigrant population, followed by Spaniards. France and Belgium are favored by the high proportion of Italians, other EEC nationals, and other north Europeans (especially Poles) among their immigrants, followed by Spaniards — who are all to be

123

counted among the adjustables. But France has a high proportion of Africans and Portuguese, who are on the low side of the adjustability index, and Belgium has a high proportion of Africans, Greeks, and Turks. The United Kingdom is well off in its European immigrants — who are mostly skilled north Europeans, Italians, and Spaniards, as well as unskilled Irish — but it has more immigrants from Asia and the West Indies who are undoubtedly lower on the adjustability index. Germany has few non-European immigrants. It has large numbers of highly adjustable Europeans — Italians and Spaniards — but also the highest proportion of Greeks and Turks who are low on the adjustability index.

◄―――

The dependent variables of adjustment include all the things which happen to the migrants after they arrive in the country of immigration (including their possible return to the country of emigration) which would not have happened to them if they had not migrated. Of course there are no data on some of the possible indexes of adjustment, but a number of unpublished and difficult-to-obtain statistics have been located which can be used to yield roughly comparable indexes of integration for the various European countries of immigration. Some data which would be relevant here — on participation of immigrants in "decompression chamber" institutions, family units, ethnic associations, and protest activities, and the extent of their reading newspapers and magazines in their language — have been presented for special reasons in earlier sections and are not complete enough to be quantified.

GENERAL MEASURES OF ACCEPTANCE AND ADJUSTMENT

Table 20 presents data on three very different measures of acceptance and adjustment. The first is the turnover rate, or the ratio of departures to arrivals within some recent time period for foreigners arriving as "permanent immigrants" (usually defined as those intending to stay at least one year, so as to exclude tourists, *frontaliers*, and seasonal workers). The figures are not exactly comparable, since record keeping and the definition of "permanent immigrant" differ from country to country, but they are sufficiently comparable to permit noting gross differences. Switzerland, because of the policy begun in 1963 to reduce the number of foreign workers, has the highest turnover rate. Luxembourg has had a decline of net immigrants also in recent years, although not as a result of policy, and hence it also has a high turnover rate. Germany has the third highest turnover rate, again because of the policy of treating most migrants as transients. Belgium and France have the lowest turnover rates. Turnover in itself is not a clear-cut measure of acceptance, since it reflects policy as well as the migrant's intention to leave the country. Over a longer period of

125

Table 20. Three Measures of Acceptance and Adjustment: Turnover of
Immigrants, Intermarriage, and Naturalization

| Country of Immigration | Turnover of Immigrants | Percentage of Cross-national Marriages | | Ratio of Naturalized to Foreign Labor Force |
		National Husband, Foreign Wife	National Wife, Foreign Husband	
Belgium	25%	2.73%	2.82%	.37%
France	25	1.12	1.34	1.61
Germany (FR) ..	62	1.65	1.09	.42
Luxembourg	68	1.27	1.50	.52
Netherlands	32	11.40	3.03	3.06
Sweden	39	2.00	2.89	6.00
Switzerland	100+	1.29	.96	.12
United Kingdom .	57	ᵃ	ᵃ	1.09

SOURCE. For Belgium: Council of Europe, Special Representative's Advisory Committee, "Problems Raised by the Return Home of Migrant Workers" (Strasbourg, April 29, 1966), p. 30 (column 1); Institut National de Statistique, *Bulletin de statistique*, No. 5 (Brussels, May 1966), p. 6 (columns 2 and 3); Institut National, *Recensement de la population* (Brussels, 1965). For France: *Commissariat général du plan d'équipement et de la productivité* (Paris, 1964), p. 7 (column 1); Institut National de la Statistique et des Etudes Economiques, unpublished figures (columns 2 and 3); Institut National, *Cahiers français, documents d'actualité*, No. 28 (May–June 1965), p. 4 (column 4). For Germany: *Amtliche Nachrichten der Bundesanstalt für Arbeitsvermittlung und Arbeitslosenversicherung (ANBA)*, 14:2 (February 1966), p. 3 (column 1); Statistisches Bundesamt, Wiesbaden, unpublished figures No. VIII/3-H40 (October 21, 1966, p. 6 (columns 2, 3, and 4). For Luxembourg: Service Central de la Statistique et des Etudes Economiques, *Annuaire statistique, 1965* (Luxembourg, 1966), pp. 47–48 (column 1); Service Central, *Statistiques du mouvement de la population, années 1953 à 1965* (Luxembourg, May 1966), Table 44 (columns 2 and 3); Service Central, *Annuaire statistique, 1965* (Luxembourg, 1966), p. 46 (column 4). For Netherlands: Centraal Bureau voor die Statistiek, *Statistiek van de Buitenlandse migratie, 1961–62* (The Hague, 1963), pp. 22–23, 54–55 (column 1); unpublished figures (columns 2 and 3); Centraal Bureau, *Statistical Yearbook of the Netherlands, 1963–1964* (The Hague, 1965), p. 16 (column 4). For Sweden: Statistiska Centralbyrån, *Allmän Manads Statistik*, 4:9 (September 1966) (column 1); unpublished figures (columns 2 and 3); Statistiska Centralbyrån, *Statistisk Arsbok, 1966* (Stockholm, 1967), p. 59 (column 4). For Switzerland: E. Duc, "Programmes for Preparing Immigrants to Return to the Home Country: Switzerland," in *Supplement to the Final Report. Emigrant Workers Returning to Their Home Country, International Management Seminar, Athens, October 18–21, 1966* (Paris: OECD, 1967), p. 6 (column 1); *Annuaire statistique de la Suisse, 1966* (Berne: Bureau Fédéral de Statistique, 1966), pp. 64 (columns 2 and 3), 110–111 (column 4). For United Kingdom: Board of Trade, *International Passenger Survey* (London, 1966), Appendix F, p. 35 (column 1); Home Office, Statistics of Persons Acquiring Citizenship of the United Kingdom and Colonies, 1965, Command 3091 (London: Her Majesty's Stationery Office, September 1966), pp. 4–6 (column 4).

ᵃ No data are available.

time, turnover would also reflect the business cycle, but this economic factor does not affect sociological use of turnover as an index of adjustment here because of the continuing prosperity and very low unemployment rate in all the countries during the entire period under study (that is, the business cycle is held constant by circumstances in these data).

Marriage between immigrants and nationals represents acceptance in probably its deepest sense, even though it affects only a small proportion of either group. Cross-national marriages were found to occur relatively most frequently in the Netherlands, by far, and were next most frequent in Belgium and Sweden. The figures given in Table 20 are not the usual marriage rates, which are the proportion of cross-national marriages to all marriages (for a given time period, usually a year), but the latter would be less useful here since they would largely be a function of the proportion of foreigners in the population. The figures in Table 20 are the number of marriages in a given recent year as a proportion of the number of foreign workers in the population, and thus hold constant the size of the foreign population, although they do not solve the problem of the effect of the sex ratio among unmarried foreigners of marriageable age (data on the latter are not available).

The high rates of intermarriage with the Dutch can most readily be explained by a combination of two sets of facts. One is the psychological openness of the Dutch people toward immigrants: they are little prejudiced and discriminatory in general toward foreigners. This point is stressed in the excellent study conducted by the (Protestant) Churches Committee on Migrant Workers in Western Europe, which also points to the positive attitudes the Sicilian immigrants in the Netherlands have toward their hosts.[1] Second, the Netherlands is the poorest among the countries of immigration, it has one of the most severe housing shortages, and it has a policy against admitting the families of immigrants and for encouraging the employment of single workers only. Thus, the Dutch get a higher proportion of single persons among their foreign workers than other countries, and they have much less hesitancy about marrying them. The result is that among the nations studied the Netherlands has the highest proportion of intermarried foreigners among its foreign population.

There is a possibly serious distortion in using the intermarriage rate as an index of acceptance or integration. When intermarriage is used as such an index one of the marriage partners is assumed to be a native, but he or she may actually be of the same nationality as the foreign spouse — having been first naturalized before getting married. This distorting influence is more likely to occur when the naturalization law is liberal. Table 9 showed that the countries with the easiest naturalization requirements are France, Germany, the Netherlands, and the United Kingdom. Since only the Neth-

erlands among these countries has a high intermarriage rate, it seems un-
likely that this rate is generally distorted by naturalization policy. There
may be some distortion for the Netherlands but it seems reasonable to at-
tribute the high rate of intermarriage for the Netherlands mainly to the
factors discussed in the preceding paragraph. A specific study of who mar-
ries whom in the Netherlands would be the only way to settle the question
factually.

The third index measured in Table 20 is the proportion of naturali-
zations (grants of citizenship) in a given recent year to the number of foreign workers in the country during approximately the same year. An earlier section noted the legal requirements for naturalization (Table 9),
and on the basis of the length of the residence requirement alone, it was
found to be easiest for a foreigner to become naturalized in France, Germany, the Netherlands, and the United Kingdom (all requiring about five
years' residence). The relative numbers actually becoming naturalized
are roughly in agreement with the legal requirements, with certain significant exceptions. Sweden has the highest naturalization rate of any country,
even though it requires seven years' residence (except for Finns and Norwegians, who need only five years). The Netherlands, France, and the
United Kingdom follow, in that order, in their rates of naturalization, and
these countries have relatively easy requirements. Germany has a low rate
of naturalization, but this may be largely due to the fact that heavy immigration is relatively new for Germany, and therefore the overwhelming
proportion of foreigners do not meet the residence requirement. Except
for the barrier of residence requirement, naturalization is a very good index of acceptance and adjustment in a foreign country.

SOCIAL PATHOLOGY

Indexes of social pathology represent adjustment (in a negative sense)
but not acceptance. The most important measure is the crime rate — calculated in Table 21 as the number of convictions of foreigners with residence permits (to exclude tourists) in a given year as a percentage of the
number of foreign workers. For several countries these statistics were
quite difficult to obtain; the authorities sometimes feel that this is a touchy
subject. Crime statistics are extremely difficult to compare: there are differences in definitions of crime in the various countries, in degrees of leni-
ency on the part of the police and the courts, in degrees of efficiency in
apprehending criminals and in producing evidence for convictions, in procedures of record keeping, and in age and sex distributions of foreigners.
For these reasons, only very large differences in crime rates should be
taken as having any significance; small differences are just as likely to be

Table 21. Crime Rates among Foreigners in Countries of Immigration[a]

Country of Immigration	Crime Rate	Note
Belgium	10.0	Number of convictions of foreigners in 1966 as percent of foreign workers in population in 1964.
France	3.5	Number of convictions of foreigners in 1963 as percent of foreign workers in population in 1963.
Germany (FR) ..	2.8[b]	Number of convictions of four foreign groups in 1965 as percent of these four foreign groups of workers in population in 1965.
Luxembourg	2.8	Number of convictions of foreigners in 1964 as percent of foreign workers in population in 1964.
Netherlands	[c]	
Sweden	0.9	Number of convictions of aliens in 1964 as percent of foreign workers in population in 1966.
Switzerland	1.2	Number of convictions of foreigners in 1964 as percent of foreign workers in population in 1964.
United Kingdom ..	0.5[d]	Number of aliens entering prisons and borstals in England and Wales in 1963 as percent of foreign work permits issued in 1966.

SOURCES. For Belgium and Luxembourg: unpublished statistics. For France: Ministère de la Justice, *Compte générale de l'administration criminelle et de la justice civile et commerciale, année 1963* (Paris, 1964), pp. 21–23, 96, 161. For Germany: Heinz-Günther Zimmermann, "Die Kriminalität der ausländischen Arbeiter," *Kriminalistik*, No. 12 (December 1966), pp. 623–625. For Sweden: Statistiska Centralbyrån, Sveriges Officiella Statistik, *Brottsligheten 1964* (Stockholm, 1966), pp. 12–13. For Switzerland: Bureau Fédéral de Statistique, *Annuaire statistique de la Suisse* (Berne, 1966), p. 530. For the United Kingdom: *Report of Proceedings in the House of Commons for 8 April 1965* (London: Her Majesty's Stationery Office, 1965), p. 96.

[a] The base figure for number of foreign workers is drawn from Table 7 unless data for a closer year to that of crime data are available.

[b] The figures used here are uncorrected ones; corrected figures are used in the text to compare foreigners with native Germans. The corrected figures would give a percentage of 2.5 instead of 2.8, but the latter figure is more closely comparable to the others in this table.

[c] Reverend Bregman, director of Landelijke Stichting Bijstand Buitenlandse Werknehmers, a voluntary association comprising church (both Protestant and Roman Catholic) and labor union groups which provides information, social services, etc., to immigrants, said: "Foreigners have probably a lower crime rate than do Dutch nationals." Several incidents of group violence have occurred over women: foreigners misunderstand Dutch girls' freedom, Dutchmen are jealous of foreigners' success with Dutch girls.

[d] These figures are for entrance to prisons and borstals, not for all convictions, and the base year is three years removed from the crime data year.

due to inadequacies of measurement as they are to any possible real differences in crime rates. For example, the lowest rate in Table 21 is for the United Kingdom, but this could be because that country has data only for foreigners actually entering prisons and borstals, ignoring the number who are on probation, whereas for other countries data reflect court convictions. Similarly, the rate for Sweden, which is shown to be the second lowest, is probably distorted by the relatively high proportion of females (who commit fewer crimes than males) in the foreign population.

The most interesting fact to emerge from the data is how low the crime rates are for foreigners in all countries of immigration except Belgium. There seems to be no way of explaining the high rate in Belgium, except possibly to note the high proportion of miners among foreign workers, but the rate should not be taken as reliable without further study. The observation of a low crime rate is general: many officials, social workers, and other informed persons in most of the countries told the author that the foreigners' crime rate was as low as, or lower than, the crime rates of nationals, especially if the distorted sex and age distributions of foreigners were held constant (foreigners tend to be concentrated in the criminal-producing ages, and most of them are males). Independent studies for the United Kingdom show that the Commonwealth immigrants (Indians, Pakistanis, and West Indians) have a very low rate of crime, especially of crime against property.[2] The Irish in Britain, on the other hand, have a relatively high rate of crime, although it is largely due to the concentration of the Irish in the young adult age group. Part of the reason for a low crime rate for European and Commonwealth immigrants in Britain is that the commission of a crime is a basis for extradition of a migrant during the first five years after arrival for the Commonwealth and Irish immigrants, and at any time before citizenship is granted for alien Europeans. Bottoms shows that only the Irish are extradited for this reason in significant numbers.[3]

A special study has been made by Zimmermann of crime statistics among foreign workers in Germany, so as to eliminate irrelevant variables and make them comparable to the statistics for Germans.[4] Statistics on crimes committed by native German workers are not comparable to the crime statistics for foreign-born workers because the latter statistics include crimes committed by non-German nonworkers; by *bona fide* tourists; and by foreign members of armed forces stationed in Germany. Using a variety of techniques to eliminate these categories, and working only with those ages 18 to 50, Zimmermann arrived at corrected figures. His table of comparable crime rates for male workers ages 18 to 50 deserves to be recorded here *in toto*, since they probably represent the most successful effort to date to make crime statistics among foreign and national workers

Table 22. Ratios of Corrected Crime Rates among Foreign and National
Male Workers, Age 18–50, West Germany, 1965

Criminal Act	Italians	Greeks	Spaniards	Turks	Total of 4 Foreign Groups	Germans
Murder; deadly assault	133	66	66	366	133	100
Attempted murder	133	183	83	517	200	100
Bodily injury with deadly outcome	250	150	50	100	150	100
Dangerous and heavy bodily injury	112	139	75	287	138	100
Rape	123	150	63	323	147	100
Obscene acts on children	163	115	63	160	135	100
Robbery and blackmail	69	77	46	163	80	100
Petty theft	69	86	54	59	68	100
Grand theft	31	28	13	18	25	100
Fraud	23	38	11	50	27	100
All criminal acts	50	72	32	88	57	100

SOURCE. Heinz-Günther Zimmermann, "Die Kriminalität der ausländischen Arbeiter," *Kriminalistik*, No. 12 (December 1966), pp. 623–625.

comparable. They are reproduced in Table 22, from which the following conclusions can be drawn:

1. For all crimes together, the four groups of foreign workers have only 57 percent as much crime as do Germans, in proportion to their total numbers.

2. This low crime rate among foreigners occurs because they commit relatively few crimes against property (robbery, theft, fraud), which are the most numerous crimes for every population group. For crimes against persons, foreigners have higher rates than Germans, and it is these crimes that get into the newspapers, even though they occur relatively infrequently. Probably the victims of most foreigners who commit crimes against persons are also foreigners, so that the Germans have very little basis for complaint against foreign workers as far as crime goes. Yet public opinion in most countries of immigration seems to hold that foreign workers are prone to crime.

3. There are considerable differences among the national groups of foreign workers in their crime rates and crime patterns. The Spaniards stand out for their low crime rate in all categories; they engage in fewer than one-third as many crimes as do Germans in Germany, and they are low even in crimes against the person. The Turks have the highest crime rate among the four foreign groups studied, and this is mainly for crimes

of passion—murder, attempted murder, and rape. There are some other special problems of crime among certain groups of immigrants which are not revealed by the statistics. For example, a small but significant number of Greeks, Turks, and Yugoslavs have been stealing automobiles in Germany to sell them at high prices in their home countries.[5]

Belgium is the only other country of immigration which has a significant number of the same four groups of foreign workers studied for Germany, and the differentials among them in crime rate showed almost the same pattern as for Germany: Italians, 5.2 percent; Spaniards, 7.5 percent; Greeks, 10.9 percent; Turks, 13.1 percent. The only difference between the rates for Belgium and Germany is that in Belgium the Italians have a lower crime rate than the Spaniards. The Italians are relatively long-settled in Belgium as compared to Germany, whereas the other three immigrant groups are mostly new in both countries. Thus, longevity of settlement as well as nationality group seems to affect the crime rate.

In sum, all the available evidence points to a relatively low crime rate for foreigners in European countries of immigration, but it does not permit any reliable conclusions to be drawn about possible differences among the countries. Yet in all countries of immigration the national public opinion seems to be that crime rates among foreigners are high. There are several reasons why the public should believe this:

1. The public considers only the occurrence of crimes, not the crime rate. They ignore the fact that foreigners are mostly males and predominantly young adults—which categories produce the highest crime rates among their own nationals also. But even the crude crime rates—ignoring sex and age—are not excessively high for foreigners.

2. Few foreigners are in a favorable position to engage in "white-collar crimes" (such as embezzlement or tax violation), and because they are more closely watched by the authorities and have less knowledge of the habits of the country, they have fewer opportunities to steal. These are among the main reasons why their crime rates are so low. But for the same reasons, they are probably more likely to be apprehended when they do commit crimes, and so foreign criminals show up worse in the statistics— in relation to their "true" crime rates—than national criminals do.

3. When foreigners commit crimes they are more likely than nationals to commit crimes against the person than against property. Crimes against the person are often violent and spectacular, and hence get into the newspapers more frequently than crimes against property do. In this sense, the newspapers and other mass media "create" the impression in the public that foreigners are criminals.

4. Fear of criminals feeds on itself. Once the public gets the impression, from a few spectacular crimes of violence, that foreigners are criminals,

its observations of any seemingly unusual behavior on the part of foreigners will reinforce the fears. Loud conversation, other seemingly aggressive
behavior, and "peculiar" customs can all serve to strengthen the nationals'
belief that foreigners have criminal propensities.

The image of foreigners as criminals undoubtedly reduces their acceptance in the countries of immigration. But the actual low crime rate among
foreigners is one clue that they are making a reasonable adjustment.

Another index of social pathology is the sickness or morbidity rate.
That is, illness is being viewed here as more than a physical condition —
it is seen as a clue to the mental and social "health" of people. Efforts to
get data on the mental illness rates of foreigners were completely unavail-
ing, but statistics were obtained on "work absences for reasons of illness"
for Germany that permit comparison between German nationals and foreigners. Workers in Germany with compulsory sickness insurance were
sampled on April 1 and October 1, 1965, and the sickness rates according to ethnic group were calculated. The results are shown in Table 23.
The data show that foreigners had lower sickness rates than German
workers, probably because they are concentrated in the younger age
groups. What is also of interest is that the foreigners did not have higher
accident rates than German workers, and in this regard younger workers
should have no advantage over older ones. Thus, from the standpoint of
absence from work due to sickness or accident, it is preferable for German
employers to hire foreign workers rather than German ones. Women have
higher sickness rates than men in all ethnic groups, but they constitute a
smaller proportion of foreign workers than domestic ones. It is also of
considerable interest for this study that the proportion of sick persons is

Table 23. Percentage of Sick Persons among Insured Workers
in Germany (representative samples)

Category	Total Insured (Domestic and Foreign)	Italians	Greeks	Spaniards	Turks
April 1, 1965					
Men	6.37%	4.75%	6.22%	5.22%	5.86%
Women	6.84	6.01	6.44	5.46	6.41
Men and women	6.49	4.91	6.31	5.28	5.92
October 1, 1965					
Men	6.15	4.82	5.76	5.12	5.75
Women	6.44	6.06	5.74	5.43	5.75
Men and women	6.23	4.99	5.76	5.20	5.75

SOURCE. *Amtliche Nachrichten der Bundesanstalt (ANBA) für Arbeitsvermittlung
und Arbeitslosenversicherung*, Nuremberg, 14:2 (February 1966), p. 12.

lowest among Italians, followed by Spaniards, then Turks, with the highest proportion among Greeks. This is the same order which informed persons interviewed by the author estimated the adjustment of the different foreign workers to be. It also approximates the order of ethnic groups according to degree of adjustment as measured by two studies of foreign workers in Belgium.[6] The criteria of adjustment used in these studies were knowledge of the language, occupational level attained, proportion of wives working, problems with food and religious observance, and performance of children in school.

Still another index of pathology is the proportion of a population receiving social assistance ("relief"). The Swedish figures permit a comparison of Finns, other Scandinavians, and other immigrants for 1964.[7] The Finns had the highest proportion on relief — 4.1 percent; the other Scandinavians had many fewer — 3.5 percent; and "all other immigrants" were lowest with 3.2 percent. It should be noted that the Finns and other Scandinavian workers were more likely to bring their families than the other immigrants, thereby increasing their chances of needing public assistance. These data confirm what the author was told in his conversations with Swedish officials — the Finns include the largest relative number of problem cases among the immigrants.

THE RETURN OF EMIGRANTS TO THEIR HOME COUNTRIES

Because the basic subject of this research is the integration of Europe, the acceptance and adjustment of emigrants who return to their home countries must be taken into account, just as must the acceptance and adjustment of these same people in the countries of immigration. It is difficult to obtain much systematic data on the returning emigrants: most countries fail even to keep a tally of their numbers, much less identify their characteristics. Not every foreigner who leaves a country of immigration is returning to his homeland; an unknown but significant proportion are moving to other countries of immigration. This is especially so for the foreign workers now being expelled from Switzerland. It is known that the absolute number of returning emigrants is growing each year: some fail or become disillusioned in the countries of immigration, and others return with a financial nest egg to buy a small business or return with acquired skills that will enable them to find good jobs. Still others return after they reach retirement age and live on their pensions; this is especially true of Italians. In general, any substantial improvement of economic and other conditions in the country of emigration (especially to be observed in the case of Italy) or deterioration of conditions in the country of immigration (such as the recession in the winter of 1966–67) will increase the return of migrants to their home countries. In a study made of returned Spanish workers, Reverend Francisco Sanchez Lopez states that the reasons given for returning were: nostalgia for country or family, 29 percent; sickness, 5 percent; hostility of host country, 4 percent; insufficient earnings (including unemployment), 27 percent; reached goals in amount earned, 14 percent; other motives, 21 percent. Of these returned migrants, 69 percent said they found jobs easily in Spain.[8]

Of forty returning Greek migrants interviewed by Elie Dimitras and Jeanne Manganara, thirty-seven said they had made a good adjustment to industrial jobs abroad, and twenty reported very favorably on the country (mostly Germany) they had been in.[9] The largest number said they returned for family reasons, but twelve indicated some failure to adapt in the country of immigration; only three came back because they knew of a decent job opportunity in Greece. Twenty actually got good jobs.

About 30 percent of immigrants to Europe return home to Greece,[10] and 7 percent to Turkey,[11] but the proportion is higher for Italy. Italy is a country experiencing significant economic development so that there are job and business opportunities for those who do return. Thus, as pointed out earlier, Italy is about to join the ranks of those European countries which were once countries with net emigration and are now countries with net immigration. The decline of Italy's net emigration and the growth in the number of its repatriates are shown in Table 24. Italy reached the peak of its post-World War II net emigration in 1961 and the number repatriated has been steadily growing except for a slight setback in 1963 and 1964.

A possible additional index of acceptance and adjustment for the countries of immigration can be derived from Table 24 by measuring the length of time between the peak year of immigration and the peak year of repatriation. If repatriation lags far behind immigration it might be said that acceptance and adjustment are high. The time lag is largest for Italian immigrants in Belgium (seven years), the United Kingdom (six years, although there were two waves of immigration by Italians which complicates matters), and France (two years). The ratio of the total repatriations to the total number of emigrants from 1955 to 1966 is similar to the turnover ratio which is found in Table 20, except the former ratio is computed for Italians alone. The rank positions of the countries of immigration are the same for both ratios, except the United Kingdom shows up better in the figures for Italians alone. In absolute numbers, Switzerland has been contributing the largest number of Italian returnees (43.8 percent of total Italian returned emigrants for the period 1958–63), followed by the Federal Republic of Germany (21.5 percent), France (17.2 percent), and Luxembourg (2.0 percent).[12] The trend data show Switzerland

Table 24. Number of Italian Emigrants and Repatriates, 1955 to 1964

Country and Total No. Italian Residents (December 31, 1964)	1955	1956	1957	1958	1959	1960	1961	1962	1963	1964
Belgium (208,350)										
Gross emigration	17,073	10,395	10,552	3,947	4,083	4,915	3,152	3,111	1,626	2,876
Repatriation	1,200	1,200	1,109	1,266	1,686	1,781	1,926	2,077	1,488	1,815
Net emigration	15,873	9,195	9,443	2,681	2,397	3,134	1,226	1,064	138	1,061
France (910,850)										
Gross emigration	40,713	87,552	114,974	72,469	64,259	58,624	49,188	34,911	20,264	15,782
Repatriation	23,712	32,675	41,637	42,821	48,822	34,388	28,884	24,632	18,382	13,086
Net emigration	17,001	54,877	73,337	29,648	15,437	24,236	20,304	10,279	1,882	2,696
Germany (FR) (403,500)										
Gross emigration	1,200	10,907	7,653	10,511	28,394	100,544	114,012	117,427	81,261	75,210
Repatriation		8,850	4,653	6,145	15,295	34,088	48,016	69,600	73,266	58,899
Net emigration	1,199	2,057	3,000	4,366	13,099	66,456	65,996	47,827	7,995	16,311
Luxembourg (20,000)										
Gross emigration	5,700	6,500	8,874	6,187	5,404	5,237	5,196	4,949	3,505	3,203
Repatriation	5,700	6,500	8,435	4,435	4,093	3,791	3,808	3,864	3,161	2,503
Net emigration	...	...	439	1,752	1,311	1,446	1,388	1,085	344	700
Netherlands (14,600)										
Gross emigration	240	2,010	2,420	311	251	1,260	3,718	1,993	922	1,036
Repatriation	4	120	121	180	113	179	610	874	814	653
Net emigration	236	1,890	2,299	131	138	1,081	3,108	1,119	108	383
Switzerland (599,900)										
Gross emigration	71,735	75,632	78,882	57,453	82,532	128,257	142,114	143,054	122,018	111,863
Repatriation	54,778	67,625	69,382	41,974	60,621	90,207	96,700	106,022	106,317	93,945
Net emigration	16,957	8,007	9,500	15,479	21,911	38,050	45,414	37,032	15,701	17,918
United Kingdom (157,600)										
Gross emigration	10,400	11,520	10,595	6,464	7,360	10,118	11,003	8,907	4,681	4,979
Repatriation	519	1,150	1,060	838	1,288	1,576	1,868	2,504	2,476	2,308
Net emigration	9,881	10,370	9,535	5,626	6,072	8,542	9,135	6,403	2,205	2,671
Other countries										
Gross emigration	1,965	3,115	2,060	458	560	921	1,214	1,413	857	1,549
Repatriation	430	2,030	1,580	347	357	404	684	1,002	781	1,001
Net emigration	1,535	1,085	480	111	203	517	530	411	76	548
Total Europe (2,308,800)										
Gross emigration	149,026	207,631	236,010	157,800	192,843	309,876	329,597	315,795	235,134	216,498
Repatriation	86,344	120,150	127,977	98,006	132,275	166,411	182,496	210,575	206,685	174,210
Net emigration	62,682	87,481	108,033	59,794	60,568	143,462	147,101	105,220	28,449	42,288

Source. Compiled from Istituto Centrale di Statistica, Annuario Statistica del Lavoro e dell' Emigrazione (Rome, 1955-64).
a Exclusive of "Other countries."

increasing its backflow to Italy (30.2 percent in 1958 to 48.3 percent in 1963) as is Germany (4.4 percent to 33.1 percent), while France decreased its backflow (30.8 percent in 1958 to 8.3 percent in 1963). These absolute figures have to be judged in the light of the total number of Italians in the respective countries, but the contrast between Switzerland and France is nevertheless sharp, and it became sharper after Switzerland inaugurated its openly restrictive policy in 1963. By 1962, 67.3 percent of the Italians in Switzerland had been there for less than one year, whereas the comparable figure for France was 38.9 percent and for Belgium 23.1 percent.[13] The percentages of Italians who lived in the country of immigration for over five years were 5.7 percent for Switzerland, 13.9 percent for France, and 46.2 percent for Belgium.

Ireland, Spain, Portugal, and Poland are also countries with long histories of emigration, but the economic and sometimes the political conditions in those countries in the mid-1960's have not been favorable to the large-scale repatriation that Italy has been experiencing. Spain's economic conditions are improving rapidly enough for its net emigration to have dropped since 1964, but this has been due more to a decrease in new emigrants than to repatriation. However, the long-run prospects are for all the European countries of emigration to follow the path of Italy. Thus, return migration will play an increasing role in the integration of Europe.

Two sets of papers have contributed significant though not systematic information on returning migrants: Council of Europe, Special Representative's Advisory Committee, "Problems Raised by the Return Home of Migrant Workers" (Strasbourg, April 29, 1966); OECD, *Supplement to the Final Report, Emigrant Workers Returning to Their Home Country, International Management Seminar, Athens, October 18–21, 1966* (Paris: OECD, 1967). Some generalizations can be drawn from these papers:

1. The main pushes to return are expulsion from the country of immigration as a result of laws restricting length of stay, inadequate housing, lack of opportunity to rise occupationally (because of formal regulations or informal prejudice), and failure to adjust. The main pulls are improvement of job or other economic opportunities, desire to return to the family, and accumulation of savings which will permit retirement (for older persons) or starting a business in the home country. Among the emigrant countries of Europe, Greece is receiving the largest proportion of forced returnees: some 50,000 Greeks (mostly employed in commerce and industry) were forced out of Egypt in the decade following 1955, and there have been in recent years a significant number of Greek refugees from the USSR and Rumania (mostly farmers) and from Turkey (mostly small business men).[14]

2. The young, unskilled, unmarried workers stay the shortest time in

the country of immigration. Some move to other countries of immigration, but most return home at least temporarily.

3. Returning home is often temporary.

4. All emigrant countries favor the return of migrants, especially skilled workers and those with capital, and several have taken steps to facilitate return by establishing favorable exchange rates (Turkey and Yugoslavia), opportunities for investment (Turkey), and reorientation and reception facilities (all).

5. Countries of immigration have different attitudes toward repatriation, though none put any obstacle in its path. France, Belgium, and Sweden have policies of encouraging permanent integration of at least a large proportion of their immigrants. The United Kingdom permits permanent residence and encourages equal treatment of foreigners, but it cannot be said to have a policy of promoting permanent integration. Germany, Luxembourg, and the Netherlands — while otherwise encouraging equality between nationals and foreign workers — have policies of encouraging repatriation after a period of time (usually three years), although the German employers in mid-1966 were reexamining this policy in favor of more permanent integration and less turnover. Switzerland — while continuing to permit the permanent integration of its old-time settlers — now requires the return of all new immigrants (usually in less than one year, and in many cases in less than three years).

6. Few returnees have acquired skills during their period abroad, but many have learned modern work habits. The immigrant countries which devote the greatest attention to training — France, Belgium, Sweden — are usually the countries which encourage permanent migration (Germany has been the main exception, since it has provided much training but has thus far not favored permanent residence).

Some of the countries of emigration make special efforts to keep in touch with their nationals working abroad for the purpose of maintaining ties, encouraging their eventual return, and facilitating their readjustment when they do return. The Spanish government is perhaps the most active in this regard. Spanish consulates in countries of immigration offer courses in the Spanish language so that children of Spanish workers are not estranged from their mother tongue. (Italian and Greek consulates offer like services.) The Spanish consulates provide information and other aids to their nationals abroad. Spanish priests are scattered through the countries of immigration to encourage the maintenance of religious and community activities. Newspapers published in Spain especially for emigrants are distributed free or at nominal cost to Spanish workers abroad. The Yugoslav government is also quite active in keeping in touch with its nationals abroad: its cultural associations help to finance branches for Yugoslav workers in other countries; they hold festivals and maintain other national customs and organize mutual aid activities. There are newspapers and magazines sent from Yugoslavia, and there is a radio program in Yugoslavia beamed to central and northern Europe in the various Yugoslav languages.

The training and experience benefits which the migrant worker is supposed to gain by his experience abroad have been questioned by authorities in the emigrant countries. An Italian official, responding to a questionnaire, wrote: "Workers who have done a full day's work and generally some overtime as well . . . prefer a rest when they finish work rather than attending training or re-training courses organized by the immigration country, and even if they do attend these courses the benefit they derive from them is in inverse ratio to their fatigue and their lack of knowledge of the language." [15] This suggests that training is minimal and experience abroad is irrelevant for the migrant returned to his home country. Further, many jobs that migrant workers obtain abroad are completely unskilled, so there is no work training or experience. But considering that probably most of the emigrants emerge from a peasant background and that their experience abroad does teach them to adjust to factory work and to urban living conditions, they do have some advantages when they return. Some returnees have accumulated a little capital and start small businesses, which may or may not be successful, but probably most returnees seek factory work where the work habits they learned in the country of immigration are appropriate even if their specific training is not. If their home countries are still very underdeveloped — as would largely be true of Greece, Ireland, Portugal, and Turkey — there would not be enough industries available to offer them employment where their skills could be used. They have to accept unskilled or agricultural employment, start small service businesses which are of little benefit to the economy, or emigrate again.

A special effort is often made to bring back those emigrants with skills which are in short supply in the home country. In 1965, for example, the Jamaican government made an appeal to the 3,000–5,000 Jamaican nurses in the United Kingdom to go home because of the desperate shortage of nurses in the home country.[16] Yet it is usually these skilled and professional workers who make the best adjustment to the country of immigration and who have the greatest amount of difficulty readjusting to the life of their less-developed home country. Various economic incentives are provided for the return of emigrants. The favorable currency exchange rate offered by Turkey has already been mentioned. Yugoslavia has eliminated the customs duty on furniture and automobiles for its returning migrants. Greece, under the Papandreou government of 1964–65, planned an extensive program of attracting emigrants home and of reintegrating them into the economy, but probably nothing has come of its five-year plan.

The transportation expenses of the returning migrant are usually paid for by the employer if the worker has fulfilled his contract (either individual contract or group contract provided for under a bilateral treaty).[17] Often the employer makes regular deductions from wages for this purpose. If the worker has broken his contract, he must pay for his own return journey. If he cannot do so, the national authorities of the immigrant country transport him to the border of his home country, the authorities of which then pay for the rest of his journey to his home town. Railroad companies (mostly state-owned in Europe) often provide reductions in fares and sometimes provide special trains, and the Swiss Railways gives reductions for transportation of belongings. Italy provides travel credit to its emigrating workers to enable them to make the return journey. The United Kingdom and the Netherlands require employers, when they apply for permission to employ foreign workers, to agree to arrange for the repatriation of the foreign workers if it becomes necessary.

Social insurance benefits often cease after the migrant worker has returned to his home country.[18] Britain is the major exception in its policy with regard to old age and industrial accident insurance: it treats returnees just as it does its own nationals who have ceased working. If the returnee has worked in the United Kingdom for three years consecutively, he is eligible to continue payments on a voluntary basis to preserve his right to retirement and widows' benefits. The Common Market countries have similar provisions for returnees to other Common Market countries only. The agreement between the United Kingdom and Ireland provides for unemployment insurance payments to unemployed returned Irishmen. Some other bilateral agreements provide for return of the worker's payments on social insurance when he leaves the immigrant country, but in most cases he loses his contributions as well as his benefits entirely. The 1960 agreement between Germany and Greece (which now sends over 80 percent of its emigrants to Germany) provides that Greeks originally accepted for Germany but unable to find work after their contracts expire will receive unemployment benefits for five months after repatriation, and that the German government will pay 60 percent of these. The compensation is only fifty drachmas (about two dollars) a day, and very few returned Greeks have claimed it — indicating that most find employment when they return to Greece.[19]

A few interesting experiments have been carried out to aid in the economic reintegration of the returning worker. A Swiss firm which manufactures saws — after an economic study to determine the most profitable way of investing excess capital — built a branch factory in Greece. While it was being built, the firm brought Greek workers to its main factory in Switzerland for training and work, and then sent them home to work in the branch.[20] Turkish workers in Germany pooled part of their savings to invest in a new firm to be established within the Turkish economic development plan, and the Turkish government gave them a rate of exchange more in accord with the free-market rate than the official rate. After this firm is established, those who contributed to its financing will be able to work there when they return to Turkey; they will then be both workers and owners in the firm. The Greek government has instructed one of the Greek credit banks to set up a special savings fund with agencies in various parts of Germany to enable migrant workers to save to purchase a house on their return home.[21] Marziale cites other examples of emigrant countries engaging in activities to attract their emigrants home: "The government of one emigration country has co-operated with employers in drawing up a list of specialised posts which cannot be filled from the country's present labour force. It then intends to offer annual contracts to its nationals working abroad, either on their return home or, before that, when their present contracts in Europe expire. Other emigration countries have organized information services, which they are constantly improving, to keep migrant workers informed of the work available to them at home."[22]

Returning to their home countries is not a shock for most migrants who have worked in other European countries, for they have been home periodically for holidays and for voting, and most of them have kept up with what is going on in the home country through letters, newspapers, and conversations with conationals. Even when they have not been notably successful in their jobs in the immigrant countries, they usually have a certain prestige when they return home. There is a problem of readjustment to work and living conditions, but it is not nearly as severe as in the case of migrants who have spent a protracted and unbroken period overseas. The degree of readjustment required is a function of several variables. If the returned migrant lives in a city he finds it generally easier than if he returns to a peasant village; if he returns to a rapidly developing society like Italy's he finds it generally easier than if he returns to a more traditional society like Portugal's or Turkey's; if he acquires a job that makes use of his new knowledge and pays him for it he generally finds it easier than if he must go back to working as an unskilled laborer. As has been observed by a Turkish student, "The social pressure of small communities, the restrictive men-women relations, the lack of entertainment facilities, all begin to be felt after the return of the employee. . . . The problems Turkish labourers will face on their return are more critical than the small difficulties they encounter when going to find employment in the West." [23] On the other hand, 83 percent of the returned Spanish workers studied by Reverend Lopez said they readapted easily to Spain (10 percent said they took a certain time to readapt; and 7 percent said they never readapted).[24] It is probable that the cultural distance between countries of immigration and emigration (measured in Table 18), which affects adjustment to country of immigration, also affects readaptation to the country of emigration by the migrant who has spent some years abroad.

PSYCHOLOGICAL PROBLEMS

Unlike adventurers who go abroad with great expectations or refugees who are escaping hazards to life and liberty, and probably unlike most overseas migrants who anticipate creating new lives for themselves in new worlds, the great majority of European cross-national migrants today do not look forward with great hope or joy to their life in another European country. Studies of samples of them show that while practically all expect to improve their economic position by migrating, they also expect to return to their home countries after a limited stay in the country of immigration.[25] This attitude apparently arms the tougher-minded among them with unconcern and cynicism toward the unpleasant aspects of what they experience in the country of immigration and enables them to maintain a healthy mental balance. On the other hand, the lack of a strong personal motive to migrate helps to create mental problems for some. One professional observer describes the latter as the "average emigrant":

He is demoralised by the difficulty of finding a job and by the precariousness of his position. He emigrates without enthusiasm or ideals to a country which is virtually an unknown world. He has to leave his wife, friends and familiar surroundings behind. He sets off without confidence, his sole object to make some money. He arrives in a place which is strange and new. He finds everything different: language, climate, food, way of life, etc. He may come across a group of compatriots, but is just as likely to be alone in the midst of foreigners. All these things have a considerable traumatic effect on the mind of this "average" man who, in both character and temperament, is always very attached to his spiritual and physical surroundings, whatever their importance.[26]

The "culture shock" which almost everyone experiences when he participates in a different society for the first time is accentuated for migrant workers because they usually come from a restricted cultural background. During the mid-1960's in the countries of immigration, the foreign worker could expect to find poor housing, an impersonal employer, shockingly high prices for the necessities of life, and — in several countries — few facilities to aid and orient him. He was typically lonely, even if he found some compatriots to associate with, and he considered the host population to be distant. All these things upset some foreign workers' mental equilibrium, and they had to be given psychiatric attention, either in the country of immigration or immediately upon their return home. In other cases some traumatic incident precipitated a mental disturbance.

Dr. J. L. Villa, former head of the Polyclinique Psychiatrique at the University of Lausanne, Switzerland, reported on some seven hundred Italians examined at his clinic between 1948 and 1958.[27] The clients were in a state of depression and anxiety, and they manifested a progressive intolerance toward certain conditions in the host country (food, climate, people). Dr. Villa reported that the sick person began to regard those around him as hostile forces.[28] Various psychosomatic symptoms appeared, and behavior tended to go to extremes of schizoid withdrawal or paranoid aggressiveness.

The director of the psychiatric hospital at Verona, Italy, made a study of fifteen migrant workers who were treated on their return home after a period abroad. They all showed the same symptoms — depression accompanied by emotional disturbances and a refusal to take part in society:

In the case of twelve of the subjects, there is a clearly defined cause-and-effect link between their behaviour (outbursts of intolerance, hallucinations, delirium and persecution mania) and their working and living environment: They are suspicious of their workmates ("They were jealous of me because I worked harder than they did"; "They were jealous of me because the boss liked me better"; "They thought I was a spy"), suspicious of their boss ("He was always keeping a watch on me") and suspicious of the local community ("The neighbors were always saying things behind my back"; "The people were driving me mad, they were always watching me"; "They threatened to kill me"; "They watched you as if they had a grudge against you," etc.).[29]

These cases are, of course, the failures among the migrants, but it seems likely that some of them might not have become mentally disturbed if they had never had to leave their protected home environments.

CONCLUSION

Unfortunately no data were available for other indexes which could measure acceptance and adjustment — such as the proportions speaking the language of the country of immigration, joining unions or other occupational associations, or having close friends among nationals. The relatively few indexes of dependent variables for which data were available are summarized in Table 25. The low scores in the table indicate the greatest degree of acceptance and adjustment. While these data are not so adequate nor the method of measuring them so precise as to permit incontrovertible conclusions, they indicate that Sweden, the Netherlands,

Table 25. Summary of Indexes of Acceptance and Adjustment[a]
in Countries of Immigration

Index	Belgium	France	Germany (FR)	Luxem-bourg	Nether-lands	Sweden	Switzer-land	United Kingdom
Turnover of immigrants	1	1	1	2	1	1	3	2
Percentage of cross-national marriages	1	2	2	2	1	1	2	[b]
Ratio of naturalized foreigners to foreign labor force	3	2	3	2	1	1	3	2
Crime rate	3	2	2	2	1	1	1	1
Lag between repatriation peak and migration peak .	1	2	3	3	3	[b]	3	1
Total	9	9	11	11	7	5–7	12	7–9

[a] The number 1 indicates the greatest degree of acceptance and adjustment.
[b] Data are not available.

and the United Kingdom have the best adjusted immigrants; Switzerland has the least well adjusted, with Germany and Luxembourg having immigrants only a little better adjusted; while those of France and Belgium are in the middle ranges of adjustment.

From 1955 through 1966 at least eight million Europeans voluntarily left their homes to take up residence and work in another country of Europe. Most of these Europeans migrated from some southern country to some northern or central country. A couple of million among them have returned to their homelands, and another significant minority (perhaps a million) have become citizens of the country to which they had migrated. At the end of 1966 there were at least five million Europeans, plus their dependents, living and working as foreigners in European countries. The economic recession in the winter and spring of 1966–67 sharply reduced the rate of migration, and while the rate might be presumed to swing upward when the recession is over, for reasons detailed in Chapter 2, the migration will probably never return to the pace it had achieved in the early 1960's: about 4 percent of the Europeans living outside the Soviet bloc had voluntarily changed countries, but both economic and social-psychological factors were operating to keep that proportion from going much higher.

This migratory movement has had effects in areas other than the economic one which largely stimulated it (and since the economic impact is not central to the problem of integration there will be no further discussion of it). Some minor effects of migration were the changes it wrought for those who had special reasons to be dissatisfied in their native countries and who used migration to avoid these dissatisfactions. Presumably, the majority of these migrants successfully escaped from individual political repressions, uncongenial dominant ideologies, unhappy marital ties which could not be legally broken by divorce, and repressive social customs (such as those restricting freedom for women). The more libertarian and democratic countries of northern and central Europe provided sanctuaries from such kinds of political and sociological restrictions, but at the same time they posed new social-psychological problems for the migrants.

More important to a study of the integration of people than economic or miscellaneous effects is the impact on migrants of the whole category of problems of adjustment to migration. The disruption of traditional patterns of behavior and accommodation to new ones — symbolized in such sociological concepts as culture shock, cultural conflict, and alienation — was probably experienced in one form or another by every migrant. Some of this was painful and damaging, especially to the tiny minority who manifested psychiatric symptoms, but in many cases it was just as constructive (in providing release from social constraints) as it was destructive. All change — including tourism — is disruptive; the question is what are the long-run and countervailing consequences of the disruption? Considering that most of the migrants were moving from a rural to an urban culture at the same time as they were crossing national (and cultural) lines, the disruption was considerable. But probably in only a small minority of cases did the long-run negative effects outbalance the long-run positive effects.

In this study it was found that while economic factors are the main ones in motivating individual workers to migrate, policy factors seem to be most important in facilitating or retarding their acceptance in the country of immigration and their adjustment to that country. This does not refer to policies excluding immigrants or reducing their numbers after they are in the country; it refers only to policies and practices toward foreigners already permitted to work in the country. There are gaps, however, in every immigrant country's organized activities to aid in the acceptance and adjustment of its immigrants — that is, a country may have an excellent program in several respects, but have little activity in other respects. Nevertheless, it is possible to discern different central tendencies among countries in the intensiveness and extensiveness of their programs. France and Sweden lead the countries of Europe in the variety and completeness of their organized efforts. At the other end, Switzerland does the least. Italy and Spain are the only emigrant countries to have significant programs to aid in the adjustment of their nationals going abroad, although Greece has also recently set up missions in several cities of Germany.

The multilateral international agreements — especially those of the EEC, Council of Europe, ILO, and Scandinavian Free Labor Market — have done a great deal to upgrade the programs and activities of their ratifying countries. While the benefits are specifically for the nationals of the member states, they tend to "spill over" and be applied to other migrants. Private employers, trade unions, local governments, churches, and voluntary associations are significantly aiding the reception, training, and adjustment of foreigners.

While progress has been made in the past decade, the inadequacies of the programs to aid cross-national migrants make an adjustment — in the light of their initial handicaps of cultural limitations, rural background, low educational level, poor vocational preparation — suggest that, by and

146

large, the life of the cross-national migrant is not a pleasant one. The public opinion polls show that a good deal of dissatisfaction with the free migration policies now prevails in most countries of northern and central Europe, as well as significant antagonism toward the migrants. The inadequacies of housing and the exclusion of the family of the worker are probably the most unpleasant features. A large number of immigrant workers are being exploited economically without compensatory social advantages or because of insufficient orientation think they are being exploited. Despite progress, and despite the efforts of several countries and many groups throughout western and northern Europe, policies, programs, and practices toward migrant workers cannot be considered a generally favorable force toward the future integration of Europe.

In policy factors facilitating the integration of immigrants, Sweden offers its workers the highest wages, for any given occupation, of any country in Europe, with Germany coming second. The occupational level of immigrants to the United Kingdom is the highest, mainly because that country no longer accepts many immigrants who are not skilled. On the nonpolicy factors facilitating the integration of immigrants, France stands in the best position. Insofar as the culture and social structure of the countries of emigration facilitate the adjustment of their emigrants, Italians have the greatest likelihood of adjustment and Turks the least, among the seven European peoples studied. The inadequate indexes used in this study suggest that the best adjustment has been made by immigrants to Sweden, the Netherlands, and the United Kingdom.

The main hypotheses stated earlier in this book were that acceptance, integration, and adjustment of foreigners into a host society is a function of the following: (1) the openness of the host society; (2) the degree of attachment the immigrants feel to their society of origin (that is, the inverse of this should be correlated with measures of integration into the host society); (3) the similarity of the cultures of the country of emigration and the country of immigration. A summary of facts relevant to these hypotheses has been assembled in Table 26. As throughout the study, no attempt will be made to weigh the diverse variables measured, but a weight of 1 is arbitrarily assigned to each.[1] This means all are being treated alike. The dependent variables — that is, the measures of acceptance, integration, and adjustment — are important ones, but they may not be enough to cover what happens to the immigrants as they are intended to do. There may also be defects in the reliability of the data themselves, although they came from official government sources. Nevertheless, the summary index of dependent variables was related to each of the summary indexes of independent variables.

The one significant correlation is that between the summary index of

147

Table 26. Summary Indexes of Independent and Dependent Variables
Related to Acceptance and Adjustment of Immigrants [a]

Variable	Belgium	France	Germany	Luxem-bourg	Nether-lands	Sweden	Switzer-land	UK
Openness of policies of immigrant country (from Table 11)[b] ...	5	1	4	6	7	2	8	3
Economic factors of immigrant country (from Table 12) ...	2	2	1	1	3	1	2	1
Attachment to culture of emigrant country, according to distribution from various countries of emigration (Table 18 interpreted by Table 7)	2	2	3	2	1	1	1	3
Differences between countries of emigration and immigration (from Table 17)	2	1	4	2	4	3	4	4
Summary of rankings for independent variables	11	6	12	11	15	7	15	11
Summary of rankings for dependent variables (from Table 25)	4	4	5	5	2	1	6	3
Summary of rankings for independent and dependent variables	15	10	17	16	17	8	21	14

[a] The number 1 is used to indicate the greatest degree of acceptance and adjustment.

[b] The indexes are rank orders based on the total score of 1–3 rankings for the variable.

dependent variables and the summary index of openness of a country's policies, practices, and programs in regard to immigrants. When the rank order coefficient of correlation for all eight immigrant countries was used, a rho measure of .47 was found, which means that there is a moderate relationship. This is a positive finding for the first hypothesis. One country is an obvious deviant in the relationship — the Netherlands. Its deviancy lies in the fact that immigrants make a good adjustment in the Netherlands, but the country's policies, programs, and practices are not very open to them.[2] This seems easy to explain: the Netherlands is the poorest immigrant country — in fact, it is only marginally an immigrant country since it has almost as many emigrants as immigrants. The Netherlands can afford to do very little for the immigrant, but Dutch public opinion is pro-immigrant, compared to that found in most other countries, and in this *informally* favorable atmosphere, immigrants make a relatively good adjustment. Public opinion has not been related statistically to the dependent index, since the measuring instruments were noncomparable. If the Netherlands is left outside the correlation, rho jumps to .73, which is a fairly high correlation for complex data such as these. Thus the first hypothesis can be considered confirmed — integration and adjustment of immigrants is related to the openness of programs, policies, and practices of immigrant countries. If there were comparable measures of the openness of public opinion, the Dutch case indicates that the indexes would be even more closely related.

But other hypotheses do not hold up to the correlation of the indexes. The facts give no reason to believe that the degree of attachment of the immigrants to their society of origin inhibits good integration or adjustment to the immigrant country (rho = 0). Nor do the facts give reason to believe that similarity of the cultures of the country of immigration and the country of emigration encourages better integration and adjustment of the immigrants (rho = .10). This is not to say these hypotheses have been disproved, but rather that the data have failed to prove them. If the true relationship should be nothing, as the crude indexes of this study suggest they are, a most valuable finding emerges, and it is one that goes against current sociological thinking: the cultural and political backgrounds of the migrants — by country, not as individuals — appear to have little or nothing to do with the kind of adjustment they make to the immigrant society, and, in a significant sense, all cross-national migrant groups — on the average for their country — start off on the same foot when they migrate. What *is* important for integration and adjustment is the openness of the *immigrant* country — certainly in its overt policies, programs, and practices, and probably in its informal attitudes as well.

An important qualification needs to be made to these generalizations.

They are based on macroscopic data — that is, information applying to all national groups. No information is presented here on individual cases or on variations among individuals. It could still be true that *some* individual migrants are very much affected by their ties to their national and local backgrounds. It could still be true that a small number of immigrants find the different climate, language, or religion of the country of immigration to be such an obstacle that they cannot make an adjustment. And it could also be true that some immigrants make an excellent adjustment even when the immigrant country is least open and most hostile (within the range examined in this study). Thus it should be emphasized that these are macroscopic, *grouped data*, that the correlations are of the type which have taken on the technical misnomer of "ecological," [3] and that the findings presented here do not apply to all individuals.

Chapter 4 contained a summary of the indexes used to measure openness of a country to immigrants as indicated by its formal policies, programs, and practices. France, Sweden, the United Kingdom, in that order, were found to be the most open countries and the Netherlands and Switzerland the least open. In subsequent chapters of this book several other measures affecting or indicating the integration or adjustment of immigrants were presented. To draw them all together creates a theoretically meaningless index, but one which may have practical utility. Such a summary of summaries, presented in Table 26, might be called an "index of favorable conditions" affecting immigrants. It shows where, among the eight countries of immigration studied, the immigrants are best off and where they are worst off. Sweden is ahead of France on this final measure, and the Netherlands and Germany rank next to Switzerland as the worst countries for the immigrant. These measures are all relative to each other: certainly no country is really very bad for immigrants; if it were, immigrants would soon cease to go or stay there. And certainly no country offers perfection for immigrants, although Sweden and France make a conscious national effort to do as well as they can.[4]

This "index of favorable conditions" for the countries of immigration harks back to one of the basic themes introduced early in this book: to what extent are the people of Europe beginning to think of themselves as Europeans and not merely as Frenchmen, Germans, or Swedes? It was assumed at the outset that if the concept of "European" is to have substance, it must take the form of European peoples accepting nationalities other than their own *as their own*. This applies to the total population of Europe, of course, but this study has concentrated on cross-national migrants and their hosts. In a very important sense, the migrants and their hosts are the best persons on whom to test the question of acceptance: their mutual presence is real, not academic or something to fill in on a questionnaire;

they are together for a substantial period of time, not for a few days of superficial tourism or convention-going; the relationships are formed under
conditions of everyday living, not on special diplomatic or professional
occasions where everyone exhibits only his best behavior. For these reasons cross-national migration provides an almost experimental situation
for judging whether European peoples are accepting each other.

This study has focused on the hosts to a greater extent than the migrants
themselves because there are more relevant data on them, and because the
hosts provide a more critical test of the acceptance of others since they
have more power and freedom than the migrants, who in a sense *must* accept the hosts. Acceptance by the host peoples does not refer to any hypo-
thetical willingness to accept all foreigners under any and all conditions.
Every nation has limits on its expansivity, and every nation must set limits
on the rate of immigration, for economic reasons if no other. What this
study has sought to determine is whether the host people, who have invited the immigrants either to take the least desirable jobs in their countries or to fill in occupational gaps which their own nationals cannot fill,
treat these migrants as people in the same sense they treat their fellow-na-
tionals. This is what is meant by "acceptance" among the host people. To
determine this an examination was made of all the host countries' policies,
programs, and practices for which objective information was obtainable,
all relevant public opinion polls, and various indexes of the adjustability
of the migrants. The conclusion is that there are gaps and faults in every
country, but that France and Sweden have made significant formal efforts
to accept the migrants. "Formal" efforts are emphasized because the public opinion poll data show a considerable rejection even in those countries,
and in France the efforts seem to include a proviso that the immigrants
must become "francisized." [5] The United Kingdom, Belgium, and Luxembourg follow behind the two leaders, with the British making an obvious
effort to face up to their shortcomings by sponsoring studies, much public discussion, and legislation. Germany's policy apparently has been to be
very formally correct in regard to the immigrants, to treat them well ma-
terially, but in no sense to accept them as equivalent peoples. The German policy is expressed in the term used to designate the migrants — "guest
workers." The Netherlands represents almost a direct contrast to France
and Germany: it does little to help the immigrants formally, but its attitudes are more open than those in most countries and the immigrants generally find it easy to adjust to the Netherlands despite the lack of formal
aids. Only Switzerland has chosen the conscious path of rejection to the
point of overt and explicit chauvinism. This is evident not only in Switzerland's restrictions on immigration, but is expressed also by the treatment
meted out to the immigrants accepted into the country. While the "re-

151

jection" is clearest in Switzerland, it exists to some extent among all the immigration countries, and few nationals of these countries think of themselves as really interchangeable with their immigrants.

About the migrants themselves there is less information. The naturalization and intermarriage rates offer important clues on the extent to which the migrants accept their hosts as interchangeable with their native nationalities, which is defined as "acceptance." But clearly acceptance means something beyond assimilation, and both naturalization and intermarriage refer to acceptance only insofar as it also means assimilation. Even if an immigrant returns to his home country and takes a spouse from among his native people, he can still accept his former hosts as "my own kind of people," and consider them as interchangeable with his own nationality for social and political purposes. This kind of opinion is difficult to measure, except very crudely by scattered references to such things as participation in cross-national voluntary associations. Very few emigrants leave their home countries with the intention of never coming back, except perhaps for a visit. But the fact that only a minority have returned is a crude index that the majority have accepted their host country as their adopted country, whether the law and those who apply it allow them to be naturalized or not. Except for those who return with bitterness or with psychological problems to their home countries, the migrants seem to show a great deal of tolerance, if not outright acceptance, of their host peoples.

The study that has been presented here lacks a real contrast or comparison, which probably could be best provided by studying migrants in Canada, Australia, and some countries of Latin America. To make this comparison would require a separate study, but it seems probable that mutual acceptance is greater among migrants and their hosts in these countries, composed entirely of past migrants, than among recent European migrants to European countries.

A few comparisons could be drawn between acceptance of cross-national migrants in Europe in the 1960's and acceptance of migrants who came from Europe to the United States in the century and a half before the quota-restriction laws of the 1920's. Yet the times were so different that the comparison is not really appropriate: the early 1900's was an era of laissez-faire for government, so the programs and practices toward immigrants were largely those of private organizations, which did much to aid the foreigners but not nearly as much as is done today by governments. It was a migration of much longer distance, and — although there is no information about whether the migrants initially dreamed of returning to their homelands — they found it much more difficult to return, even for a holiday. Other profound differences could be specified.

Mutual acceptance was dominant in the immigration to America in the pre-1921 period. There were those Americans who insisted that the immigrants adapt to an "American" cultural norm, those who looked forward to a more cosmopolitan "melting pot," and those who favored an equalitarian cultural pluralism. But there were practically none who insisted that the migrants return to their homelands after a period of labor here — even at the height of the agitation for putting restrictions on further immigration, and even at the highest pitch of racist hatred. Different conceptions prevailed on how the European immigrant was to become an American, but there was no doubt that he could become an American and that he should have full legal and political rights as an American. There was a norm of acceptance that made integration ultimately inevitable — despite many personal hardships attending the process.

There are no comparative, systematic data on the adjustment of these early migrants, but the historical studies of Marcus Hansen, Oscar Handlin, and others suggest that most immigrants to America quickly thought of themselves as permanent Americans, even though many retained a sentimental and cultural loyalty to the "old country" and adopted assimilation as their personal goal. There was also a transfer of political loyalty, which has yet to be measured among the intra-European migrants of the 1960's. Some of the immigrants to America, especially the Italians, returned to their homelands, but there is no evidence that this involved repudiation of the United States: some returnees were trapped by European wars and new American immigration restriction laws into staying in the homelands when they originally had intended to go back to the United States after a holiday or settlement of family affairs. The European immigration to the United States was a successful, integrative migration, if the evidence of history can be trusted. This study raises the question whether there has been as much mutual acceptance among European migrants and their hosts in Europe in the past decade. The findings would seem to indicate that there is not, although cross-national migration has not increased hostility; rather, it has decreased it to some extent. Integration and acceptance among Europeans, to the extent that it exists among Americans, will probably not occur without substantially more political and economic integration backed by cooperative intergovernmental policies.

APPENDIX A

SELECTED NEWSPAPER ARTICLES
On Conditions for Foreign Workers

◄───

In this appendix are presented two series of articles that appeared in leading newspapers of Yugoslavia and Turkey describing living and working conditions of emigrants in Sweden and in Germany. As noted in the text, Sweden is one of the countries most favorable for foreign workers today, yet the conditions described (probably fairly accurately) are quite unfavorable. These articles no doubt created deep impressions on the minds of ordinary citizens, and perhaps affected international attitudes more than do international economic and political exchanges on a high level. The newspaper features translated below represent fairly typical "case materials" of their genre, which are not readily accessible to most English-speaking scholars. Yugoslav and Turkish nationals employed by the American embassies in Belgrade and Ankara courteously translated them for the author.

Excerpts from the Series "Yugoslav Workers in the World: Sweden" by Jug Grizelj, Appearing in the Yugoslav Newspaper Vecernje Novosti *(Belgrade), December 24–January 2, 1967*

According to the police data thirty-nine Yugoslavs crossed the Swedish frontier on December 9 this year. I was the only one who had a room in a hotel, who was met at the station, and who did not shiver at the thought of the coming day.

Incidentally, I met almost all, actually thirty-five of the thirty-eight, citizens of Yugoslavia who came to Sweden on the same day. After a thirteen-day stay thirty of them had a permanent job which in no case was adequate and the remaining eight, mostly hungry, exhausted, and unshaved, were without a job and prepared to accept any work to earn some money for food. All thirty-eight Yugoslavs arrived in Sweden with tourist passports and no one had a job provided in advance.

According to Yugoslav statistics there are 16,000 Yugoslav workers (without families) in Sweden; according to Swedish statistics there are 11,927.

I spent fifteen days in Sweden and visited big industrial centers in Stockholm, Malmö, and Göteborg. I met over two hundred Yugoslavs, sat in restaurants where they ate, entered their homes, saw the factories where they work. I talked to Swedish journalists, workers' union officials, social workers, and writers who were mostly absorbed by the theme of Swedish emigration. That is why I am able to say that people who think Sweden is a promised land are no more right than the ones who believe that Yugoslav workers are slaves in Sweden. Millions may be earned there but they cannot be found on

157

pavements; Swedish apartments are cosy and warm but Yugoslav workers rarely live in them. The Yugoslav worker is praised but he is also ignored sometimes; Swedish girls are beautiful and they like dark-haired men, but they "do not carry a bed on their backs" as I have heard many Yugoslavs say.

I met a Yugoslav who has five million old dinars in the bank and lives in a large modern apartment in the fashionable part of Malmö but I also saw the following words written in Macedonian on the wall of an airport toilet: "Damn the foreign country." I met a group of workers who earned a thousand crowns a month and I met four Yugoslavs who tried to collect some money to buy tickets for the train back as they could not find a job for over a month.

Yugoslavs in Sweden can be found in the following places of work:

Hospitals, technical institutes	311
Administration	45
Commercial business	31
Mining	26
Farms, forests, gardens	58
Transportation	136
Industry	9,451
Various services	1,766
Other jobs	97
Total	11,927

Out of 12,000 workers in Sweden there are only 400 who have finished secondary school, 20 who graduated from the university, and the remaining 11,-500 are manual workers, mostly unskilled.

Let me tell you about the "importers" of Yugoslav workers to Sweden. Vlada V. is a famous importer from Nis. His services are not cheap: for transport by his own car from Nis (a town in southern Serbia) to Malmö he charged 200,-000 old dinars and for a bed in a cold room in his apartment in Sweden he charged 50,000 old dinars. For four days Vlada ate and drank at the expense of his protégés and then he told them that he could not find them a job, which he had promised to do and for which they had paid him. Ninety-six percent of Yugoslavs come into Sweden this way.

This is what Stipe Sikić from Split, now staying in Malmö told me: ". . . I saw three of them appearing. 'You are looking for a job?' they asked me. 'Yes,' I answered thinking how lucky I was to run into them. They said they would find me a job and a place to live. Of course, they asked for six hundred crowns. I was ready to pay. . . . Suddenly I saw the letter 'U' [for *Ustacha*, a right-wing extremist movement, anti-Tito] on his coat. Then one of them asked: 'Are you really one of us?' 'What do you mean?' I said. 'Are you a Croat?' 'I am a Croat, I am a Yugoslav,' I said. 'Are you crazy or something? From now on Yugoslavia does not exist for you; here I am your Tito and your mother. You will either join us or. . . .' I understood, and the next day early in the morning I packed and ran away."

Some ran away and some did not. Practically, there are only two ways to get a job here: by accepting offers extended by *Ustachas*, who call themselves "uncles," or by using Vlada V.'s services.

The average Yugoslav worker in Sweden earns nine hundred crowns a month (250,000 old dinars). But let us see what is the cost of living and what are his monthly expenses:

158

350 crowns — minimum for food
130 crowns — minimum for apartment
100 crowns — minimum for various expenses
___
580 crowns

He is able to save three hundred crowns monthly if he does not spend a single crown for cigarettes, cinema, and restaurants.

We should divide Yugoslavs who go to Sweden into two main groups: really good workers who want to earn money; and the ones who are attracted by the interesting far country, and who are adventurers and often criminals. Fortunately, the number of the members of the first group is much the greater, but the other gives all Yugoslavs a bad reputation. Very often Swedish newspapers write about the "brave deeds" of these Yugoslavs: for example, three Yugoslav emigrants, Karlo Starcevic, Nikola Konstantinov, and Zeljko Rakosa, robbed the Anders Bank in Malmö and were caught. The headline of a Swedish newspaper about this robbery was "Yugoslavs Know How to Rob a Bank besides Knowing How to Wash Dirty Dishes."

We will be able to mention later the names of many Yugoslavs who entered the Swedish police records because of stealing or running away from Sweden without paying for a car bought on credit, which became a real "Yugo-mania."

In spite of these facts Yugoslavs represent useful and valued manpower in Sweden. Ragnar Walstrom, the chief of the Department for Foreign Manpower said: "I may say without a reserve that the workers from your country are good and that they will always be welcome here. They are excellent workers with exceptional ability to accommodate. Unfortunately, we have troubles with the ones who do not come through the mutual Yugoslav-Swedish Employment organization which provides job and housing for your workers but with tourist passports. They become a difficult problem both for us and for you. . . ."

Nicolas Browning, an American engineer in a Volvo factory, said: "As a rule Yugoslav workers understand so quickly every new job given to them that one often believes that the qualifications and education of these men are much greater than what they tell us."

I visited several factories. Yugoslavs working in them were very happy to see a Yugoslav journalist but they did not stop their work for a moment.

Svetislav Dimitrijevic, a waiter at the Malmö airport, said: "During the eight-hour working day, I do not stop to smoke a cigarette because guests must not wait. How funny, when I only think how I worked in Belgrade." Aleksandar Mitrovic, an electrician in a Fiat garage in Malmö, reported: "In Nis, I worked approximately two hours a day. Here I do not stop for a moment. Swedish workers are almost jealous of my salary."

Malmö is a nice city of 250,000 inhabitants near the sea and the Danish frontier. It has several beautiful squares but there are several ugly ones too, one of them being Gustavplaz, the place where all the Yugoslav smugglers, criminals, and "managers" gather.

It is very difficult to get an apartment in Sweden. But Vlada V. and Rosha can manage to get one for you. Actually, a number of families living in old apartments move to new ones. Vlada V. and Rosha go to the Swedish office for the distribution of apartments and with their stories which would break a

159

bulldog's heart about children sleeping in cold railway stations, they break the heart of the clerk. So they get keys and then "give" them to Yugoslavs who are looking desperately for apartments. They ask in return (they say for furniture) some two thousand crowns or so.

Is the recent report of a Tanjug correspondent about terroristic organizations of *Ustashas* in Sweden a true one? Are the stories of Yugoslav workers about fascist organizations and bands whose activity is not forbidden by Swedish police a little exaggerated? Is the existence of Yugoslav workers really jeopardized?

In the Swedish Embassy in Belgrade we were told that there was no reason to dramatize the issue, for those were "little and isolated phenomena." A similar attitude was taken by the officials of our Secretariat for Foreign Affairs. However, since I talked to more than two hundred Yugoslavs in Sweden and to many Swedes, I feel obliged to state that *Ustasha* organizations exist; they terrorize our workers, threaten, blackmail, and undertake organized actions of pogroms, revenge, frightening, and "punishment." I have a great deal of proof for this statement and I can mention a number of names of *Ustashas* who have participated in such actions. I talked to outstanding *Ustasha* leaders. That is why I am surprised that responsible Swedish authorities as well as Yugoslav ones are not informed about these frightening facts. I wondered why the Yugoslav Embassy in Sweden has not informed our Secretariat for Foreign Affairs about the events in Sweden. The answer is more or less known: who could inform the Yugoslav Secretariat for Foreign Affairs when not a single Yugoslav in our embassy in Stockholm can read Swedish newspapers, which are full of stories about fascist activity as well as statements by police which say that nothing is known about the activity of some terrorist organizations? Not a single Yugoslav clerk in our embassy either speaks or reads Swedish and the counselor whose duty is to read the daily press and be in contact with public life does not even speak English. Not only this, but they are also so occupied by daily duties that they are not able to visit Malmö and Göteborg where several thousand Yugoslav workers live.

And Swedes are only too glad to accept such an attitude on the part of our officials in Stockholm. This is very convenient for them, especially when the idea of quiet compromise under any circumstances in the interest of good relations between the two countries is accepted only by the Yugoslavs, while the Swedish press is not often very tolerant and objective about Yugoslav workers.

These are the words of Mr. Ove Lin, a Swedish writer, historian, and journalist, and a very important member of the leading Social Democratic party: "You keep silent. You do not react to the ridiculous thesis of the newspapers and the naive statements of the police, and so you leave the impression that you have nothing to say."

The number of physical and blackmail attacks on Yugoslav citizens by *Ustashas* is increasing: there have been several hundred in the last three months.

The following is a passage from the best and biggest newspaper of southern Sweden, *Schnallposten*, of November 27, 1966: "It is known to all Swedish citizens that during the last several months hundreds of Yugoslavs have received threatening letters signed by the *Ustasha* organization 'Croatia.' It is also known that Yugoslav citizens are threatened with death if they do not pay a certain amount of money monthly from their salary to this extremist emigrant organization, and that the ones who refused to pay were roughly maltreated."

Who are these maltreated Yugoslavs and what do they say? (The names are not given in full at the request of the people involved.) M. K. from Malmö had his apartment totally demolished by *Ustashas* four days before we came: "Everything started in the factory during the break when I asked an emigrant not to offend my country and Tito in my presence. . . . Two days later I received a threatening letter signed by 'Croatia' which I immediately delivered to the police. This is a part of it: 'You dirty jerk. You would do better to work and earn food for yourself and your hungry family than to spread Tito propaganda. Many who did the same have been quickly punished. Do not repeat this. If you do, you won't be alive very long.' "

"Did you go to the Yugoslav Embassy in Stockholm to ask for protection?"

"I went several times to Stockholm and to Copenhagen. They advised me to be quiet. Hurry up, they say, earn money and return to your country."

The beaten-up A. feels helpless: "Up to that day I believed that it was not true that Swedish police did not want to defend us. Now I know it for sure. Although I was beaten for ten minutes, not a single policeman appeared, yet in other cases they are always at hand. I am absolutely demoralized. . . ."

M. M. from Kockmos refused to pay what they asked, which was not a small sum of money. Several days later three *Ustashas* came to his apartment and attacked him and his wife. He was in the hospital for eight days.

Let us not mention the mysterious disappearance of Yugoslavs, murders in daylight, and similar tragic events.

As for the *Ustashas*, they live in fashionable quarters under almost luxurious conditions. We visited one of them, the ex-*Ustasha* lieutenant from Tuzla, I. Mirazinovic, whom I interviewed while he acted as a sociologist in the Yugoslav-Swedish Emigration Institute. I asked him about the position of our workers in Sweden. Mirazinovic was a member of the Scandinavian *Ustasha* movement "Drina" led today by General Drinjamin, better known to Yugoslavs as the murderer Luburic. He has withdrawn from public life, has three big car agencies, and does the translations for the Swedish police.

We asked him to read a statement given by the well-known Tomislav Klobucar, the leader of the organization HOP, actually "Croatia," to a noted Swedish journalist: "Yugoslavs who have come here lately speak a lot against us, so that even the press has started writing that my society stands behind all this. This is absolute nonsense. 'Croatia' as well as HOP is a cultural-discussion institution, like a club, whose task is to write and focus on the present situation in Croatia for whose independence we fight." (*Schnallposten*, November 27, 1966.)

Mirazinovic said, "Nonsense, they are told from time to time to make such statements so that 'Croatia' and HOP will be left alone."

"Who tells them?"

"Well . . . I don't know. . . ."

"[*Ustashas*] are fascist organizations . . . appearing with purely fascist slogans and methods, absolutely the same as in World War II," said Mrs. Uli Heden, chief of the Department in the Employment Bureau, one of the rare

Swedes who does not think that the *Ustasha* is a cultural and national liberation war organization.

What are the names and ages of these men who fight so persistently for the
"liberation of Croatia"?

Mile Stojic is one of the leaders of this movement in Malmö, who stayed in
Trieste recently and bought twenty revolvers there. It has been verified that
Mile Stojic is a war *Ustasha*, as are Ilija Marincic, Nikola Senic, and Franc
Turka, who are very careful not to appear in public. Nikola Senic and Franc
Turka participated in the attempted kidnapping of the Yugoslav chargé d'af-
faires in Stockholm.

Eleven Yugoslav sailors working on a Greek boat were shipwrecked and almost drowned. They came barefoot and almost naked to a hotel some hundred
kilometers from Stockholm. I asked for a car from our embassy in Stockholm,
and since I heard that nobody went to see them, I proposed that a member of
our diplomatic mission should come too. I was told very politely that, unfortunately, the car had to be used for a reception which was taking place in
another embassy. Let me add this: when I said to the Yugoslav chargé d'af-
faires that urgent action should be taken to gather money and buy clothes for
the Yugoslav sailors, he said it was customary that the sailors be helped by the
neighboring villages. Nobody thought that this was perhaps a human duty and
an obligation of one Yugoslav toward another Yugoslav.

*Excerpts from the Series "The Lonely Migrants of the North: Turks" by Orhan
Türel Appearing in the Turkish Newspaper* Milliyet *(Istanbul), December 25–
29, 1966*

Sweden is the most developed country in the world. The standard of living
is high. The people living there are so comfortable that they don't worry about
daily problems. They don't know the meaning of hunger. For many centuries
nobody has died of hunger in Sweden. But, in the year 1966, Hasan Uygun
surprised everybody by dying of hunger.

Serafim Lasarett, a young doctor working at one of the biggest hospitals in
Stockholm, called his friend Anika Hangström, a journalist. "You may put
this in your paper, Anika. For the first time in Sweden, a man has died of
hunger." The correspondent of the north's greatest newspaper, *Expressen*, was
baffled. She couldn't comprehend what she had heard. As her mind worked
frantically and she tried to decide what to do, she walked to the window. It was
a sunny day, rare in Stockholm. Everybody — young, old, children, grown-ups
— was trying to get some warmth from the sun. Lovers walked arm in arm.

Yes, Sweden doesn't have many sunny days. One day in autumn when the
weather was icy cold, Serafim Lasarett received a patient. This was a quiet and
tired-looking man with very light clothing. At first the doctor didn't pay much
attention to the patient; then, with knitted eyebrows, he motioned the man to
come in. The dark man was led to the room for serious cases. After a thorough
examination, he was hospitalized. In spite of great efforts, the man died quietly
in his sleep. That same day, the doctor who diagnosed Hasan Uygun's disease
as "acute asthenia and insufficiency of the heart caused by malnutrition,"
picked up the telephone.

Anika Hangström, after hanging up the phone, felt very sad. The death of a young man, thousands of kilometers away from home, in Sweden, had made her very sad. Without losing time, she investigated the problem thoroughly and wrote a series of articles in *Expressen*.

Anika concluded her article as follows: "His family in Kulu was notified of the sad event. At present there are four hundred people in Sweden who are from the same village as Hasan. Even before Hasan was hospitalized, Hikmet, from the same village, had moved in and taken over Hasan's bed in the dismal quarters. According to Hasan's friends, his family will split up. His children, who are between 3 and 15 years old, will have to leave home to earn their living because Hasan had sold everything to come to Sweden. Probably his daughter, who is 12 years old, will have to marry an older man to bring some money to the family."

After the explosion caused by this article, many journalists went to Turkey to visit Hasan's village, Kulu, which is not far from Ankara.

"I am from Kulu. Yes, brother, Kulu is where I am from."

This will be the answer you'll get when you ask our countrymen, tired and depressed from unemployment, whom you'll meet on the streets of Sweden. You will hear Kulu later from the police, from the employer, and from other people concerned. Columnist Lars Berglund of Stockholm's daily *Dagens Nyheter* describes Ahmet Özcan's life as follows: "The roof of Ahmet Özcan's new house couldn't be finished because Ahmet had to go to Sweden since he couldn't make money on his cornfield. He was prepared to wash dishes there. Naturally he sold his cornfield when he left Turkey. He left behind a wife, four children, an uncompleted house, and many debts. This happened two months ago. But Ahmet still is not rich from what he earned washing dishes. He was able to find neither a job nor a roof over his head. His family moved to live with a relative."

The first day I arrived in Sweden, I went to find out why four hundred Turks from Kulu came to live in Sweden. As I was thinking, "Why not from Istanbul, Ankara, or Malatya?" I was confronted with another interesting problem — the modern concentration camp. I was puzzled. A concentration camp in Sweden? As I later found out, the place called the concentration camp was the garret of a villa in Huddinge where the people from Kulu were staying, and this was the name that the Swedish press used to describe the living conditions.

I immediately set out to this place with my friend Lill Valfridsson. What I had in mind was to see this dismal garret and have a chance to talk to Hasan Uygun's friends.

It wasn't hard to find the place. I immediately spotted the villa to the right of the hill. It was made of black wood and had two stories. The first thing that caught my eye at the entrance of the villa was a handmade sign which read "Taking pictures is forbidden." The dormitory which housed seven people was a very small room but ice cold. The only furniture in the dormitory was a row of bunkbeds; there were no closets, not even hangers on which to hang clothes. I met Abdullah Aytekin, again from Kulu, there.

We became very good friends with Abdullah. Before I asked him any questions he came up with the answers. "It was a big mistake to come to this place, but we didn't know. We cannot go back without earning at least 5000 TL, the money to get back our fields."

The landlady of the villa houses about fifty people in the two-story house. It

163

is said that she makes a profit of 21,000 TL a month. She now has a Chevrolet Impala, a car seen very rarely on Swedish streets. She sometimes has two people sleeping in the same bunk which is only 80 centimeters wide. The place is ice cold. The landlady cut off the heat a long time ago. The place doesn't have a kitchen. The electricity and water supply is limited. As a whole the villa is horrible and not livable. The only reason the Turks keep on living there is that they are afraid of not being able to find other sleeping quarters.

This is the scene in Sweden. Most of the Turks who come to this country are farmers around fifty years of age and know no foreign language. It is impossible for them to work at public business places. The ones that work eighteen hours in a restaurant have nervous breakdowns. Hacibey hanged himself; Halil Girgin had to be put in an asylum.

The Turkish Embassy in Sweden seems to have encouraged the workers to come to Sweden. When the Turks started becoming a social burden to Sweden, the director of the employment agency wrote a letter to the Turkish Embassy asking them to discourage workers who wanted to come to Sweden.

The British newspaper *Financial Times* calls Sweden the most expensive country in the world. It is a dream to save money in Sweden and send it home. The Swedish authorities housed only twelve of the Turkish workers.

Now not only the workers in Sweden but in West Germany as well are restless. Germany, not wanting to lose its prestige with Turkey, is still importing Turkish workers, but is playing a very sad trick in the end. Many of the workers are discharged at the end of the month because they are unqualified.

According to some the crisis in Germany is temporary, but to others it is permanent. In Cologne there is an information agency for Turkish workers. The workers are stationed most of the time at the cafés near the agency. Especially on Saturday nights you can watch the folk dances and hear the folk songs at these cafés. Soon the workers will have to come back, even though the German government gave permission to the unemployed to stay in Germany for six months. But, according to one worker, "You cannot live in Germany even six days if you are not employed." The problem is not solved by bringing these workers back to Turkey. The next and bigger problem is what to do with them in Turkey. It is time for the authorities to put on their thinking caps and start concentrating on this problem.

APPENDIX B

Appendix B. Synoptic Table of Differential Laws Governing Foreign Workers in the Countries of Immigration, 1965

Prepared by T. Stark "Situation of Migrant Workers from Countries of the EEC as Compared with That of Workers from Other Countries," International Institute for Labour Studies, Symposium on Migration for Employment in Europe, mimeographed (Geneva, October 12-15, 1965), pp. 9-14.

EMPLOYMENT

Class of Rights	EEC Workers Employed in EEC Countries	Workers from Non-EEC Countries					
		FRANCE	GERMANY	BELGIUM	NETHERLANDS	LUXEMBOURG	SWITZERLAND (all foreign workers)
Access to employment	Free access to wage-earning employment actually offered.	Access according to vacancies, after worker has obtained residence and employment permits.	Access to employment in a particular occupation, subject to residence and employment permits or, for workers recruited officially, identity card and contract.	Access according to vacancies after application by employer.	Access according to vacancies and trend of labor market; application for permit may be made by worker or employer.	Access to specified employment after issue of permit to the employer (not the worker).	Access in conformity with national economic and social interests and with the extent of foreign overpopulation.
Bilateral labor agreements		Spain (1961) Portugal (1963) Yugoslavia (1965) Morocco (1963) Tunisia (1963) Mali (1963) Mauretania (1963) Senegal (1964) Algeria (1964)	Spain (1960) Greece (1960) Turkey (1961) Morocco (1963) Portugal (1964)	Spain (1956) Greece (1957) Turkey (1964) Morocco (1964)	Spain (1961) Portugal (1963) Turkey (1964)	Portugal (1962)	All EEC countries (except Luxembourg) Spain (1961) Austria (1950)
Placement (public service)	Help without discrimination.	Help without distinction of nationality.	Free help for all foreign workers.	Only the agreement with Turkey gives a right after 3 years' work with the family and 5 years' without.	Help to foreign workers.	Help without distinction of nationality.	Only workers with an establishment permit can use the public service, except the French (equality with Swiss) and Italians (after 5 years' residence).
Prolongation of employment	Automatic prolongation after 1 year.	Renewal of employment permit if the labor market allows.	Prolongation from year to year.	Prolongation for 6 months at a time up to 2 years.	Prolongation for the same period within the duration of the residence permit.	Prolongation at the employer's request.	Period of prolongation decided in each case in conformity with economic and social interests and degree of overpopulation.

166

Class of Rights	EEC Workers Employed in EEC Countries	Workers from Non-EEC Countries					
		FRANCE	GERMANY	BELGIUM	NETHERLANDS	LUXEMBOURG	SWITZERLAND (all foreign workers)
Unrestricted changing of place of work	Unrestricted changing after 2 years.	General regime: resident at least 10 years and admitted before the age of 35; OECD regime: Greeks and Spaniards after 5 years' employment.	After 2 years in the same occupation; not restricted to a particular undertaking.	General regime: after 10 years' residence, or if family resides in Belgium, 5 years' residence; OECD regime: for Greeks and Spaniards.	Foreign workers employed for at least 5 years are automatically free to change their place of work.	After at least 5 years' residence and continuous employment in Luxembourg.	General regime: authorities free to decide. Bilateral regimes: Italy, Germany, Austria—after 10 years' residence; France, Belgium, Netherlands, etc.—after 5 years' residence. OECD regime: entitlement to permit to continue working after 5 years.
Unrestricted changing of occupation	Unrestricted changing after 2 years.	General regime: after 13 years' residence; OECD regime: Greeks and Spaniards after 10 years' working.	After 5 years' work, for 3 years; and after 10 years, unrestricted.	Same conditions as for changing the place of work.	Foreign workers employed for at least 5 years are automatically free to change their occupation.	After at least 5 years' residence and continuous employment in Luxembourg.	Same conditions as for changing the place of work.
ADMISSION OF FAMILY							
Principle	Free admission of family (without time limit or distinction of nationality).	Encouragement to establish family.	Admission provided for in agreements for Greeks, Portuguese, and Spaniards (Moroccans and Turks not mentioned) without time limit.	Under agreements: Turks, 1 month; Spaniards, established workers; Greeks, no time limit.	Admission according to reception and lodging facilities (reunion of family not mentioned in agreements).	Admission free.	Admission after workers' 3 years' continuous residence in Switzerland. For Italians, 18 months.
Dependents	Spouse and children under 21; ascendants and descendants supported; persons living under the same roof.	Spouse; boys under 18, girls under 21; ascendants and collateral relatives if supported.	In principle, spouse and children under age. Nothing on this subject in the agreements.	Spouse; unmarried children living under worker's roof; ascendants if Greek or Turkish (under agreements).	Spouse and children under age.	Descendants and ascendants in direct line.	Spouse and children under age.

Class of Rights	EEC Workers Employed in EEC Countries	Workers from Non-EEC Countries					
		FRANCE	GERMANY	BELGIUM	NETHERLANDS	LUXEMBOURG	SWITZERLAND (all foreign workers)
Conditions for admission	Obligation to have family lodging.	Medical supervision of the family; normal lodging (according to the region).	Family lodging and residence permit.	"Sufficient" housing.	"Suitable," i.e., independent housing; after at least 2 years' work and a contract for at least 1 year.	No conditions mentioned.	The same conditions as for the worker himself—above all, adequate accommodation.
Employment of family	Free on ordinary conditions for EEC workers (reply to actual offer).	Subject to conditions for non-EEC workers as regards prolongation, changing, etc.	Subject to conditions for ordinary authorization.	Subject to the same conditions as for the worker.	Employment permit given automatically to wife and children.	Subject to ordinary conditions for the workers in question.	The same conditions as for the worker.
Traveling expenses of family	According to provisions of national legislation.	Expenses paid from French frontier to place of residence, but some differences in bilateral agreements.	Advance or contribution by the employer may be provided for in agreement with him.	Voluntary repayable advances by certain employers.	Expenses paid by the worker himself.	Expenses paid by the worker (possibly with help from the employer).	Expenses paid by the worker (possibly with help from the employer).
HOUSING							
Access to housing	Equality of treatment with nationals (according to national legislation).	Inequality of treatment in practice owing to housing shortage.	Housing shortage. Loans for housing construction granted to employers and workers.	No housing shortage. Housing facilities granted to workers recruited in contingents.	Foreigners treated equally with Dutch in the allocation of housing.	No special regulations for non-EEC workers.	In practice, lodging hard to find.
FAMILY ALLOWANCES							
Right to allowances outside the country	Every wage-earner from an EEC country.	Only Algerian, Portuguese, and Spanish workers.	Only Greek and Spanish workers (excluded are Turks, Yugoslavs, Portuguese, and Moroccans).	All foreign workers, without distinction of residence.	All foreign workers, without distinction of residence.	Only Portuguese, Spanish, and Yugoslav workers.	Workers employed in all cantons but 1 (Appenzell Outer-Rh.), but differences in nature and amount as compared with Swiss.

Class of Rights	EEC Workers Employed in EEC Countries	Workers from Non-EEC Countries					
		FRANCE	GERMANY	BELGIUM	NETHERLANDS	LUXEMBOURG	SWITZERLAND (all foreign workers)
Dependents	Legitimate, legitimized, natural, and adopted children, both of the worker and of his spouse, living at home.	As for EEC, but up to the age fixed by the legislation of the country of origin.	Children, grandchildren, brothers, and sisters—living together.	Children of worker or his spouse or both if dependent.	The first and second of the worker's legitimate, natural, or adopted children.	Legitimate, legitimized, and recognized natural children, and orphans who have lost both parents.	According to cantonal legislation. In Geneva, legitimate, natural, and adopted children, siblings, and foster children.
Beginning of right	According to national legislation.	If the worker has at least 2 dependent children.	At least 2 children. Condition: annual income of parents not exceeding 7200 DM. From third child onward no income limit.	From the first child onward.	From the first child onward.	From the first child onward.	According to cantonal legislation. In Geneva, from the first child onward.
End of right	According to national legislation.	Allowances are paid up to 15 years; for apprentices 18 years, for students 20 years. Spaniards up to 14 years.	Up to 18 years (students up to 25 years).	Up to 14 years; for students and apprentices, up to 21 years.	Up to 16 years; for students and apprentices, up to 27 years.	Up to 19 years; for students and invalid dependent children, 25 years.	Up to 15 years; for students and apprentices, up to 25 years.
Duration of payment abroad	No time limit.	Spaniards receive allowances during 6 years; Portuguese, 2 years.	Spaniards receive allowances during 6 years; Greeks, 2 years.	During 6 years from the admission of the workers (no time limit mentioned for Greeks and Turks).	No time limit.	No time limit.	No time limit.
Amount	Up to the amounts provided by national legislation.	For those living in France, according to the French regime. For Spaniards, lump sum per child. For Portuguese, according to Portuguese allowances.	Amounts fixed by the German Act of 1964.	The amounts applying in the country in which the children are brought up. But the Belgian rate applies during the six months before the children's arrival in Belgium.	The amounts provided under the Netherlands regime.	Lump sums per child.	According to cantonal legislation. In Geneva, uniform monthly allowance per child.

Class of Rights	EEC Workers Employed in EEC Countries	Workers from Non-EEC Countries					
		FRANCE	GERMANY	BELGIUM	NETHERLANDS	LUXEMBOURG	SWITZERLAND (all foreign workers)
		SOCIAL SECURITY					
Principle	Equality of treatment for persons residing in EEC countries; cumulation of all insurance periods in EEC countries; transfer of benefits to another EEC country.	Application of French regime if worker satisfies conditions laid down in French legislation. Cumulation and transfer as under social security agreements.	Equality of treatment for residents. Bilateral regime for Greeks, Spaniards, and Turks.	Equality with Belgians for persons residing in the country; other conditions according to social security agreements.	Generally, equality for persons residing in the Netherlands; other conditions according to social security agreements.	Equality with Luxembourg workers; other conditions according to social security agreements.	Equality with Swiss for resident workers; other conditions according to social security agreements.
Unemployment	Cumulation of insurance periods; transfer of unemployment allowances on transfer of residence.	Spain (1957) Greece (1958) Portugal (1957) Yugoslavia (1950) Equality for persons residing in France. Because of nature of assistance, transfer excluded.	Greece (1961) Spain (1964) Turkey (1964), etc. Equality for residents. Cumulation of insurance periods for Greeks, Spaniards, and Turks. Transfer of unemployment allowances on change of residence.	Spain (1956) Greece (1958) Yugoslavia (1954) Only workers with an employment permit enjoy the same benefits as Belgians. No exportation of unemployment allowance.	Spain (1962) Yugoslavia (1956) Equality for persons residing in the Netherlands. If Spaniards or Yugoslavs have been subject to the legislation of their country, the insurance periods are cumulated.	Spain (1963) (not ratified) Yugoslavia (1954) Equality for persons residing in Luxembourg. It is assistance and so not exportable.	All EEC countries. Spain (1959) Yugoslavia (1962), etc. Only persons with an establishment permit can be admitted to unemployment insurance; Italians after 5 years' residence.
Sickness	Cumulation of insurance periods; right of family to medical benefits in kind abroad; cash benefits and medical care on change of residence (no time limit).	Cumulation for the 4 countries signatories to social security agreements; medical care of family, but only Greeks and Spaniards, and duration of benefits limited to 3 and 6 years respectively; transfers allowed for sickness during paid holidays, or with authorization of the fund.	Cumulation of insurance periods and benefits for family in country of origin for above-mentioned nationals.	Cumulation for Greece, Spain, Yugoslavia; medical care for family (limited if nonresident).	Cumulation; medical care for family remaining in own country; transfer of benefits on change of residence (with consent of the fund) only for Spaniards and Yugoslavs.	Cumulation of insurance periods and transfer of benefits for Spaniards and Yugoslavs.	No compulsory sickness insurance and no right of members of the family to benefits in their own country (except canton of Lucerne).

Class of Rights	EEC Workers Employed in EEC Countries	Workers from Non-EEC Countries					
		GERMANY	FRANCE	BELGIUM	NETHERLANDS	LUXEMBOURG	SWITZERLAND (all foreign workers)
Maternity	Benefits in kind (care) for the spouse even if she is in another country.	Cumulation of insurance periods and medical care as for sickness insurance.	Cumulation of the woman's insurance periods and medical care for her; same groups and time limits as for sickness insurance. No maternity allowance if the child is not declared French.	The worker's wife is assimilated to persons in sickness insurance.	Consent to change of residence may be given, even before confinement.	For the moment, cumulation for Yugoslavs only.	No maternity insurance outside Switzerland, and no confinement allowance for foreign workers.
Invalidity	Cumulation of insurance periods; transfer of invalidity pension abroad.	Cumulation of insurance periods and transfers for Greeks, Spaniards, and Turks.	Cumulation for 4 groups of countries signatories to agreements; transfer for same 4 groups.	Cumulation for the 3 above countries; for nationals of Greece, Spain, and Yugoslavia, transfer as though they resided in Belgium.	Cumulation of insurance periods for Spaniards and Yugoslavs; transfer on change of residence for the same two nationalities.	Cumulation and transfer only for Yugoslavs.	Invalidity benefits only if the worker has resided in Switzerland for at least 15 years or has paid contributions for at least 10 years.
Old age	Cumulation of insurance periods; transfer of old-age pension to country of origin on change of residence.	Retirement age 65 for men, 62 for women; cumulation and transfers only for the 3 nationalities mentioned above.	Retirement age 60 (20 percent of wages) or 65 (40 percent); cumulation and transfers only for the 4 groups of countries signatories to the agreements; old workers' allowances for the same 4 groups after 15 years' work; apart from bilateral regimes, benefits only in proportion to contributions paid.	Retirement age 65 for men, 60 for women; cumulation and transfers of pensions for the above 3 countries (with some restrictions).	Retirement age 65 for men and women; cumulation and transfers of pensions for the above 2 nationalities.	Retirement age 65 (but may be 62); for the moment cumulation of insurance periods only for Yugoslavs.	Retirement age 65 for men, 62 for women; cumulation and transfers only if they have resided in Switzerland and have paid contributions for at least 10 years; Belgian, French, and German nationals after 5 years; Italians and Yugoslavs after 1 year.

Class of Rights	EEC Workers Employed in EEC Countries	Workers from Non-EEC Countries					
		FRANCE	GERMANY	BELGIUM	NETHERLANDS	LUXEMBOURG	SWITZERLAND (all foreign workers)
Occupational accidents	Medical care provided in a country other than the one in which the accident occurred; transfer of pensions on change of residence.	Medical care only for Spaniards if transfer authorized beforehand; transfer of pensions for 4 mentioned groups, otherwise right to capital equal to 3 years' pension.	Medical care and pensions possible in a country other than that of employment for Greeks, Spaniards, and Turks.	Provisions restricting rights of foreigners cannot be applied to Greek, Spanish, and Yugoslav workers.	For Spaniards and Yugoslavs as though the accident had occurred in their own country; transfer of pension for the above 2 nationalities.	Medical care and transfers authorized for Greeks, Portuguese, Spaniards, and Yugoslavs.	This insurance is compulsory in Switzerland, and agreements with the EEC countries and Spain provide for medical care in the other country.
MEDICAL-SOCIAL ASSISTANCE							
Provisions	Under the European medical and social assistance convention of 1953, all EEC nationals are entitled to hospitalization, care at home, and invalidity and old-age allowances.	Only Greeks and Spaniards have special regimes. For other workers: free access to hospital; care at home after 3 years; allowances for invalids after 15 years' continuous residence.	Under the German legislation, right to medical and social aid, and aid to mothers and the tuberculous.	Only Greeks benefit under the 1953 convention.	Only Greeks benefit under the 1953 convention.	Only Greeks benefit under the 1953 convention.	Not signatory to the European convention of 1953. The obligation to maintain a destitute foreign worker until his repatriation applies only to Italians and Spaniards. For the French, free medical aid and aid to aged invalids.
APPRENTICESHIP AND VOCATIONAL TRAINING							
Apprenticeship of young persons	Equality with national workers.	Equality and special pretraining courses for young persons. Special centers for Africans.	No mention in bilateral agreements. Courses provided only by employers.	No special provisions for young persons.	Equality with Netherlands nationals.	Free access to official centers subject to knowledge of language.	All young workers whose parents have an establishment permit enjoy the same rights as the Swiss, but pay a higher entrance fee.
Training for adults	Equality with national workers.	Access to extent that vacancies permit for Spaniards, Portuguese, Yugoslavs, Moroccans, Tunisians, and Senegalese.	No mention in bilateral agreements. Courses provided only by employers.	Access to accelerated training and retraining for adults.	Equality with Netherlands nationals.	Free access to official training centers.	Finishing courses are also open to adult foreigners.

Class of Rights	EEC Workers Employed in EEC Countries	Workers from Non-EEC Countries					
		FRANCE	GERMANY	BELGIUM	NETHERLANDS	LUXEMBOURG	SWITZERLAND (all foreign workers)
REPRESENTATION IN THE UNDERTAKING							
Competent institutions	Body representing the workers.	Works committees; delegates of personnel.	Works councils; economic committees.	Works councils; trade union delegations.	Works councils.	Workers' delegations.	Workers' committees (only in some undertakings); no legislation.
Electorate	Equality of treatment with nationals.	Employment in the undertaking for at least 5 years.	18 years of age and possession of civil rights.	Possession of employment permit for at least 2 years.	1 year's employment in the undertaking.	6 months' continuous employment in the undertaking.	No legislation.
Eligibility	Equality after 3 years' employment in the undertaking.	Only EEC workers.	21 years of age and 1 year's employment in the undertaking. Foreigners not eligible.	No eligibility for works councils; for delegations, 10 years' residence.	3 years' employment in the undertaking (equality with EEC workers).	Only Spaniards and Yugoslavs who have been employed 1 year in the undertaking (but quota for foreigners).	No legislation.
TRANSFER OF WAGES TO FAMILY							
Provisions	Regulated by the European Monetary Agreement of August 5, 1955.	Freedom to transfer all net basic wages for all workers without distinction.	Freedom of transfer under the German exchange regulations.	Part of savings according to regulations. For Greeks and Turks, transfer of wages allowed according to agreements.	Agreements with Portugal, Spain, and Turkey allow unlimited dispatch of savings.	No restriction on amount.	No restriction on amount.

NOTES AND INDEX

NOTES

PREFACE

1. See, for example, European Community Institute for University Studies, *University Research and Studies in European Integration*, No. 3 (Brussels, 1966).

THE MEANING OF INTEGRATION

1. Jacques-René Rabier, "L'Information des Européens et l'intégration de l'Europe" (Brussels: Université Libre de Bruxelles, Institut d'Etudes Européennes, 1965); Jacques-René Rabier, "L'Opinion publique et l'Europe" (Brussels: Université Libre de Bruxelles, Institut de Sociologie, 1966); Gallup International Poll, *L'Opinion publique et l'Europe des six* (Paris: Institut Français d'Opinion Publique, 1962); Reader's Digest Poll, "Products and People," 1963; "L'Opinion publique et l'Europe," *Annuaire Européen*, 10 (1962), p. 46; International Research Associates, "L'Image de l'Europe unie dans l'opinion publique" (Brussels, December 1966); "8000 jeunes ruraux nous disent . . ." (Louvain, Belgium: MIJARC, 1966); "Les Français et l'entrée de la Grande-Bretagne dans le marché commun," *Le Monde* (Paris), January 24, 1967, p. 3; Gallup International Poll, "Big (British) Majority Keen on Joining Europe," *Daily Telegraph* (London), December 12, 1966, p. 18.

2. Seymour Martin Lipset, *The First New Nation* (New York: Basic Books, 1963).

3. Some Italians raise the question whether the Italian people have yet, by and large, accepted Italian nationality, or whether provincial and local loyalties are stronger. It is an interesting question, but no attempt will be made to answer it here. See *The Economist*, 222 (March 18, 1967), pp. xxvi–xxviii.

4. S. N. Eisenstadt, *The Absorption of Immigrants: A Comparative Study Based Mainly on the Jewish Community in Palestine and the State of Israel* (London: Routledge and Kegan Paul, 1954).

5. Jerzy Zubrzycki, *Polish Immigrants in Britain* (The Hague: Martinus Nijhoff, 1956), pp. 165–175.

6. See the chapter by Robert H. Beck in the forthcoming Minnesota collaborative volume, *The Changing Structure of Europe: Economic, Social, and Political Trends* (Minneapolis: University of Minnesota Press, 1970).

7. See the chapter by John G. Turnbull in *ibid.*

CROSS-NATIONAL MIGRATION

1. One of the best studies of individual motives for emigration is B. P. Hofstede, *De Gaande Man* (The Hague, 1958), summarized in "The Motives of Emigration," *International Labor Review*, 81:1 (January 1960), pp. 74–81. Also see G. Beijer, N. H. Frijda, B. P. Hofstede, and R. Wentholt, *Characteristics of Overseas Migrants* (The Hague: Government Printing Office, 1961).

2. L. Danieli and A. Brandt, "Employment of Foreign Workers in Some Western European Countries. A Statistical Picture," in International Institute for Labour

Studies, "Conference on the Migration of Workers to Europe" (Geneva, 1965), p. 4.

3. "Evolution générale de la population française," *Population*, 20:6 (November–December 1965), p. 1118. See also J. L. Rognaut and J. Schultz, "Les Rapatriés d'Afrique du Nord dans l'Hérault (1954–1964)," *Société languedocienne de géographie. Bulletin trimestrial*, 2nd series, Vol. 35 (July–December 1964), pp. 283–417; Christine Toujas-Pinèda, "Les Rapatriés d'Algérie dans la région Midi-Pyrénées," *Revue géographiques des Pyrénées et du Sud-ouest*, 36 (December 1965), pp. 321–372.

4. Information from Centraal Bureau voor de Statistiek, The Hague.

5. USIS daily radio bulletin, American Embassy, Paris, May 25, 1967.

6. Y. Altug, "Turkish Aspects of Migration for Employment in Europe," in Institute for Labour Studies, "Conference on the Migration . . ." p. 8.

7. *Ibid.*

8. Beijer, Frijda, *et al., op. cit.*, p. 85.

9. See the chapter by Philip Raup in *The Changing Structure of Europe* (Minneapolis: University of Minnesota Press, 1970).

10. Economic efficiency or rationality is not simply a question of achieving maximum output, it also involves value problems concerning the composition of output — public services versus private consumption, heavy-goods investment versus consumption-goods investment — and the equitable distribution of that output. Here these problems will be ignored and rationality will be defined in terms of achieving maximum output.

11. Figures for 1946 are from Institut National de Statistiques et d'Etudes Economiques, *Annuaire statistique, 1951*, Vol. 58, Partie Internationale, p. 353. Figures for 1965 are from unpublished OECD statistics.

12. Robert Descloîtres, *The Foreign Worker: Adaptation to Industrial Work and Urban Life* (Paris: OECD, 1967), pp. 19–20.

13. An excellent history of cross-national migrations is contained in Donald R. Taft and Richard Robbins, *International Migrations: The Immigrant in the Modern World* (New York: Ronald Press, 1955). For the specific period of World War II, see Joseph B. Schechtman, *European Population Transfers, 1939–1945* (New York: Oxford University Press, 1946). Also see W. D. Borrie, *The Cultural Integration of Immigrants* (Paris: UNESCO, 1959).

14. Germany allowed Poles to come as seasonal laborers and as miners. Poland, along with Italy, was a leading emigrant country in the pre-World War II era. Jerzy Zubrzycki (*Polish Immigrants in Britain* [The Hague: Martinus Nijhoff, 1956], p. 27) states that of the 1,485,600 "permanent" emigrants between 1919 and 1938, 348,200 returned — leaving a permanent net emigration of 1,137,400. Many of these were dependents rather than workers only. The classic study by W. I. Thomas and F. Znaniecki, *The Polish Peasant in Europe and America* (Chicago: Badger Press, 1919), examines the causes within Poland for the extensive emigration largely in terms of the breakdown of primary group controls.

15. For example, France returned some 117,000 Poles to their home country during the depression years 1931–35 (see Zubrzycki, *op. cit.*, p. 28). During the occupation years, 1940–45, the Pétain government deported many foreigners, some of whom were sent to slave-labor camps in Germany (see Taft and Robbins, *op. cit.*, p. 188). Probably under the influence of Hitlerism, some xenophobia developed in France during the 1930's and 1940's (see J. M. Domenach in *Espirit*, 34:4 [April 1966], p. 529). Also see J. Doublet, "Les Mouvements migratoires en Europe," *Revue Internationale des sciences sociales*, 17:2 (1965), pp. 304–317.

16. La Documentation Française, *Les Travailleurs étrangers en France. Notes et études documentaires*, No. 3057 (January 23, 1964), p. 15.

17. On the post-World War II refugees, see Taft and Robbins, *op. cit.*, Ch. 11; Jacques Vernant, *The Refugee in the Post-War World* (New Haven: Yale Univer-

sity Press, 1953); H. B. M. Murphy, *et al., Flight and Resettlement* (Paris: UNESCO, 1955); Louis W. Holborn, *The International Refugee Organization: Its History and Work, 1946–1952* (Oxford, 1956); Joint Statistical Project on European Migration (CIME, ILO, OEEC, and UN), *A Decade of Post-World War II European Migration* (Geneva, 1958). For more general discussions of post-World War II international migration, besides Taft and Robbins, see Brinley Thomas, "International Migration" in P. M. Hauser and O. D. Duncan, *The Study of Population: An Inventory and Appraisal* (Chicago: University of Chicago Press, 1959), pp. 510–543; Anthony T. Bouscaren, *International Migrations since 1945* (New York: Frederick A. Praeger, 1963); Brinley Thomas, *Migration and Economic Growth* (Cambridge: Cambridge University Press, 1954).

18. Taft and Robbins, *op. cit.*, pp. 271–272.

19. Norman Pannell and Fenner Brockway, *Immigration: What Is the Answer?* (London: Routledge and Kegan Paul, 1965), pp. 7–14.

20. Alain Girard and Jean Stoetzel, "Français et immigrés," in Institut National d'Etudes Démographiques, *Travaux et documents*, Cahier No. 19 (Paris: Presses Universitaires de France, 1953–54). Also see Leo Bogart, "Les Algériens en France, adaptation réussie et non réussie," *Travaux et documents*, Cahier No. 20 (1954). The 1947 law eliminating restrictions on Algerians was repealed in 1962 when Algeria became independent.

21. "Evolution générale . . ." p. 1118.

22. Some Algerians entered illegally with the aid of false passports, to the extent that, in late 1966, the French authorities were planning to set up a dormitory in Nice where those apprehended for illegal entry could be sheltered while awaiting repatriation (see *Le Monde* (Paris), November 1, 1966, p. 14).

23. G. Tapinos, "L'Immigration étrangère en France de 1959 à 1964," *Population*, 20:4 (July–August 1965), pp. 675–686.

24. Pannell and Brockway, *loc. cit.*

25. Descloîtres, *op. cit.*, p. 24.

26. "L'Immigration portugaise," *Population*, 21:3 (May–June 1966), pp. 575–576; "L'Immigration portugaise," *Hommes et migrations*, Cahier No. 105 (1966), p. 203.

27. John A. Jackson, "Experience with Emigrants Returning to the Home Country: Ireland," in *Supplement to the Final Report, Emigrant Workers Returning to Their Home Country, International Management Seminar, Athens, October 18–21, 1966* (Paris: OECD, 1967), p. 1.

28. Robert C. Doty, "Europe's Migrant Workers Are Facing Job Crisis," *New York Times* (International ed.), February 27, 1967, pp. 1, 5.

29. *Migration Today*, No. 5 (December 1965), p. 62.

30. *Ekonomska Politika*, October 5, 1966, p. 1320.

31. In 1958 the British government was reported to favor sending 200,000 trained technicians a year to Commonwealth countries, provided the outflow was spread over age groups. It was their contention that these emigrants tighten the political and economic ties between their new homelands and Britain (see *New York Times*, March 1, 1958, p. 31). The British government after 1958 apparently took no action on this; in fact, their position seems to have reversed.

32. National Science Foundation, *Scientific Manpower from Abroad* (Washington, D.C.: Government Printing Office, 1962); OECD, *Resources of Scientific and Technical Personnel in the OECD Area*, 3rd International Survey (Paris: OECD, 1963).

33. Overseas Migration Board, *White Paper, 1964* (London, December 1965).

34. Inter-Agency Council on International Educational and Cultural Affairs, *Report* (Washington, D.C., 1966) — cited in *New York Times* (International ed.), May 2, 1967, p. 6.

35. *New York Herald Tribune and Washington Post*, May 2, 1967, p. 7.

36. See, for example, *New York Times* (International ed.), March 3, 1967, p. 2.

37. *New York Herald Tribune and Washington Post,* May 2, 1967, p. 7. Also see *The Economist,* 223 (May 6, 1967), p. 589.

38. In France, for example, foreigners may not be civil servants, lawyers, or sellers of liquor, and they may be pharmacists or social workers only if they hold a diploma from a French professional school (or are recognized by an official as having training equivalent to that provided by a French professional school). See M. T. Pouillet and J. M. Bouttier, "L'Accueil officiel," *Espirit,* 34:4 (April 1966), p. 590.

39. Solomon Barkin, "The Foreign Worker in Europe," *Britannica Book of the Year, 1966* (Chicago: Encyclopedia Britannica, 1966), pp. 281–283.

40. Instituto Centrale di Statistica, cited in Churches Committee on Migrant Workers in Western Europe, *The Return of Migrant Workers* (Geneva, 1966), p. 29.

41. *Ekonomska Politika,* November 12, 1966.

42. United Nations, Office of Social Affairs of the European Office, *European Seminar on Social Welfare Programmes for Migrant Workers, Madrid, April 2–10, 1964* (Geneva, 1965), p. 12.

43. Barkin, *op. cit.,* p. 282.

44. Roger Girod, "Travailleurs étrangers et mobilité sociale en Suisse," *Revue économique et sociale,* 24 (May 1966), pp. 149–171.

45. Conversation with the staff of the Institute for International Politics and Economics, Belgrade, Yugoslavia, January 4, 1967.

46. Attilio Oblath, "Recent Developments and Future Prospects of Migration in Europe," in Institute for Labour Studies, "Conference on the Migration . . ." p. 5.

47. The predictions made here will be very general in nature, and hence "safer" than predictions which are specific. These general predictions are based on economic, occupational, and demographic trends rather than on stated policies and plans voiced by governments. The latter are often publicized partly for political reasons, and are thus unreliable for predictive purposes. This has been shown by the sudden disappearance of demand for foreign labor when the small economic recession of the winter 1966–67 occurred: up to the very eve of the recession, countries of immigration were announcing huge manpower "needs," and yet a few weeks later were curtailing foreign immigration. Some countries of emigration, like Greece, announce that they will need all their unskilled labor because of coming economic development, but it is doubtful that their development will occur so rapidly.

48. See the section on public opinion in Chapter 5.

49. Bernard Nossiter, "North Europe Cutting Foreign Labor Needs," *New York Herald Tribune* (International ed.), December 2, 1966, p. 3; Robert C. Doty, "Flow of Workers from Southern Europe to the North is Halted," *New York Times* (International ed.), February 27, 1967, p. 1 (Doty estimates that by January 1967 at least 100,000 were sent back — because of unemployment — to their home countries); Bernard Nossiter, "Europe's Joblessness," *New York Herald Tribune* (International ed.), March 13, 1967, p. 4 (Nossiter points out that while some migrant workers have been forced to return, others held jobs which nationals of immigrant countries refused to accept unless economic conditions got much worse, and thus were "sheltered").

A THEORY OF ACCEPTANCE OF MIGRANTS

1. On trade union policies toward foreign workers see Solomon Barkin, "Trade Union Policies and Programmes for National Internal Rural Migrants and Foreign Workers," in International Institute for Labour Studies, "Conference on the Migration of Workers to Europe" (Geneva, 1965), pp. 6–14; Attilio Oblath, *Inter-*

national Differences in Factors Affecting Labour Mobility (Geneva: ILO, 1965), pp. 192–195.

2. Solomon Barkin, "Trade Union Policies and Programmes for National Internal Rural Migrants and Foreign Workers," *International Migration*, 4:1 (1966), pp. 17–18.

3. The French do not permit occupational freedom to Portuguese immigrants for thirteen years; see G. de Rochcau, "Intra-European Migration in the Last Three Years," *Migration News*, 14:1 (January–February 1965), pp. 6–11.

4. A number of the polling agencies have asked questions designed to test prejudice, and the ones in Germany and Sweden have lately attempted more systematic polls. But detailed observations and measurement of discrimination — relatively advanced in the United States — have been carried out in Europe only in the United Kingdom, by Anthony Richmond, Michael Banton, Ruth Glass, John Rex, and Robert Moore, the publications of the Institute of Race Relations, and many others. See A. Sivanandan and Margaret Scruton, "Register of Research on Commonwealth Immigrants in Britain" (London: Institute of Race Relations, March 1967). In France there is the earlier work of Girard and Stoetzel, Jean Treanton, and the continuing reports of the Centre Nord Africain. In the Netherlands, Switzerland, and West Germany there have been some studies, but they do not compare in quantity with those published in the United States or the United Kingdom.

5. France provides a partial exception here: most of the French people manifest a certain tolerance of deviation, but they also seem to regard cultural deviation as an opportunity for "francisation," and both of these factors aid acceptance of the immigrants.

6. Francesco Alberoni and Guido Baglioni, *L'Integrazione dell'immigrato nella società industriale* (Bologna: Società Editrice Il Mulino, 1965).

7. Shotaro Frank Miyamoto, "Social Solidarity among the Japanese in Seattle," *University of Washington Publications in the Social Sciences*, 11:2 (December 1938), pp. 75–76.

8. Robert E. Park, *The Immigrant Press and Its Control* (New York: Harper and Brothers, 1922).

9. On the role of the voluntary organization in aiding the adjustment of immigrants, see William S. Bernard, presentation to the UNESCO Havana Conference, quoted by W. D. Borrie, *The Cultural Integration of Immigrants* (Paris: UNESCO, 1959), pp. 59–62.

10. Milton M. Gordon, *Assimilation in American Life* (New York: Oxford University Press, 1964), pp. 106, 242. E. K. Francis of the University of Munich hypothesizes that these secondary ethnic group institutions develop only to the extent that the host country and the country of emigration are different in culture (personal conversation, November 25, 1966).

11. Arnold and Caroline Rose, *America Divided* (New York: Alfred A. Knopf, 1948), Ch. 7.

12. Gordon, *op. cit.*, p. 264.

13. S. N. Eisenstadt, *The Absorption of Immigrants: A Comparative Study Based Mainly on the Jewish Community in Palestine and the State of Israel* (London: Routledge and Kegan Paul, 1954), p. 9.

14. *Ibid.*, pp. 12–13.

15. Gordon, *op. cit.*, p. 71.

THE INDEPENDENT VARIABLES: OPENNESS OF
POLICY TOWARD MIGRANTS

1. "Foreign Workers: A Problem of Social Adaptation," *OECD Observer*, No. 25 (December 1966), pp. 11–14.

2. See K. Lewin, "The Free Movement of Workers," *Common Market Law Re-*

view, 2:3 (December 1964), pp. 300–324; Ulrich Erdmann, "Internationale Be-mühungen um den Abbau fremdenrechtlicher Beshränkungen in Europa" (unpub-lished manuscript, Juristische Fakultät, Universität Göttingen, 1966).

3. The treaty provisions and subsequent adaptations are summarized in Gordon L. Weil, *A Handbook on the European Economic Community* (New York: Fred-erick A. Praeger, 1965), pp. 259–265.

4. EEC press release, No. 2549, November 8, 1966, p. 6.

5. *Le Monde* (Paris), April 8, 1967, p. 21; EEC press release, "Toward Com-plete Freedom of Movement for Workers," IP(67)53, Brussels, April 13, 1967.

6. EEC press release, April 13, 1967.

7. *Migration Today*, No. 5 (December 1965), p. 57.

8. G. de Rochcau, "Intra-European Migration in the Last Three Years," *Migra-tion News*, 14:1 (January–February, 1965), pp. 6–11. Also see the treaty between the Netherlands and Spain, April 8, 1961, and the one between the Netherlands and Portugal, November 22, 1963.

9. OECD Council, "Application in 1964 of the Council Decisions Governing the Employment of Nationals of Member Countries," C(66)18, pp. 9–11.

10. The most comprehensive discussions of Swiss migration problems and poli-cies are *Rapport de la commission chargée de l'étude du problème de la main-d'oeu-vre étrangère* (Berne: Office Fédéral de L'Industrie, des Arts et Métiers et du Tra-vail, 1964); Kurt B. Mayer, "The Impact of Postwar Immigration on the Demo-graphic and Social Structure of Switzerland," *Demography*, 3:1 (1966), pp. 68–89.

11. *U.S. News and World Report*, March 15, 1965, pp. 71–72. Even wealthy per-sons and free-lance foreign newsmen were asked to leave the country in 1965 and 1966.

12. *New York Times* (International ed.), February 11–12, 1967, p. 4.

13. See, for example, the statement of the secretary of the Christian trade union federation, quoted in *Migration Today*, No. 5 (December 1965), p. 58. Also see *New York Times* (International ed.), February 11–12, 1967, p. 4, for mention of opposition to government policy from French-speaking businessmen.

14. United Nations, Office of Social Affairs of the European Office, *European Seminar on Social Welfare Programmes for Migrant Workers, Madrid, April 2–10, 1964* (Geneva, 1965), p. 17.

15. Home Office, *Immigrants from the Commonwealth*, Command 2739 (Lon-don: Her Majesty's Stationery Office, August 1965).

16. T. Stark, "Situation of Migrant Workers from Countries of the EEC as Com-pared with That of Workers from Other Countries," in International Institute for Labour Studies, "Conference on the Migration of Workers to Europe" (Geneva, 1965), p. 1.

17. Alfred Caron, "Migrant Workers in Belgium and Their Vocational Train-ing," *Migration Today*, No. 7 (November 1966), p. 27.

18. United Nations, *European Seminar on Social Welfare Programmes* . . . p. 19.

19. *Migration Today*, No. 4 (March 1965), pp. 17, 35.

20. *Migration Today*, No. 5 (December 1965), p. 56.

21. I. Erixon, "Adaptation and Training of Rural Manpower Moving from Pop-ulation Surplus Areas to Industrial Regions and Countries," MS/S/65.128 (OECD, 1965), pp. 3–4.

22. C. P. Kindleberger, "Integration v. Nationalism in the European Economy," *The Reporter*, December 2, 1965, p. 39.

23. C. P. Kindleberger, "Mass Migration, Then and Now," *Foreign Affairs*, July 1965, pp. 647–658.

24. The work of the nongovernmental organizations is very important in social welfare programs, but since information about them is difficult to get and the pro-

grams themselves are often irregular, only passing references to them can be made here.

25. Lionello Levi Sandri, *Social Policy in the Common Market, 1958–65* (Brussels: European Community Information Service, 1966), p. 3.

26. *Ibid.*, p. 4. Sandri, who is a vice-president of the EEC Commission, however, states that the Social Fund has not had the impact expected and also has run into political opposition from the council because of its supranational character. Vocational training is handled on a national basis, with the Social Fund paying 50 percent of the cost retroactively (the remaining 50 percent is often divided according to an agreement between the country of emigration and the country of immigration). The Social Fund may also be used to pay for resettlement of workers whose firms have been negatively affected by modification of trade barriers and other development programs within the EEC. Most resettlement is within the country affected, not cross-national, and the country requesting Social Fund allocations for resettlement must pay half of the costs.

27. *Migration Today*, No. 8 (March 1967), p. 53.

28. Sandri, *op. cit.*, p. 7.

29. Exchanges of information have also been sponsored by the ILO, through several conventions and resolutions, and by UNESCO, through its conference at Havana in 1956 (reported in W. D. Borrie, *The Cultural Integration of Immigrants* [Paris: UNESCO, 1959]). The Office of Social Affairs of the European Office of the United Nations, in cooperation with Swiss authorities, convened an expert group at Mont-Pelerin in Switzerland in 1962, and a more extensive seminar at Madrid in 1964. The OECD held international conferences at Gröningen in 1960 (see H. Krier, *Rural Manpower and Industrial Development, Adaptation and Training* [Paris: OECD, 1961]); at Paris in 1961 (see G. Barbichon, *Adaptation and Training of Rural Workers for Industrial Work* [Paris: OECD, 1962]); at Wiesbaden in 1963 (see *Adaptation of Rural and Foreign Workers to Industry, Final Report, International Joint Seminar, Wiesbaden, December 10–13, 1963* [Paris: OECD, 1965]); and at Athens in 1966 (see *Emigrant Workers Returning to Their Home Countries, Final Report, International Management Seminar, Athens, October 18–21, 1966* [Paris: OECD, 1967]). The studies, conversations, reports, and periodicals of the International Catholic Migration Commission (see its periodical *Migration News*, and its Migration Informative Series No. 4, *Catholic Migration Activities*), the World Council of Churches (see its periodical *Migration Today*), and the Intergovernmental Committee for European Migration (see its periodical *International Migration*, and Paul Ladame, *Le Rôle des migrations dans le monde libre* [Geneva: Droz, 1958]), have also had a considerable intellectual impact on those private persons and public authorities who provide various services to migrant workers. For information about these organizations, also see OECD, Division of Social Affairs, "Etude de politiques et mesures d'ordre pratique: organisations internationales," MS/S/2657/13 (Paris, October 23, 1964).

30. The point of view of this paragraph has also been guided by Sandri, *op. cit.*, p. 10.

31. Information for this paragraph has been taken from Martin Schnitzer, *Programs for Relocating Workers Used by Governments of Selected Countries*, US Congress (89th) Joint Economic Committee (Washington: Government Printing Office, 1966), pp. 70–73. Also see European Community Information Service, *Social Policy in the ECSC*, Community Topics No. 20 (Brussels, 1966).

32. *The Economist*, 223 (May 27, 1967), p. 933.

33. British Information Services, *The Council of Europe* (London: Central Office of Information, 1966), p. 11.

34. Erixon, *op. cit.*, pp. 18–19.

35. This paragraph is based on Jacques Jean Ribas, *Social Security in the Euro-*

pean Community (Brussels: European Community Information Service, 1965), pp. 10–13.

36. The EEC alone has a full volume of regulations pertaining to migrant workers moving exclusively within the six nations (*Sécurité sociale des travailleurs migrants, état au 1ᵉʳ janvier 1965*) and three volumes of *Tableaux comparatifs des régimes de sécurité sociale*, 3rd edition (1964).

37. United Nations, *European Seminar on Social Welfare Programmes* . . . p. 22.

38. EEC Commission, Direction de la Sécurité Sociale et des Services Sociaux, "Suites données à la recommandation de la commission aux états membres concernant l'activité des services sociaux à l'égard des travailleurs se déplaçant dans la communauté," 6936/1/V/64-F (Brussels, 1964), pp. vi–vii.

39. Robert Descloîtres, "Adaptation of Foreign Workers to Industrial Work and Urban Life," MS/S/66.167 (OECD, June 1966), pp. 112–113.

40. Robert Descloîtres, *The Foreign Worker: Adaptation to Industrial Work and Urban Life* (Paris: OECD, 1967), pp. 102–110.

41. *New to Sweden*, unpublished English translation of Svenska Institutet, *Ny i Sverige* (Motala: Bröderna Borgströms AB, 1965), pp. 55–56, 81.

42. This and the next paragraphs are summarized from Descloîtres, "Adaptation of Foreign Workers . . ." pp. 122–125, 133–140.

43. United Nations, *European Seminar on Social Welfare Programmes* . . . pp. 44–60.

44. For national policies on permitting foreign workers to participate on industrial committees, see Council of Europe, Special Representative's Advisory Committee, "Draft Monograph on the Participation of Immigrants in the Life of the Firms in Which They Work," RS82 (Strasbourg, April 20, 1966).

45. On earlier restrictionist policies of unions, see Borrie, *op. cit.*, pp. 172–173.

46. There are some exceptions, for France at least. See *Migration Today*, No. 6 (May 1966), p. 49.

47. François Olivieri, "Foreign Workers in Luxembourg," in *Joint International Seminar on Adaptation of Rural and Foreign Workers to Industry, Wiesbaden, December 10–13, 1963, Supplement to the Final Report* (Paris: OECD, 1965), p. 116.

48. Solomon Barkin, "Trade Union Policies and Programmes for National Internal Rural Migrants and Foreign Workers," in Institute for Labour Studies, "Conference on the Migration . . ." p. 14.

49. Council of Europe, Special Representative's Advisory Committee, "Problems Raised by the Return Home of Migrant Workers" (Strasbourg, April 29, 1966), p. 5.

50. Margaret S. Gordon, *Retraining and Labor Market Adjustment in Western Europe*, US Department of Labor, Manpower and Automation Research, Monograph No. 4 (Washington: Government Printing Office, 1965), pp. 113–114.

51. *La Vie sociale*, No. 5 (1966), p. 237.

52. M. P. Guillen, "Programmes for Preparing Immigrants to Return to the Home Country: France," in *Supplement to the Final Report. Emigrant Workers Returning to Their Home Country, International Management Seminar, Athens, October 18–21, 1966* (Paris: OECD, 1967), pp. 3–4.

53. Caron, *op. cit.*, pp. 28–30.

54. Council of Europe, "Problems Raised . . ." p. 10.

55. *Migration Today*, No. 8 (March 1967), p. 61.

56. *Ibid.*, p. 63.

57. Unless otherwise indicated, facts in this and the following three sections have been taken from Descloîtres, "Adaptation of Foreign Workers . . . " pp. 80–102, 141–150, 165–168; and from International Catholic Migration Commission, "Über die Situation der Auswandernden Arbeiter aus Ländern der EWG und Jener Ausserhalb der EWG," CCMIE/XIV/D/2, mimeographed (Geneva, 1965).

58. A survey by the Council of Europe, "Problems Raised . . ." p. 2, finds that "there is a definite connection between the information given to emigrants before they leave home or as soon as they reach the immigration country and their chances of adjusting themselves to their social and work environment in their new country."

59. *Migration Today*, No. 8 (March 1967), p. 60.

60. For a general statement on French facilities for the reception of immigrants, see Haut Comité Consulatif de la Population et de la Famille, *L'Accueil des étrangers en France* (Paris: La Documentation Française, 1963).

61. "Foreign Manpower in Switzerland," *International Labour Review*, 87 (February 1963), p. 140.

62. See the report of the Swedish joint team to Germany and the Norwegian joint team to Germany and Switzerland in OECD, *National Missions Reports No. 1 and No. 2* (Paris, 1966). Also see Walter Ritter, "Gleichbehandlung und Kündigungsrechtsproblems in Zusammenhang mit der Beschäftigung von Ausländern," *Arbeit und Recht*, 14:2 (1966), pp. 34–36.

63. An excellent source of information on language instruction for immigrant workers is Council of Europe, "Special Aspects of the Problem of Teaching Languages to Migrant Workers" (Strasbourg, September 10, 1964).

64. A private association in Belgium, the Centre d'Initiation pour Réfugiés et Emigrés, receives some government subsidy to conduct language courses, but not many courses are offered nor are they well attended. The CIRE also has an orienting function for immigrants, which was very important when most of the immigrants were refugees.

65. Inga Gottfarb, "La Nouvelle légion," *Suède d'aujourd'hui*, 3:26 (1965), pp. 26–31.

66. Elie Dimitras, "International Migration," in *Joint International Seminar . . .* p. 82.

67. *Migration Today*, No. 8 (March 1967), p. 58.

68. *Joint International Seminar . . .* pp. 124–125, 173; International Catholic Migration Commission, *Survey on Families of Migrant Workers in Six European Countries* (Geneva, no date).

69. This paragraph is based on interviews with officials of the education ministry.

70. *La Vie sociale*, No. 5 (1966), p. 237.

71. Erixon, *op. cit.*, p. 7.

72. *Migration Today*, No. 3 (December 1964), p. 27.

73. Council of Europe, "Problems Raised . . ." pp. 3, 18.

74. *Migration Today*, No. 3 (December 1964), p. 30.

75. *Migration Today*, No. 8 (March 1967), p. 56.

76. Catholic Migration Commission, *Survey on Families . . .*

77. Council of Europe, Special Representative's Advisory Committee, "The Effects of the Housing Problem on the Psychology of Migrant Workers and Their Adjustment to the Social Environment of the Host Country" (Strasbourg, March 25, 1964), Part II, p. 6. This report (in two parts) is the best single source of information on immigrant housing in Europe in the 1960's.

78. Stark, *op. cit.*, p. 4.

79. Haut Comité, *L'Accueil* . . . p. 74.

80. Council of Europe, "The Effects of the Housing Problem . . ." Part I, p. 14.

81. C. Calvaruso, "Le Logement des travailleurs italiens dans le canton de Genève," *Migration News*, 3:2 (March–April 1964), pp. 5–6.

82. EEC Commission, "Suites données . . ." p. 7.

83. Council of Europe, "The Effects of the Housing Problem . . ." Part I, pp. 36–38.

84. *Ibid.*, pp. 26–29.

85. *Ibid.*, pp. 39–45.

86. *Ibid.*, pp. 50–54.

87. J. Doublet, "Les Conséquences sociales des mouvements migratoires en Europe," in Institute for Labour Studies, "Conference on the Migration of Workers . . ." p. 9; G. Peslouan, "L'Expérience de l'industrie du bâtiment en matière de logement des travailleurs," *Migration News*, 3:1 (January–February 1964), pp. 4–7.

88. Descloîtres, "Adaptation of Foreign Workers . . ." p. 165.

89. This is Milton Gordon's term; see *Assimilation in American Life* (New York: Oxford University Press, 1964), pp. 105–106.

90. Catholic Migration Commission, *Survey on Families* . . .

91. Descloîtres, "Adaptation of Foreign Workers . . ." p. 167.

92. Roberto Motta, "Towards a Study of Alienation amongst Some Foreign Workers in the Netherlands" (master's thesis, Institute of Social Studies, The Hague, November 1964).

93. The Prague radio beams broadcasts to Germany every day in Italian and Spanish — native music, news from home, and propaganda — and the Budapest radio does the same in Turkish and Greek (*New York Times*, December 23, 1965, pp. 1, 12).

94. Interview with Madame Camille Gilon, director of the Service Provincial d'Immigration et d'Accueil, February 22, 1967.

95. In Belgium, for example, there is the *Sindikalni Glasnik* for Serbo-Croats and Slovenes, *Emek* for Turks, *Praca* for Poles, *Magyarok* for Hungarians, *El Ibero* for Spaniards, *Sole d'Italia* for Italians, *Protoporos* for Greeks, and *Buleten* for Ukrainians — mostly sponsored by the Christian trade union organization of Belgium. The Belgian Ministry of Employment and Work, with the collaboration of the Coal Federation of Belgium and the Embassy of Turkey, publishes, for example, the *Turk Iscileri Bülteni* for Turks. In Switzerland all 247 firm newspapers have a page or two in Italian or Spanish (see E. Duc, "Programmes for Preparing Immigrants to Return to the Home Country: Switzerland," in *Supplement to the Final Report* . . . p. 18).

96. In Munich, Germany, a biweekly Turkish-language newspaper is published by a Turkish immigrant; in London Greek-language weekly newspapers are published by two rival political groups of Cypriots. Scores of other examples could be given.

97. Secretariat d'Etat à l'Information, "Liste des journaux et périodiques étrangers ou de langue étrangère édités ou imprimés en France," mimeographed (Paris, no date).

98. Interviews with embassy officials in Brussels.

99. Borrie, *op. cit.*, pp. 81 *passim*.

100. United Nations, *European Seminar on Social Welfare Programmes* . . . pp. 58–59.

101. An excellent study of this community, Sparkbrook, has been written by John Rex and Robert Moore, *Race, Community and Conflict: A Study of Sparkbrook* (London: Oxford University Press, for the Institute of Race Relations, 1967).

102. *The Economist*, 222 (March 11, 1967), p. 911.

103. *Migration Today*, No. 4 (March 1965), p. 39.

104. Political and Economic Planning (PEP), *Race Discrimination in England* (London, 1967); see *The Economist*, 223 (April 22, 1967), pp. 319–320.

105. Opinion Research Centre, "*Sunday Times* Poll," *Sunday Times* (London), May 7, 1967, p. 41.

106. In Switzerland classified ads in the newspapers for rooms to rent sometimes carry the line "Italians excluded" or "foreigners not admitted." In France the author has personally witnessed Negro would-be customers turned out of restaurants and refused the rental of vacant apartments.

107. International Catholic Migration Commission, *The Family: A Guarantee of Successful Migration*, Migration Informative Series No. 2 (Geneva, no date).

108. A. Berten, "L'Etablissement des travailleurs migrants et de leur famille en Belgique," *Revue du travail* (December 1966), pp. 1–24.

186

Notes

109. Descloîtres, *The Foreign Worker* . . . pp. 141–142.
110. Churches Committee on Migrant Workers in Western Europe, *Enquiry Related to the Return of Migrant Workers* (Geneva, 1966), p. 47.
111. Council of Europe, "Problems Raised . . ." p. 18.
112. Interviews with personnel of German Employers' Association, October 1966.
113. Information for this paragraph is taken from Descloîtres, "Adaptation of Foreign Workers . . ." pp. 159–164.
114. In Belgium in the province of Liège, where foreign workers are concentrated, two schools have remedial classes, but all schools have "after-school sessions" to help foreign children with their homework (interview with Madame Camille Gilon, February 22, 1967). For an excellent discussion of the problems of immigrant children in Belgium, with comparisons for France and Switzerland, see F. Picard, "L'Intégration des enfants étrangers dans l'enseignement d'une grande ville," Centre d'Etudes et de Documentation Sociales de la Province de Liège, *Bulletin*, No. 9 (October 1965), pp. 475–491.

In England the government has sponsored research at Leeds University on techniques of teaching English to immigrant children. Special centers to teach immigrant school children English are described in Eric Butterworth, "The Presence of Immigrant School Children," *Race*, 8:4 (January 1967), pp. 247–262.

In France the special language and vocational courses for teen-age immigrants in France are dealt with in Marcelle Trillat, "French and Pre-Vocational Training for Young Immigrants in France," *Migration Today*, No. 4 (March 1965), pp. 20–23.

For Switzerland see Lischer, "Les Enfants des travailleurs étrangers et l'école," mimeographed (Geneva: International Catholic Migration Commission, no date).
115. *New to Sweden*, p. 72. In a letter to the author, Mr. Sven Enander, deputy superintendent of schools in Stockholm, wrote:
The instructions issued by the Swedish National Board of Education in December 1966, concerning additional lessons for foreign pupils are:
(1) The responsibility for arranging supporting lessons for foreign children is on the School Board (i.e., local school authority).
(2) The supporting lessons are intended to enable the pupils to make the most of their compulsory education in the Swedish school. Thus the aim of the supporting lessons should be:

> to prevent, if possible, that the pupil's time for studies is unnecessarily wasted because of his lacking knowledge of Swedish. This will be possible if study-guidance and books and study-matters are provided in the pupil's mother tongue.
> to facilitate the pupil's entry into the school by a good introduction consisting of an elementary instruction and training in understanding and speaking the Swedish language and general information about the new environment.
> to give special help in subjects in which the curriculum of the previous school and that of the Swedish school are very different.

It is also provided that the measures for pupil-welfare aim at these pupils' social accommodation at school and in the circle of colleagues of the same age. It is important that the teachers give regular information to the parents and that the relations between the school personnel and the parents are good.
(3) Swedish can very well be taught in classes consisting of pupils with different native languages. The teacher ought to be of Swedish nationality. The groups should be rather small (3–5 pupils) and, as far as possible, homogeneous as regards age and knowledge of Swedish. Communities with a rather great number of foreign pupils are recommended to start a permanent "clinic for Swedish language" where

187

a teacher is working all day. Otherwise it might be difficult to obtain the differentiated instruction with short, frequent training periods which is typical for clinical training — that is in cases where the supporting training of Swedish is not given by the regular class-teacher.

(4) Supporting lessons can also be devoted to studies in the pupil's native language during a couple of weekly periods under the guidance of teachers knowing the pupil's native language. Books and other materials in the pupil's native language used during these lessons must be acknowledged by the local School Board. The pupils in each group, during these lessons, can be more heterogeneous as regards age and level.

The foreign pupils should be allowed to use books and other matter in their own language in their individual work also within the regular classes.

116. Stark, *op. cit.*, p. 3. In at least one school in England (in Islington, London), the authorities have hired a Cypriot teacher to teach Greek to Cypriot schoolchildren, on the demand of their parents. See Elspeth Huxley, *Back Street New Worlds: A Look at Immigrants in Britain* (London: Chatto and Windus, 1964), pp. 86–87.

117. Centre d'Etudes . . . *Bulletin*, No. 9, p. 480.

118. Mayer, *loc. cit.*

119. *Migration Today*, No. 5 (December 1965), p. 60.

120. Facts in this paragraph are taken from Stark, *op. cit.*, pp. 5–6.

121. Data for this paragraph come from Council of Europe, "Problems Raised . . ." pp. 14–15.

122. From *New to Sweden*, pp. 13–24.

123. Also see the detailed commentary to the table prepared for the Catholic Migration Commission, "Über die Situation . . ."

124. Duc, *loc. cit.*

125. Roger Girod, "Travailleurs étrangers et mobilité sociale en Suisse," *Revue économique et sociale*, 24 (May 1966).

126. Prime Minister Harold Wilson mentioned this possible issue in his speech to Parliament formally proposing application for membership in the Common Market (May 8, 1967). See *New York Herald Tribune and Washington Post*, May 9, 1967, p. 1; also see the preceding debate in Parliament on this matter (on May 4, 1967), as reported in *Times* (London), May 5, 1967.

127. Arnold M. Rose, "Voluntary Associations in France," in *Theory and Method in the Social Sciences* (Minneapolis: University of Minnesota Press, 1954), Ch. 4; Arnold M. Rose, "Voluntary Associations in Sweden," *Archives internationales de sociologie de la coopération*, No. 20 (July–December, 1966), pp. 41–75.

128. This is not to suggest that all or most immigrants have these drawbacks, but it is characteristic of proportionally more migrants than nationals of immigrant countries. There is some sparse information available that indicates the migrants from some countries include a higher proportion of those with an urban background and better education than the general nonmigrating population of those countries.

129. The author heard frequent reports that — especially in Germany, Switzerland, Italy, and Greece — a large proportion of the migrant workers are turning to communism. Also see Council of Europe, "Draft Monograph . . ." p. 11, and B. Ch. Sjollema, "Return Migration and Development Aid," *Migration Today*, No. 5 (December 1965), pp. 19–20.

THE INDEPENDENT VARIABLES: NONPOLICY FACTORS
AFFECTING ACCEPTANCE AND ADJUSTMENT

1. Gunnar Myrdal, Richard Sterner, and Arnold M. Rose. *An American Dilemma: The Negro Problem and Modern Democracy* (New York: Harper, 1944).

2. Alain Girard and Jean Stoetzel, "Français et immigrés," in Institut National d'Etudes Démographiques, *Travaux et documents*, Cahier No. 19 (Paris: Presses

Universitaires de France, 1953–54), p. 33. The exact quotation, which loses a great deal when translated, reads: "Les français ont pu ne pas souhaiter la présence d'immigrés, mais l'admettre en pratique, et réserver ainsi aux étrangers un accueil moins hostile qu'ils ne l'eussent eux-mêmes imaginé. . . . Les germes des tensions à l'égard des immigrants coexistent dans la conscience collective avec la possibilité de les réduire." (The French have been able to not want immigrants in their country but to accept them in practice, and thus to reserve for foreigners a reception which is less hostile than they themselves [the French] might have imagined. . . . The germs of tensions with regard to immigrants coexist in the collective conscience along with the possibility of reducing them.)

3. René Clémens, Paul Minon, and Gabrielle Vosse-Smal, *L'Assimilation culturelle des immigrants en Belgique: Italiens et Polonais dans la région liègeoise* (Liège: Imprimerie H. Vaillant-Carmanne, 1953), Section V.

4. W. D. Borrie, *The Cultural Integration of Immigrants* (Paris: UNESCO, 1959), pp. 169–173.

5. Made available through the courtesy of the Steinmetz Institute of Amsterdam.

6. Data made available through the courtesy of Max Barioux, director of the Service Sondages et Statistiques.

7. Roland Sadoun, "Les Français et le problème juif," in Institut Français d'Opinion Publique, *Le Nouvel Adam*, No. 5 (1966), p. 8.

8. Roberto Motta, "Towards a Study of Alienation amongst Some Foreign Workers in the Netherlands" (master's thesis, Institute of Social Studies, The Hague, November 1964).

9. Tomiko Tanaami, "A Study about the Integration of Portuguese Workers in the Netherlands" (master's thesis, Institute of Social Studies, The Hague, May 1966).

10. The survey was kindly made available for use here by Dr. Jan Stapel, director of the Netherlands Institute for Public Opinion. The first set of figures is from Report No. 855 (August 29, 1961); the second set is from Report No. 862 (October 2, 1961).

11. Made available through the courtesy of Sten Hultgren of the Svenska Institutet för Opinionsunder sökningar.

12. Hardi Fischer, "Wege zur wissenschaftlichen Erfassung der Situation der ausländischen Arbeitskräfte in der Schweiz," in *Zum Problem der ausländischen Arbeitskräfter in der Schweiz* (Zurich: Industrielle Organisation, 1961).

13. ENMID Institute, *ENMID-Informationen*, 17:49 (Bielefeld, Germany, December 6, 1965), p. 13.

14. H. Minta, "Incidence of Migrant Labour on the German Labour Market," in International Institute for Labour Studies, "Conference on the Migration of Workers to Europe" (Geneva, 1965), p. 13.

15. Based on *IFAS Report für die Presse* (Bad Godesberg, October 3 and November 9, 1966).

16. *ENMID-Informationen*, p. 32.

17. Results made available through the courtesy of the Steinmetz Institute of Amsterdam.

18. Reverend Francisco Sanchez Lopez, "Six années d'emigration espagnole en Europe," International Catholic Migration Commission, CCMIE/XVII/F/12, Tables 3, 6, 9, 12.

19. Nermin Abadan, *Bati Almanya' daki Türk Iscileri ve Sorumlari* (Ankara: State Planning Organization, 1964), pp. 19–219, translated and summarized in several sources in German, French, and English. See, for example, Robert H. Eldridge, "Emigration and the Turkish Balance of Payments," *The Middle East Journal*, 20:3 (Summer 1966), pp. 296–316; Richard Haar, "Expérience allemande avec la main-d'oeuvre turque," *Migration News*, 4:6 (November–December 1965), pp. 4–7;

Nermin Abadan, "Studie über die Lage . . ." *Arbeitsplatz Europa*, Europäische Schriften Heft 11 (1967), pp. 102–124.

20. Translated from Menie Gregoire, "Politique française de l'immigration," *Espirit*, 34:4 (April 1966), pp. 570–584.

21. John Rex and Robert Moore, *Race, Community and Conflict* (London: Oxford University Press, for the Institute of Race Relations, 1967), p. 62.

22. Benjamin Tonna, "Fattori di integrazione familiare e socioculturale in due gruppi italiani emigrati," *Studi emigrazione*, I:1/2 (February 1965), pp. 18–42.

23. The official Swiss commission has noted this change. See *Le Problème de la main-d'oeuvre étrangère* (Berne, 1964), p. 9.

24. "State" is used here to mean the political structure, no matter in whose hands it may currently rest; "government" means here the specific political party or individuals in control of the state.

25. D. José Farina Jamardo, "Evolution of Spanish Emigration in Europe," in *Supplement to the Final Report, Emigrant Workers Returning to Their Home Country, International Management Seminar, Athens, October 18–21, 1966* (Paris: OECD, 1967), p. 9.

26. Abadan, *op. cit.* (see Haar's summary).

27. Elspeth Huxley, *Back Street New Worlds: A Look at Immigrants in Britain* (London: Chatto and Windus, 1964), pp. 74, 80.

28. Abadan, *op. cit.* (see Haar's summary).

THE DEPENDENT VARIABLES: WHAT HAPPENS TO PEOPLE

1. (Protestant) Churches Committee on Migrant Workers in Western Europe, *Enquiry Related to the Return of Migrant Workers* (Geneva, 1966), pp. 72, 77.

2. Summarized in A. E. Bottoms, "Delinquency amongst Immigrants," *Race*, 8:4 (January 1967), pp. 357–383.

3. *Ibid.*, p. 379.

4. Heinz-Günther Zimmermann, "Die Kriminalität der ausländischen Arbeiter," *Kriminalistik*, No. 12 (December 1966), pp. 623–625.

5. *The Economist*, 222 (January 7, 1967), p. 59.

6. Viviane Serteyn, "Mon expérience de stage dans un service d'accueil pour étrangers," and Jacqueline Janclaes, "Etude de quelques facteurs d'adaptation des travailleurs nord-africains et turcs dans la province de Liège" (theses for Le Service Provincial d'Immigration et d'Accueil de Liège, 1966). These theses used the same questionnaire for Italians, Spanish, Turks, and North Africans, but not for Greeks.

7. Statistiska Centralbyrån, *Sveriges Officiella Statistik: Socialvård* (Stockholm, 1966), p. 47.

8. Reverend Francisco Sanchez Lopez, "L'Intégration dans la société espagnole de migrants de retour de pays européens," International Catholic Migration Commission, CCMIE/XVII/F/14, p. 3.

9. Reported in Ionnis Mitsos, "Returned Emigrants to Greece," *Supplement to the Final Report, Emigrant Workers Returning to Their Home Country, International Management Seminar, Athens, October 18–21, 1966* (Paris: OECD, 1967), pp. 10–11.

10. *Ibid.*, p. 3.

11. United Nations, Economic Commission for Europe, *Economic Survey for Europe, 1965* (Geneva, 1966), p. 34.

12. Magda Talamo, "The Backflow of Italian Emigrants in the Context of Migratory Movements," *Supplement to the Final Report* . . . p. 7.

13. *Ibid.*, p. 28.

14. Mitsos, *op. cit.*, p. 4.

15. Council of Europe, Special Representative's Advisory Committee, "Problems Raised by the Return Home of Migrant Workers" (Strasbourg, April 29, 1966), p. 8.

16. B. Ch. Sjollema, "Return Migration and Development Aid," *Migration Today,* No. 5 (December 1965), p. 17.

17. Council of Europe, "Problems Raised . . ." pp. 22–24.

18. *Ibid.,* pp. 24–27.

19. Bernard Kayser, "The Situation of the Returning Migrants on the Labour Market in Greece: Results of Surveys," *Supplement to the Final Report* . . . p. 2.

20. *Ibid.,* p. 29.

21. Franco Marziale, "Dynamics and Characteristics of 'The Returns,' " *Supplement to the Final Report* . . . p. 19 (quoting newspaper *To Vima,* March 18, 1965).

22. *Ibid.*

23. N. H. Neyzi, "Experience with Emigrants Returning to the Home Country: Turkey," *Supplement to the Final Report* . . . pp. 10, 12.

24. Lopez, *op. cit.,* p. 9.

25. See, for example, the reports of Talamo, Mitsos, and others in *Supplement to the Final Report* . . . See also (Protestant) Churches Committee on Migrant Workers in Western Europe, *Enquiry Related to* . . .

26. Council of Europe, Special Representative's Advisory Committee, "The Return of Emigrants to Their Home Countries and the Problems It Raises," RS74 (Strasbourg, February 22, 1965), p. 5.

27. J. L. Villa, M.D., "Psychology of Migrant Workers and Their Adjustment to the Social Environment of the Host Country" (Strasbourg: Council of Europe, 1962). Also see the report of Dr. Villa's work in the United Nations, Office of Social Affairs of the European Office, *European Seminar on Social Welfare Programmes for Migrant Workers, Madrid, April 2–10, 1964* (Geneva, 1965), pp. 25–34. This report also refers to other psychological studies conducted in Switzerland. For an independent but similar report, see M. A. Psaras, "Projet d'étude sur le comportement psychique des travailleurs migrants et leur adaptation au milieu social du pays d'accueil," RS43 (Strasbourg: Council of Europe, 1963).

28. Villa, "Psychology of . . ." p. 9.

29. Council of Europe, "The Return of Emigrants . . ." pp. 5–6.

THE INTEGRATION OF PEOPLE

1. If there are a large number of variables, partly true in this study, there is mathematical support for using the arbitrary weight of 1. See Louis Guttman in Paul Horst, *The Prediction of Personal Adjustment* (New York: Social Science Research Council, 1941), pp. 251–364.

2. France is also somewhat of an exception — but to a smaller extent and of an opposite nature. France's immigrants do not have the highest integration and adjustment even though it is the most open country in terms of its policies, programs, and practices. The reason would again appear to lie in public opinion — which in France is not always hospitable toward immigrants.

3. They should be known as "grouped-data" correlations. Ecological refers to a theoretical viewpoint which interprets social facts in terms of location and distance. It is true that ecology works with grouped data, but not all grouped data are ecological. There is nothing "ecological" about the present study, for instance. Ecology was a branch of sociology and geography for thirty years before the misnomer "ecological correlation" arose in the late 1940's.

4. In Sweden public opinion polls indicate that the people cooperate more than in France with their government, big employers, and big trade unions in a conscious national effort to be pro-immigrant.

5. In the mid-1960's the Swedes were having a great debate about whether they should encourage the immigrants to be like Swedes or let them be like anyone they wanted to be. The very existence of such a debate indicates a degree of openness in Swedish society that no other European country had achieved at that time.

Migrants in Europe

Recruitment: of migrants, 69–72
Refugees: as migrants, 7–8, 20
Religion: as a factor in adjustment, 117, 121
Remittances: of migrants, 28–29
Rex, John: study on race in Great Britain, 115
Rose, Arnold M.: difference between opinion and behavior, 100

Sauvy, Alfred: on demography, 21
Service des Sondages et Statistiques: poll on Common Market, 101–02
Social security: regulated by treaty, 47, 48, 56–60, 61–64; family allowance provision of, 84; cessation of, 140
Spain: emigration from, 17–20, 22–23; treaty with Switzerland, 48–49; restriction of emigration from, 55; attitudes toward migration in, 111–12, 120; and its nationals abroad, 138
Stark, T.: table on laws, 89, 166–73
Statistics: lack of uniformity in, 15–16
Sterner, Richard: difference between behavior and opinion, 100
Stoetzel, Jean: on French attitudes toward foreigners, 100
Sweden: number of immigrants in, 17–20, 22–23; treaty with Yugoslavia, 47–48; aid to migrants in, 64; attitudes toward immigrants in, 107–08; limitations on aliens in, 88–89
Switzerland: statistics in, 16; number of immigrants in, 16–20, 22–23; treaty with Spain, 48–49; statutes on migration in, 50; restriction of immigrants to, 50–52; attitudes toward immigrants in, 108–09, 116

Treaty of Rome: establishing European Social Fund, 57–59
Turel, Orhan: article by, 162–64

Turkey: emigrants from, 22–23; remittances to, 28; restriction of emigration from, 55; attitude of immigrants from, 112; newspaper article from, 162–64

Unions: voting rights in, 65–66. See also Labor force
United Kingdom: refugees in, 8, 20–21; statistics in, 16; number of immigrants in, 16–20; restrictions on migration in, 50, 52–53; programs against prejudice in, 78–79; attitudes toward immigrants in, 104–05
United Nations: High Commission for Refugees, 8
United States: assimilation in, 4, 153
Ustachas: in Sweden, 158, 160–62

Villa, J. L.: report on psychiatric problems, 143
Vocational training: in Sweden, 47; sought by underdeveloped countries, 54–55; for migrants, 66–68; availability of, 97–99; failure of, 139
Voluntary associations: to aid migrants, 72–74, 77–78, 94
Vosse-Smal, Gabrielle: mentioned, 100

Work permits: regulation of, 46, 49, 50, 53–54

Yugoslavia: emigration from, 22–23; remittances to, 27; treaty with Sweden, 47–48; and its nationals abroad, 138–39; newspaper articles from, 157–62

Zimmermann, Heinz-Günther: study on crime, 130–32
Zubrzycki, Jerzy: mentioned, 5, 100

194